ADVANCES IN HUMAN ECOLOGY

Volume 3 • 1994

EDITORIAL ADVISORS

ADVANCES IN HUMAN ECOLOGY

Editor: LEE FREESE
Department of Sociology
Washington State University

**Published in association with the
Society for Human Ecology**

VOLUME 3 • 1994

 **JAI PRESS INC.**

Greenwich, Connecticut   London, England

CONTENTS

LIST OF CONTRIBUTORS

John H. Bodley

Department of Anthropology
Washington State University

C. Dyke

Department of Philosophy
Temple University

Lee Freese

Department of Sociology
Washington State University

Jeremy Pratt

Institute for Human Ecology
Santa Rosa, CA

Allan Schnaiberg

Department of Sociology
Northwestern University

Jonathan H. Turner

Departament of Sociology
University of California,
Riverside

PREFACE

EDITORIAL POLICY

This series publishes original theoretical, empirical, and review papers on scientific human ecology. Human ecology is interpreted to include structural and functional patterns and changes in human social organization and sociocultural behavior as these may be affected by, interdependent with, or identical to changes in ecosystemic, evolutionary, or ethological processes, factors, or mechanisms. Three degrees of scope are included in this interpretation: (1) the adaptation of sociocultural forces to bioecological forces; (2) the interactions between sociocultural and bioecological forces; and (3) the integration of sociocultural with bioecological forces.

The goal of the series is to promote the growth of human ecology as a transdisciplinary problem-solving paradigm. Contributions are solicited without regard for particular theoretical, methodological, or disciplinary orthodoxies, and may range across ecological anthropology, socioecology, sociobiology, biosociology, environmental sociology, ecological economics, ecological demography, ecological geography, and other relevant fields of specialization. The editor will be especially receptive to contributions that promote the growth of general scientific theory in human ecology. No single volume will represent the full range the series is intended to cover.

CONTENTS OF VOLUME 3

The first two papers address a central problem in human ecology: how human ecological and social organization are bound together by means of human economic organization. C. Dyke begins with an analysis of connections between technological growth and economic cycles, using the framework of the new interdisciplinary sciences of complexity. The new framework renders some classic problems now ordinary and uninteresting, and Dyke shows how and why the foci of explanations have to be adjusted to comprehend the interactive dynamics of technology and world economy. Allan Schnaiberg focuses on a central feature of the modern economy, its treadmill of production, and he explains how this produces and sustains modern political-economic conflicts about competing human uses to which ecosystems are put. Schnaiberg's argument is extensively illustrated by examining patterns of environmental conflict and attempted resolutions that have appeared in the recent experience of the United States.

Two papers follow that present contrasting human ecological perspectives on long-term growth in the complexity of sociocultural systems. Jonathan H. Turner develops a sociological explanation with his theory of the process of the assembling of populations—a process Turner traces to the interactive cycle in which power is concentrated and production expanded, each escalating the other. John H. Bodley develops an anthropological explanation with his theory of human cultural development and change. Bodley argues that, historically, three distinct cultural processes correlate with three distinct scales of culture, and that a conscious reordering of the hierarchy of culture-scale processes is necessary because the modern scale is ecologically unsustainable.

The next two papers explore concepts of evolution, with completely different ends in view. Jonathan H. Turner tries to integrate into a general model of macrosocial differentiation two thematic anologies to natural selection: (1) the Darwinian selection analogies of organizational ecology, and (2) the non-Darwinian selection analogies of Herbert Spencer and Émile Durkheim. Next, I try to show that the task of explaining evolutionary change in sociocultural systems is insurmountable if traditional social science or conventional biological concepts are employed (by anology or homology). I argue that the concept of adaptation to environments provides too weak a paradigm.

The last paper, by Jeremy Pratt, is a comprehensive review of multifarious programs, having both scientific and policy objectives, that have recently proliferated to address human ecological interactions. Pratt examines and compares the self-definitions and objectives of the major programs, identifies common themes, finds that all of them are calling for human ecology, but not by that name, and that few of them seem to be aware of their intellectual roots. While deploring the innocent reinventing of human ecology as a field of investigation, Pratt assigns the cause to the field's own failure to provide a basis for the applied science now so fervently in demand.

THE WORLD AROUND US AND HOW WE MAKE IT:

HUMAN ECOLOGY AS HUMAN ARTIFACT

C. Dyke

ABSTRACT

Technology is one of the major shapers of human ecology. On the basis of recent work, it looks as if an understanding of the integrated role of technology in world economy lies at the intersection of ideas in the theory of economic cycles (Schumpeter and followers), evolutionary theory, and theories from nonlinear dynamics and others of the new "sciences of complexity." The paper begins to synthesize these strands. On this basis, some common phenomena, puzzling from traditional points of view, come to look quite ordinary and expectable from the new points of view.

INTRODUCTION

For the last fourteen thousand years or so, we humans have been making a continuous and concerted effort to surround ourselves with a world of our

Advances in Human Ecology, Volume 3, pages 1-22.
Copyright © 1994 by JAI Press Inc.
ISBN: 1-55938-760-2

own making. No one standing on the corner of Wall Street and Broadway could doubt that we've made a certain amount of progress in the effort. Standing there, we may begin to wonder why we do it, but there's no doubt that we do.

We can also wonder *how* we manage so successfully to surround ourselves with a world of our own making. The one-word answer to the "how" question is "technology," of course, and that means that if we want to understand the history of our world-building, we have to understand the course of our technological activity. Indeed, the search for such understanding is currently a prominent part of the agenda of several disciplines and subfields. This paper attempts to collect and synthesize a certain amount of present-day thinking on the subject.

We arrive in the middle of an ongoing discussion. Matters have gotten quite complicated by this time. Our technological activity is inextricably embedded in our economic activity. We understand both economic and technological activity as evolving dynamical interactions between people, institutions, and "nature," where "nature" is simply a catch-all word collecting all those aspects of our world that are not humans or their institutions. Furthermore, our efforts to know, understand, and explain something like our technology are *themselves* evolving dynamical interactions, intrinsically tied up with the very technology we hope to understand. Consequently, several strands are going to have to be twisted together in this paper, because several strands are twisted together in the phenomena we wish to study. Fortunately, it's possible here at the beginning to identify the strands we'll be working with.

First, there is the ongoing line of thought (call it Schumpeterian after a nodal figure) directed toward understanding the impact of technology on economies. Next, it is part of the Schumpeterian insight that technology is deeply implicated in "driving" economic cycles, so the second strand is the line of thought examining economic cycles as pervasive but badly understood phenomena. But cycling is a phenomenon now best understood by means of the resources of nonlinear dynamics and nonequilibrium thermodynamics, so we have to introduce a few fibers from those fields. Of course when we do so, we'll see that the explanatory patterns we work out look somewhat different from those we may be used to in traditional investigations. In fact, seeing that our explanatory habits have to change is absolutely essential for winding all the threads together, so the longest section of the paper will address these issues. Finally, as I mentioned, all this takes place in a context of evolution. Technology is evolving; the world economy is evolving; our investigative and explanatory activities are evolving. So, the final strand we must introduce comes from the subfield of evolutionary economics. A well worked out Darwinian account of economic evolution has been advanced, and we will be able to move forward by examining its insufficiencies. The hope is that when we have finished twisting all the strands together, we will have a grasp on one end of a rope strong enough to hang onto as we try to understand our making of the world we make. Of course, there's always the chance that given enough rope....

There is a substantive point to all this as well. We are currently being told again, as we were by Daniel Bell and his fellow travelers in the 1950s, that we are at the end of the age of ideology. What this would mean from the point of view of the sciences of complexity is that we now are fairly certain that those located at the ends of the old ideological spectrum were each trying to inflate half a balloon. What remains when we've left behind the ideology is the realization that the history of the production process is a dynamical organization and reorganization of labor and technology. When this process is conceptualized in terms of self-regulating markets stabilizing at a moving point equilibrium, explanatory efforts are frustrated; but what frustrates equilibrium theorists is exactly what interests the dynamicists. Similarly, the theory of the revolutionary end of capitalism now looks to be the heroic denial of the conditions of a rapidly growing human population trying to build a world fast enough to support its existence.

CONFRONTING COMPLEXITY: EXPLANATION VERSUS RATIONALISM

We need to look at the general considerations with respect to explanatory pattern right away, for *this* strand will continue all the way through. What I say here is no more than a theoretical summary of what is implicit in recent work on complexity. The second generation of complexity theory is at hand. The first generation produced chaos theory, better thought of as the maturation of nonlinear dynamics; Mandelbrot's theory of fractals; and Prigogine's investigation of the thermodynamics of systems far from equilibrium. We've seen the pictures; we may even have begun to get a feel for a world that is deterministic yet unpredictable. At the very least we've been tuned to look for complex patterns rather than simple regularities.

Always lurking at the edges of first generation complexity theory was the realization that within nonlinear dynamics and nonequilibrium thermodynamics were explanations for the emergence of stable structures, including living things. The picture is a "This is the house that Jack built" one. The singularity at the beginning of the universe yields the right stuff to "build" stars (eventually), yielding the right stuff to "build" planets (eventually), yielding the right stuff to "build" organic molecules, and eventually organisms. Now, all that has to be figured out is how the "building" goes on.

The first generation of complexity theorists had made some guesses (some of them reasonably educated ones, some not) about how complex stable structure could emerge under the right conditions. The second generation has gone beyond the guesses to the stage of theory, hypothesis, and simulation.

Start by thinking of scientific explanations as rigorously constrained narratives, stories about why things happen written primarily in the language of mathematics. Enlightenment science, Newtonian/Cartesian science at root, taught us how to write responsible stories about the flight of ballistics objects of all sorts. These are still amazingly successful stories—in a restricted realm. In this century, quantum mechanics has been developed to provide the stories of very small things and very high energies. It, too, is extremely successful. But up until recently, the stories told by these theories were simplistic in a particular way: They were linear. Linearity shows up in different ways for different phenomena. For "building," linearity shows up as a picture of piling up building blocks in a strictly additive way. Anything complex is thus considered as a stuck-together combination of smaller things. This story is fine for things that are actually made in this building block way, but it turns out that there are lots of things the story doesn't fit, and, in fact, the building block story is the *whole* story for practically nothing.

So the second generation of complexity theorists is working on new sorts of stories of synthesis. These stories often involve differentiation, mutually transforming interaction, and elaborated generation from "seeds" of various sorts. The near-slogan that these things happen at the edge of chaos is a precise elaboration of the general intuition that nothing very interesting happens under conditions of extreme stability (rocks), and the interesting things that happen in conditions of ultra-extreme instability are too transient to result in anything that captures our attention. At the edge of chaos, seedlike things happen that trigger cascades of ever more elaborate structuring. Of course, we also have a number of recent semi-popularized accounts (e.g., Waldrup 1992; Lewin 1992) at hand to give us an overall sense of what these new lines of investigation are all about. There is no doubt whatsoever that over the next few years, the techniques and results of the new sciences of complexity will be woven into our understanding of ecointeraction and, especially, ecointeractive dynamics, that is, evolutionary processes.

Naturally, there is no such certainty about what we will actually find out as we begin to think in the new ways. The broad outlines are fairly clear; the details, subject to serious contention. Those (and there are many) stamping their petulant feet for the instant gratification of completed science are going to have to put up with a delay while people do some serious work. Meanwhile, we can start to retune our stock of intuitions, hunches, hypotheses, and reasonable expectations about complex systems so as to be ready to evaluate new work as it comes forth. For, the *first* result of the investigation of nonlinearity, nonequilibrium, and their consequences is that many of our old expectations about how "things work" need to be revised.

What I will do here is work on some of the necessary retuning. It has to be emphasized at the earliest possible moment that nonlinearity and nonequilibrium are the *norm*. Linearity is the *exception* in real-world phenomena ranging from cosmology through biology to social systems. We have to see exactly what we leave behind when we replace the once-normal expectations grounded in an assumption of linearity with the new normal expectations grounded in the recognition of nonlinearity. In particular, we will never model technological change intelligently until we stop thinking of it as an exogenous input offering additive increments to an otherwise self-standing economic system whose trajectory is simply shifted up a bit as the result of the input. That is, technological introduction is not to be thought of as a perturbation that temporarily moves an economy away from an equilibrium to which it subsequently returns. We must *expect* that the coupling of technological innovation to the rest of the economy will be an interactive endogenous *restructuring* connection. Such interactive restructuring is absolutely common in the evolutionary trajectories of systems of all sorts, and there is no reason to think that socioeconomic systems will prove to be exceptions.

Interactive structured restructuring is always going to defeat attempts to explain in terms of the relation between an independent and a dependent variable, or make such explanations unhelpful or beside the point. But the claim that the search for explanation is not the search for an independent variable is bound to make traditional social scientists (and, indeed, traditional scientists in many fields) begin to feel uneasy. For the tradition of linear mechanism inherited from the Enlightenment, and typified, perhaps, by the allegiance to "Humean causation," is fervently committed to precisely the pattern of explanation being denied. Since I've had a lot to say about this elsewhere (Dyke 1988, 1990a, 1990b), here I'll simply summarize matters.

The overall logical situation—contrast space, as Alan Garfinkel (1981) would say—is this. Within traditional linear mechanism, if I am accused of providing the wrong explanation, then I am being accused of having identified the wrong causal condition and am urged to replace it with the right one. The situation being urged here, in the context of nonlinearity, is quite different. In this mode, we accuse (some straw man, let us suppose) of providing a wrong explanation not because the wrong causal condition is being offered (there is no *right* replacement), but because no causal condition of the appropriate linear sort is ever going to be found. The *conditions* to look for are arrays of local and global spacial patterns that shift temporally. There will be one or more *control* variables, but changing them incrementally need not produce Humean outcomes, that is, lawlike regularities. Changing a control variable may do nothing, or it may change the conditions of interaction in such a way that an apparently colossal change of pattern occurs (for, apparently, "little reason at all"). This, after all, *is what nonlinear coupling means*.

Linear mechanism looked like an adequate explanatory recipe just as long as a set of fixed conditions could be specified (or, more often, assumed), providing the background against which the "causal" variable played out its lockstep linear game. An Eleatic world; simple behavior. But except in extraordinary circumstances, no such set of fixed background conditions can be specified or assumed to hold. In a world characterized by nonlinear interactivity, backgound conditions are always fluctuating—and fluctuating beyond the range of traditional Eulerian equilibrium—since sensitive to initial conditions. A Heraclitean world; the "independent variable" never finds the same river to step in twice; complex behavior.

Note that the failure to find independent variables is just as acute in systems that are completely deterministic, and the finding of them can be guaranteed only in the sense that any initial value of a variable maps onto a consequent value. In fact, it was Poincaré's (1957) discovery that mappings produced homoclinic tangles that began what we know as modern nonlinear dynamics. The usual nonlinear dynamical system produces mappings under the control of a parameter, and examining the behavior of the system is as much a matter of understanding what happens when you vary the parameter as it is a matter of figuring out which initial assignments produce which consequent assignments. The latter is, of course, the pure Humean strategy.

A handy example we can use to further the contrast is the very fundamental process of making a white sauce. Some of the sauce-making conditions can be fixed, and are not initial-conditions-sensitive. The materials are two tablespoons of butter, two tablespoons of flour, and one cup of milk. The tolerances are not tight, and the range where scaling makes no difference is quite large. That is, you can make about a cup or about a gallon without varying the proportions of the ingredients. The order of "steps" is also fixed: melt the butter, add the flour and cook it a little, then add the milk. There are two interactive parameters, however, and this is where the dynamics lie. They are the amount of heat applied, and the whisking rate. A good sauce depends on coupling the right heat to the right whisking rate. There are three dynamical regimes: (1) Not enough heat. If you're timid about turning the heat up to a minimum threshhold, you'll never get a good sauce. You can whisk the merry bejeezes out of it, but the butter will separate, the flour will clump, and you'll be unhappy. (2) At the other end of the parameter ranges, we have too much heat. You just can't whisk fast enough for a long enough time to keep the sauce from sticking and burning. (3) The Goldilocks range where there is neither too little nor too much heat. You can get pretty good sauce anywhere in this range. At the lower heat end, you have to be careful not to whisk too vigorously or you'll froth the milk rather than melding the ingedients smoothly together. It will also take quite a lot of time, not always the best situation during a busy cooking session. So you have to dare turn the heat up a bit, and be willing to whisk attentively. In fact, the best sauces are probably made with the heat turned up a bit more than is comfortable. Then the ingredients marry and cook the best. But the whisking responsibility is a grave one. (This is why, while you can make a tolerable white sauce without a whisk, you must have a whisk to make a good one.) So the two parameters, heat and whisking rate, go up together, making their interaction a plausibly linear one—in range 3—as well as making it possible to be a good cook.

Now, how are we to deal with all this from an explanatory point of view? I suggest the following. Nothing we do in making the sauce makes the sauce. The sauce makes itself under the conditions we establish enabling it to do so. Nothing we do is an "independent variable" resulting in some predictable change in some "dependent" variable. Or, more accurately, if we set up the explanatory format in such a way that we create the appearance of such a straightforward connection, then we do something quite silly, that misses the most important and interesting things about the making of the sauce.

Now, notice the nature of the preceding claim. Nowhere have I said that an explanatory schema involving an independent and a dependent variable in apparent Humean relationship *cannot* be set up. Indeed, I assume that one can, and trivially so, since the trick of cooking a sauce is to keep things in a linear range. *Recipes,* for the neophyte, in fact try to produce a scheme that approaches the Humean one as closely as possible, as do all sets of instructions intended to enable you to do something without understanding what you're doing. Writers of software manuals get really good at providing such linearized instructions, as do the designers of software themselves. Constrain ambient conditions enough to lock a system into a linear range, and you'll always be able to produce the Humean scheme, and the consequence semblance of explanation. But, with rare exceptions, this tack simply suppresses all the interesting dynamics. After all, this is *exactly* what the instruction booklet *is meant* to accomplish, in the service of cookbook instruction.

At this point, the dedicated rationalist is up in arms, especially if dedicated to a species of rationalism that requires any sound explanation to be the unique explanation. Trading on Alan Garfinkel's conception of explanation, I've dealt with this requirement at length elsewhere. Here I'll simply say that even when a mathematical model of the $y = f(x)$ sort is the basic heuristic, nothing forces us to cast our results in the form of a Humean narrative. No a priori argument to the effect that we must do so succeeds except by fiat.

Note, also, that the claim that the sauce makes itself if we provide the right conditions, far from being an obscuring claim, is far more illuminating than most alternatives. For it points us to the chemistry of milk, butter, and flour as a next topic of culinary conversation. At that level, we could become still more enlightened about the process of sauce making, and examine the chemical dynamics hidden in the words "cook," "meld," and "marry." I forebear, except to remark that the ingredients are not operating in a linear range, and our condition-creating efforts are designed to keep the system far from equilibrium while it cooks (and at the *appropriate* equilibrium thereafter).

In addition to the explicit rejection of the Enlightenment "causal" picture, there are two interesting messages in this approach to the explanation of sauce making. The first is directly corollary to the rejection of the Enlightenment picture and links closely to recent feminist critiques of that picture. For we find that we can understand the Master Chef as one who, in respect for the bounty of nature, provides the conditions that enable the various ingredients to combine with one another so as to be especially tasty. Once we have that image, we can rethink the "master" scientist, along lines suggested to us by Keller (1983), Haraway (1991), and others. Instead of the master manipulater, the scientist becomes the nurturing enabler of complex physical process in contexts where it can be observed, measured, and understood. (If this sounds hyperbolic or excessive, it may be time to examine the assumptions and habits causing it to seem so.)

The social sciences could gain considerable benefit from this way of looking at things because it narrows the distance between "experimental" sciences and sciences that have to make do without experiments. The experimentalist is seen as maneuvering the world into position for investigation, not (necessarily) manipulating it to specification. The degree of maneuvering possible varies from case to case, even within the deeply experimental sciences themselves (Hacking 1983). The room for maneuver then shades off through sciences such as geology, astronomy, and ecology. There is no radical break along the way— especially in these days when sophisticated simulation is possible.

Second, the account of sauce making bears an obvious message with respect to our understanding of ecointeraction and technological "intervention." We can, of course, think of ourselves as "rational agents" intervening in natural processes as master manipulaters of the world around us. But we could as well think of ourselves as providing circumstances within which natural processes are enabled—or, more frequently, disabled. Nothing *compels* either conception. No rationalist a priori is available to provide the requisite necessity. By the same token, and for the same reasons, there is no compulsion to insist upon a Humean model of causality as *the* prioritized or unique pattern of explanation. But let me emphasize what should be obvious. The rejection of a Humean narrative as the prioritized explanatory pattern does not involve the rejection of mechanism as a fundamental pattern (so long as we understand that not all mechanisms are linear); nor does it involve the abandonment of the mathematical resources we have accumulated (on the contrary); nor does it involve the abandonment of determinism (though it involves the abandonment of the certainty of predictability). Humean metaphysics has to be *added* to the explanations the sciences normally provide. It isn't an intrinsic part of them.

BEGINNINGS AND ENDS

As we change our attitudes toward explanation in the light of nonlinear systems far from equilibrium, there is another issue to be addressed, the distinction between start-specific and finish-specific processes. Start-specific processes are the familiar "Humean" or "Newtonian" ones associated with classical mechanics, and mechanism in general—wrongly, of course, in my view. The best (generic) example is the ballistics trajectory. Given Newton's Laws and the muzzle velocity of a projectile, we can predict where that projectile will be at any time as it carries out its (unimpeded) trajectory. The possibility of prediction implies that the initial conditions uniquely determine future trajectory.

Finish-specific processes are ones for which we know the end point, and explain in terms of the end point, but the end point isn't associated with a unique starting point. The best cases are simple thermodynamic ones—two gasses becoming randomly mixed after a while, etc. We can predict eventual random mixture with fair certainty, but the prediction isn't based on the knowledge of any specific starting point. As a matter of fact, if we sample the system along the way to equilibrium, we'll find that our ability to guess at the starting point deteriorates as time goes by, without effecting our confidence in the end point. This is certainly not true of the ballistics trajectory. The claim of the Newtonian mechanics is that information does not deteriorate over the course of the trajectory. This, after all, is essential for the claim that the process is a reversible one.

We could, of course, try to make a big deal out of the distinction between start and finish specificity—thump on it as if it were the distinction between mechanism and teleology. This would be a mistake. Finish specificity need have nothing at all to do with purpose, for example. Furthermore, virtually nothing that happens is completely start-specific or completely finish-specific. One important asymmetry is, of course, that the second law of thermodynamics guarantees that, eventually, everything is finish-specific. But to say this is to realize how little specific finish-specificity can be.

The simple mechanistic ideal was to show that everything that happens is start-specific. We now know that this ideal can be maintained only under really bizarre constraints. In fact, we know that determinism, another ideal of classical mechanism, can be maintained far more easily than start specificity. For, chaotic systems are not start-specific unless the start is specified to a degree of accuracy unattainable in cosmic time, hence start specificity is physically meaningless with respect to them. Yet, since mechanism is most usefully defined in terms of differential equations of the appropriate sorts, chaotic systems can, of course, be characterized as mechanistic since they are characterized by deterministic equations. To bring the matter around full circle, some determistic equations, or sets of such equations, are start-specific, and others are finish-specific. Mathematics is nicely neutral with respect to the issue. In fact, if there really were "reversible" processes of the sort the Newtonian idealizations model, then it would not be possible to even distinguish between start and finish specificity with respect to them.

What are *not* nicely neutral are modern rationalist theories of causality. To a first degree of approximation, premodern rationalism required finish specificity and modern rationalism requires start specificity. (There is no postmodern rationalism.) In particular, modern rationalism holds out the ideal of deductive consistency and completeness as the mark of a truly successful project of scientific explanation. As Robert Rosen has pointed out many times, this commits the rationalist to *identify* causality with deduction. That is, when a rule is sought to associate a causal language with a mathematical formulation, an isomorphism must be chosen and the causal language adjusted accordingly. Rosen has shown how arbitrary this choice is (especially in biology). For our purposes here it's enough to point out that the post-Enlightenment rationalist scheme then requires strict start specificity in the presence of laws of alethic force as the conditions for the mapping wanted. The obvious canonical example, of course, is "Hempel-model" explanation.

The remaining attraction of start-specific systems to be reemphasized is their deep connection to aspirations of manipulation and control. The beauty of the ballistics trajectory is that with adjustments to speed of muzzle exit and direction of aim, the gunner can hope to drop the projectile on target. This beauty has contributed substantially to the attraction of the start-specific paradigm within social sciences under pressure to produce beneficial social results. So, the search for manipulable initial conditions with "lawlike" links to determined outcomes has characterized the positive social sciences throughout their histories. The connection with an underlying "Enlightenment optimism" about the tractability of social progress is obvious. As we will see, the search for manipulative control may not be an entirely intelligent one— even in the realm of technology itself. One would think that the very nature of technology as progressive instrumentality would mean that technology would need to be embedded in start-specific science. But I think we will be able to see that the situation is opposite: that technology's natural home is within basically finish-specific historical processes.

CYCLES, THE MOST COMMON STRUCTURES

Schumpeter's (1934, 1939) theory of technology is based on the observation that technology and economic cycles are intrinsically connected. The first step in our understanding of this is to recognize that all systems operating nonlinearly and far from equilibrium have lumpy histories rather than smooth ones. They are characterized by symmetry breakings, bifurcations, periodicities and quasi-periodicities. On this basis, the observation that economic systems seem to embody cycles points to intrinsic nonlinearity. Thus, the detection of cycles of various periods is centrally connected with the move to nonlinear models, and research demonstrating the reality of such cycles is an important part of the shift in normal expectations. The behavior described in the following can be taken as typical, and a sort of orienting benchmark as we move on:

> With energy input, self-organization can occur in self-assembled membranes or tissues. (Self-organization refers to processes of morphogenesis in a tissue or of dynamical activity in a membrane.) Turing showed chemical morphogens could cause a self-assembled tissue to exhibit waves that change in space and time. These waves self-organize within the self-assembled tissue, which would be homogeneously quiescent in the absence of the morphogen dynamics. The key to morphogen dynamics is energy input, which results in autocatalysis coupled to feedback inhibition. Section 4-4 showed how such mechanisms can cause constant-in-time input to result in nonharmonic, time-dependent dynamic behavior—a consequence that cannot happen in a linear system. Thus the emergent properties of nonlinear, driven, dissipative systems appear in at least three distinct ways: self-assembly, autocatalysis, and self-organization. Each manifestation is a consequence of energy flow; however, energy flow alone is not sufficient because the particular energy type and the particular substances involved determine the emergent properties (Fox 1988, p. 155).

Cycles, temporal oscillations, are the most commonly studied structural features of nonlinear nonequilibrium systems because they are most commonly present. Very few dynamical systems have been found that *do not* have oscillatory regimes. Thus, it's not surprising that oscillations have been observed in economic systems as well for centuries. In the twentieth century, most of the major attempts to account for economic cycles have used the work of Schumpeter as a starting point. Schumpeter proposed the introduction of new technologies as the key "factor" driving economic cycles. Subsequent theorists have concerned themselves with two questions: why technologies drive cycling; and why the periods should be so regular, as they seem to be. A recent contributor is Brian Berry (1991). I first summarize Berry's findings, then compare them with those of some other key theorists.

On a relatively sophisticated analysis of available economic data, Berry finds not only the long-noticed 50-odd-year Kondratieff period, but also two subperiods within it at the so-called Kuznet periods of about 25 years. Thus, in a 50 year period, there are two peaks and two valleys. Berry also finds one subcycle to be an inflationary growth cycle, and the other to be a deflationary growth cycle, so the Kondratieff is not a redundant concept. The details, as important as they are, won't concern us here since the conclusions to be drawn are the same for quite a range of scenarios. For our purposes, the salient point is Berry's understanding of the dynamics:

Technically, *there are long waves and cycles because the process is endogenous*: the essence
of a cycle is an internal dynamic that gives rise to repetition. The motions result in *timing
against an internal clock,* timing that is only approximately scaled to natural time. Ample
evidence of *recurrence* has been provided....there is sufficient evidence for a long wave
theory. Because the mechanisms are endogenous, however, such a "theory" will surely have
an unfamiliar form, with cause and consequence reversing roles at different times in a system
of feedback loops that result in extreme boom and bust (Berry 1991, p. 128).

We first have to note that Berry thinks he has detected chaos through his
methods. This is, strictly speaking, not true. It's really quite hard to show that
an empirical system is chaotic; for example, how we would ever be able to
find negative Liapunov exponents in the system Berry constructs is anybody's
guess. But my claim is that the crucial distinction is not between what can
formally be shown to be chaotic and what cannot, but between what is linear
and what is not. For, it's the latter dividing line that has the important impact
on our normal expectations and normal investigative techniques. The major
contrast is between an economy that finds a "moving" point equilibrium and
one that does not. Furthermore, from a practical point of view, it might not
be very significant even if the system were chaotic. It's all a matter of how
the questions we want answered are related to the time scale at which the system
is chaotic. For instance, we know that Pluto's trajectory is chaotic, but over
any given astronomer's lifetime that doesn't come to much. For most purposes,
it's more useful to treat Pluto's orbit as slightly noisily periodic.

Furthermore, Pluto's dynamics are fairly well isolated, while as Berry,
Mokyr (1990), and Hall/Preston (1988) all are careful to point out, economies
are very interactively involved with other social systems—and climatological
systems, for that matter—no matter how we decide to draw their boundaries.
So if Berry's analysis of the data really does exhibit Kondratievs and
subperiods, it's that pattern we ought to try to explain, and not, for example,
try to find the "system of equations" whose asymptotic behavior is some sort
of strange attractor.

It is worth noting, however, that finding the Kondratieffs and subperiods
indicates that, like most other phenomena, economic systems have a
characteristic scale or, as a dynamicist would say, a characteristic first return
time. Investigation of characteristic scales is largely in its beginning stages, so
it would be foolish to speculate on the scale determinants here. It's far from
foolish to note the fact, however, since far from introducing another mystery,
it assimilates at least some social phenomena to phenomena in other realms
and guides the sorts of questions to be asked.

We can now bring Hall and Preston (1988) into the picture, and note that
they agree with Berry that the cycles are *endogenously* generated:

We think that clusters of key interrelated technologies, developing through backward and
forward linkages, are the real triggers of long waves; therefore the aim should be to try

to identify them. We believe that they tend to come forward at points when the returns from existing investments are declining. We accept the theory that as a result there is likely to be a disjuncture between the optimal application of the new technologies and the prevailing socio-economic mode of organization; thus, the development of initial innovations, and still more their general diffusion, may well be delayed by years or even decades; only when the two are again brought into harmony will the long wave upswing begin. Further, since the changes in organization are crucial they may permit the "rejuvenation" of industries based on older technologies, which may therefore go through more than one Kondratieff upswing. However, the pace of this resolution may vary from country to country and from region to region....

If the transition from one Kondratieff to the next requires not merely clusters of hardware innovations but transformations of the whole socio-economic framework, then in a sense the whole process is endogenous: the underlying mechanism is indeed the laws of motion of capitalism, represented by a falling rate of profit, which eventually must trigger not merely a set of technological innovations but also changes in the economic, social, and political superstructure (Hall and Preston 1988, pp. 25-26).

Now, we have to be a bit careful about the issue of endogenous and exogenous causation. At a crucial point, the discussion got thoroughly tangled in debates among latter-day Marxists and their critics about whether capitalism is a self-righting, self-regenerating system (identified with endogenous causation), or whether it would take a revolution (exogenous cause) to rescue it from its final dive. Expressed this way, the issue is spurious, for it assumes from the start, and on both sides, that economy is isolated and operating near equilibrium. Looked at this way, an eternally viable capitalism would have to be a perpetual motion machine. Not a likely prospect in anyone's view.

What is *right* in the insistence that "causation is endogenous" is the perception that cycles are a normal feature of the (nonlinear) dynamics. What is *wrong* is then to go on to look for the endogenous independent variable that drives the cycles. Talk of endogenous cause is also wrong because economies, like virtually everything else, are open systems operating between a source and a sink, and from that point of view the dynamics are driven by the influx of matter and energy. This does *not* make the incoming matter and energy independent variables in the standard linear sense, of course. Assessing the role of technology in economic evolution, Joel Mokyr says:

There are no one-line explanations here, no simple theorems. It is hard to think of conditions that would be either necessary or sufficient for a high level of technological creativity. A variety of social, economic, and political factors enter into the equation to create a favorable climate for technological progress. At the same time, a favorable environment may itself be insufficient if the new technological ideas fail to arise. The dynamic of this evolutionary process generated a rich historical pattern of long periods of stasis or very gradual change, punctuated at times by clusters of feverish progress in which radical inventions created new techniques with an abruptness that does not square with the adage that Nature does not make leaps (Mokyr 1990, p. 299).

THE EVOLUTIONARY SCENARIO

With the suspicion by the several authors that no independent variable is likely to be found to account for the temporal structures they have identified, we have landed right in the middle of an important current controversy concerning evolutionary theory. Darwinian fundamentalism is being challenged in several spheres by the theoreticians of complexity, who offer various evolutionary scenarios in contrast to the orthodox Darwinian scenario. Evolutionary economics, indeed, has *its* fundamentalist Darwinians, Nelson and Winter (1982; Dosi et al. 1988). In a series of works they, too, have pursued a line of thought that attempts to work out the Schumpeterian insights on technological advance. In addition, the scenario they offer is quite straightforwardly Darwinian. Contrasting their theory with theories of complexity is an obvious way to assess the impact of the latter.

The Darwinian scenario Nelson and Winter put forward imagines particular technological "advances" as phenotypes subjected to selection by a market economy. The introducers of technologies are considered to be carrying out a rational search pattern within a phase-space of cost-benefit possibilities in order to locate regions of marginal superiority. The scenario is a straightforward "survival of the fittest" one, with superior technologies eventually replacing earlier inferior ones.

Darwinian theory is by now orthodox and ever safe. Its safety lies largely in its ad hoc unassailability, that is, its capacity to generate what critics like Gould have called "Just-So Stories." In hindsight, it's always easy to say that one technology has outcompeted another on the simple ground that it survives while the other has disappeared. But this strategy is exactly what produces the trivializations of Darwinism. As I have argued before (Dyke 1988), the Darwinian explanations worthy of our attention are those that establish the closure conditions for differential survival. In fact, Mokyr is pretty good on this point, realizing that under many conditions two or several techniques can thrive together for long periods, because they don't, in fact, compete with one another. The clearest cases are those in which geographical separation of economies withdraws the conditions for direct competition. The next clearest cases are those in which traditional social practices are still strong enough to stand up against the economic totalization of value. The third sort of case, interesting for the sociological questions it raises, is that in which status boundaries are erected to protect and perpetuate historical techniques. Arts and crafts movements and prestigious producers of traditionally made "reproductions" are the obvious examples. Not only do these phenomena have their (marginal, of course) economic place, but they often become a significant component of the process of social distinction that produces and reproduces a system of class fractions (Bourdieu 1984).

So, what these cases show us is that the conditions of competition can't be *assumed,* but must on one hand be created and on the other hand made explicit when a Darwinian explanation is offered. Mokyr sees this through a glass darkly. In the historical survey that takes up most of his book he is sensitive to this complexity, but he doesn't handle it very well in his theoretical account. In particular, what he doesn't see is that to make the usual economistic assumptions is to beg all the evolutionary questions. That is, it is to decide a priori at which level the operative dynamics are working.

As I have shown elsewhere (Dyke 1988), with respect to biological evolution, it is all too easy to confect surface bookkeeping that seems to indicate a competitive game. But it's almost impossible to confect a surface bookkeeping that is *uniquely* associated with competition. This means, in the case at hand, that newly arising technologies can *always* be made to look like Darwinian competitors. Indeed, they can be thought of that way by the innovators themselves, and by analysts with a particular point of view. But it doesn't follow that the eventual explanation we ought to accept is the Darwinian one.

In particular, the concept of "searching" embedded in the Nelson/Winter model is an interesting one but, I think, misplaced—just as it would be in biological evolution. The major cause of the misplacement involves the tendency to confuse finish specificity with purposiveness. The searching that goes on in noisy nonlinear systems takes place as "random" fluctuations. In most cases, these are *thermo*dynamic fluctuations, relevant to what happens at other dynamical levels but explanatorily decoupled from them.

One of the common scenarios is the following: (1) Per Bak (Bak, Tang, and Wiesenfeld 1988) has identified criticality at the edge of chaos as the locus of autocatakinetic events. (2) But a system in a chaotic regime is always at the edge of chaos; there are periodic trajectories infinitely densely in chaotic attractors, thus infinitely close to any chaotic trajectory. (3) Shinbrot, Grebogi, Ott, and York (1993) have shown that on the basis of (2) a chaotic system may be capable of being "tuned" to some period, and the method of tuning is the introduction of fluctuations. That is, structure (in this case, temporal structure) is a consequence of a system's being induced to explore its state space through fluctuations.

So, Nelson's searchings look like rational behavior when looked at from the point of view of orthodox economic thinking. From a dynamical point of view we recognize that the system reads these searchings as noise. What looks to be under rational control need not, in fact, be under rational control. Similarly, changes in biological populations can look as if they are "under the control" of selection mechanisms but in fact not be at all the result of selection pressure at the organismic level. One of the usual indications that the orthodox Darwinians see the point here is that they shift over (usually belligerently) to burden-of-proof challenges at this point, as if their story were somehow the solidly legitimated one. It's not. The exact same dialectical move is, of course, standard in the social sphere where rational choice theory pretends to scientific entrenchment rather than the ideological hegemony it actually enjoys. Burden-of-proof moves are point scorers, but they never lead us to learn very much.

However, the priority given to rational choice explanation gives us a chance to think of one of the more intriguing consequences of nonlinearity in social contexts: the apparent ubiquity of "unintended consequences." First, we have to reflect that the traditional rationalist patterns of explanation involve a stylized scenario in which consequences are rationally predictable outcomes of value informed plans. The scenario imagines a Rational Economic Man (REM) producing something with the prospect of bringing it to market, where he will, on the basis of rational pricing decisions, trade it for other goods in such a way that his gains are maximized subject to the ambient constraints of the market. Any confidence that the scenario of the REM will work out as planned must be based on the assumption that the system of production and trade will remain in a linear regime. Under such circumstances, unintended consequences can be discounted as the result of unfortunate imperfections—theoretically eliminable and practically adjustable. For in the REM scenario, the engine that runs the economic dynamics is the rational behavior of the economic actors themselves. The conceded *ubiquity* of unintended consequences is simply lamented.

From the point of view of the sciences of nonlinearity, on the other hand, "unintended consequences" are a fully expected feature of the dynamics, and it would be as silly to try to explain global systematic behavior on the basis of the plans of REMs as it would be to explain the formation of Benard cells on the basis of the behavior of individual molecules. Now we must be careful here. The point is *not* that the behavior of individual REMs (or molecules) is *irrelevant* to what's happening in the system. Further, there is no thought of denying that in both cases, in the very special circumstances of linear behavior very near equilibrium, a reduction of sorts can be performed in which either statistical mechanics or orthodox REM theory can indeed provide explanations. The point, rather, that ought to be clear by now, is that neither Benard cells nor modern economies operate within the linear range. Far from equilibrium, the wannabee REMs of the modern economy can hardly expect global outcomes to be confined to the range they would be confined to if the system were operating in the linear range. *Many* aspects of the economy will look like unintentional consequences. To return to Nelson and Winter, then, there is a big difference between conceptualizing technological innovation as a rational search and conceptualizing it as random fluctuation that may or may not be captured in a global dynamics. From the point of view of the economy, it could well be the latter, irrespective of what the innovators themselves may think.

TECHNOLOGY: THE EXPLORATION OF PHASE SPACE

Now, we can move to a more concrete look at ways of connecting theoretical insights with what we actually see happening. Here is where the methodological situation laid out earlier has to be respected, for we know that we cannot expect to make concrete predictions in the ways we are used to when dealing with simplicity. Instead, what we can do is put forward a set of reasonable expectations (Dyke 1990b) about patterns of phenomena that will characteristically show up and the kind of spatio-temporal structures we are likely to see. These reasonable expectations constitute the sort of hypotheses we must learn to work with as we explore nonlinear systems operating far from equilibrium.

In the presence of technological innovation, above all, cycles as gradients are created and exhausted, giving rise to conditions under which new sorts of fluctuations can occur under new circumstances of capture. Furthermore, to confirm the suspicions of Berry, Mokyr, and Hall/Preston, there is no point in looking for the independent variable, the "start" of a cycle, in the microbehavior. Technology doesn't start things; demand doesn't start things. They, along with the rest of the "economic" activities we are familiar with, are interactive parts of a system within which, as Berry put it, cause and consequence reverse roles at different times. Prime movers are not to be found.

The perception that an economy is a system of gradients is, of course, far from a new or idiosyncratic one. In fact, it's ubiquitous in the standard talk of cash flow, competitive advantage, balance of payments, and much else in orthodox economic theorizing. The evolution of an economic system is thus, among other things, the history of gradients, their appearance and disappearance, changes in their spatial and temporal locations, the rates at which they transfer matter and energy, and the rates at which they produce equilibria. Technological advance is relevant to economic evolution insofar as it affects the history of gradients.

Following Schumpeter's typology will help here. The Adam Smithian effects of technology, the facilitation of flow, are most visible, because advances in transportation technology directly effect the rates of flow along well-established gradients or allow flows along new gradients. In this vein, we might class as one of the historically most important technological advances the development of financial instruments in the age of the great fairs (Braudel 1984). For they clearly enabled the expanded exploitation of long-range gradients. In these cases, that which flows remains the same. *Where* it flows and the *rate* at which it flows are affected. A next sort of technological advance produces material or energy gradients that did not exist before. The development of the aluminum industry in this century is a good example of this sort of advance, one of hundreds that could be cited. Here, we are talking precisely about *what* flows. The third sort of technological advance is that which introduces new competing techniques into already existing flows. Typically, these innovations affect rate of flow indirectly by affecting price.

Each of the three species of technological advance can operate within a linear range. Then, talk of rate change, opening of new directions of flow, and even the establishment of new gradients can be confined to considerations of additivity. But each of the species can also operate in a nonlinear range, and in this case structural changes can be expected. Obviously, this is a direct analogy with what can be expected of an ecosystem. Or, rather, continues to be an analogy, since ecosystems are virtually always conceptualized as natural economies.

The shifting and rearrangement of gradients, then, is one of the things we can confidently look for in the long-term behavior of the world economy. From this point of view, Fernand Braudel, as I have said before (Dyke 1990a), was one of the first thinkers tuned to a nonlinear dynamical conceptualization of the world economy. (As far as I know, this tuning was empirically and intuitively based. He *noticed* what a dynamicist would *look for*.) He draws our attention to an intriguing phenomenon that can provide us with a final test for our intuitions as well as an example of the sort of hypothesis we can expect to see more of as the new sciences of complexity move forward. For as long as world capitalism has been decently well established—that is, for as far back as it makes much sense to look for Kondratievs and the like—the economy has not only cycled, it has precessed. Roughly, on the evidence of Braudel and yesterday's newspaper, its center (which can be specified rather precisely in terms of financial activity) has moved from Genoa to the Low Countries to London to New York, and is now located somewhere on the western rim of the Pacific Basin. For somebody focused on sources and sinks, this makes perfectly good sense. The search for the creation and maintainance of gradients is, in economic terms, above all a search for new raw material and cheap labor as sources, and a search for terminal consumers as sinks. From that point of view, migrating colonialism is as expectable as the introduction of technique.

Whatever the retrospective advantages and disadvantages of the historical movement of the center of the world economy, we can say with certainty that it was never the object of rational strategy in those terms. As usual, this is not to deny that rational strategies directed at other ends had something to do with the result. In the same way, the spread of climax forest in abandoned land can't be assigned to the rational strategies of the flora involved. Ultimately, the two phenomena are to be understood in terms of the system imperative of maximum rate of entropy production (Swenson 1989). But we can get a bit closer to an account of the specifics.

As nation after nation has joined the world economy, at least since the early beginnings of the capitalist era early in this millenium, the characteristic pattern has been that the nation finds a niche in this economy by (1) exploiting a natural advantage (classic economic lore), and (2) gaining control of some of its important boundary conditions. The most important, and surely most conspicuous, boundary conditions early on were the conditions of the reliability of trade. This is documented thoroughly with respect to two aspects: military strength to secure trade, and technical achievements in transportation both on the sea and on land. The first is, of course, continuous with the ancient pattern carried through the medieval period by the Islamic traders. The second is the modern reprise of something that had stagnated for centuries. The two "paradigm" cases of this are the Venetian Republic (Lane 1973), and the British Empire in its heyday.

However, the boundary condition most crucial for the advent and growth of modern economies is labor supply. So much is a matter of agreement from one end of the ideological spectrum where capital is defined as the capacity to command labor, to the other where the history of capitalism is identified as the class struggle engendered by the organization of the industrial labor force.

Technique organizes labor. This is a truism visible in the transitions that took place at the advent of the factory system, the advent of the assembly line, and the advent of automation and robotics, but discernible at less spectacular levels with nearly every technological advance. At every stage of technological advance, the labor force has to be reorganized (and redisciplined) to some extent or other. The changes in the typical worker's way of life attendant on the reorganization can range from minimal to catastrophic—from retraining to migration (Dyke 1988, ch. 10). The maintenance of discipline, political order and at least minimal "allegiance" require that any successive reorganization couple workers into the production process in a way that satisfies their short-term needs and provides at least the illusion of supporting their long-term aspirations. In the modern state, this means that the labor force must have access to commodity markets, as Henry Ford saw so perceptively. As terminal consumers, the labor force also provides an important sink, of course.

If the population remained stable and aspirations were modest, it might be possible to get such a system to operate in a linear range. But one of the main ways technology feeds back into the system is through the promotion of population growth. Increased populations have to be coupled into the system of consumption. (When it isn't possible to do so by involving them in the production system, you do so by putting them into make-work maintenance, such as the service industry or the military, or by explicitly instituting a welfare system.) So any national economy has to grow either to "provide jobs" (the only remaining viable bit of political rhetoric in countries with mature economies) or provide the dole—hence the modern welfare state. This has all been going on within a small range of variations and styles for nearly a millenium.

From a dynamical point of view, it is no surprise that the well-known cycles discussed by Berry, Hall/Preston, and Mokyr occur. But the way to describe them, in general, is in terms of the successive creation and gradual disappearance of gradients. The story of these gradients in terms of return on investment isn't *wrong,* but it doesn't go to the dynamical heart of the matter.

Second, the multiple couplings of the work force into the economy are themselves the source of pervasive nonlinearity. This has, in fact, been investigated theoretically by Goodwin and his Sienese colleagues (Goodwin, Kruger, and Vercelli 1983), and by Gabisch and Lorenz (1987). They show, for example, how the equations for the Tobin curve produce periodic and chaotic regimes. Looked at from a more thermodynamic perspective, the multiple couplings of the work force create and dissipate gradients. This is more straightforward than it sounds, for what it means is that the profitability of investment depends heavily on labor costs. This is no surprise, even for the orthodox. This is what motivates the Tobin curves in the first place. On the Schumpeterian view, of course, it also drives the search for technology.

We can now imagine a space of labor force reorganizations and technological advances *possible* for a given "unit" in the economy, where "units" is the word for whatever structures have emerged historically. In our world, more often than not the units we are concerned with happen to be nation-states, at one scale, and firms at another. "*Possible*" is in italics to remind us that we need to consider it "realistically" rather than from an a priori point of view (see Dyke 1988). Once the gradients available in that possibility space are exhausted, new ones have to be found. That means that the system of constraints and enablements producing the possibility in the first place have themselves to change. (Notice that when stated at this level of generality, this is the handwaving replacement for the old questions about endogenous and exogenous cause referred to by Hall and Preston. The advantage is that this formulation is neither trapped at this level of generality, nor stuck with finding a linear causal factor [see above]).

The traditional way of renewing gradients, either by finding sources of cheap labor or avoiding the extreme costs of replacing production infrastructures (the snail shells nations carry around with them), is to colonize in one form or other. In the very early days of capitalism, this meant finding new sources of trade goods and new markets. Under industrial capitalism until the end of the Second World War it meant colonization *tout court.* Now, it means a complex of asymmetric investment and trade. So, the internal dynamical pattern of an economic unit is one of cycles, as we have seen. And these cycles spread to the extent of the significant couplings between economic units, now worldwide of course. But superimposed on this is the Braudelian precession—no Spenglerian or Toynbeean romantic march of destiny, but a normal succession of systems adjustments to a succession of rearrangements of gradients.

The hypothesis is that no national economy can indefinitely sustain the gradients that brought it to the fore. These gradients are transferred elsewhere as the conditions of possibility for the ascendency of new nations. The *point* of the hypothesis is that the phenomenon is the absolutely mundane and expectable consequence of the sort of system in play. Exactly analogous phenomena occur in ecosystems for the "same kinds" of reasons. The perceived ordinariness—when it is seen from the point of view of the dynamics of complex systems—of what from a traditional point of view seems spectacular and mysterious, is surely one of the reasons for giving the new sciences of complexity their innings. For this same shift from mystery to ordinariness has characterized many scientific advances, signal among them the movements of the planets in the heavens. Of course, we always do lose the romance of things as we understand them. The moon isn't a goddess, but a big rock. The world economy isn't a triumph of human reason, but a big, lumbering, clumsy, thermodynamic engine.

REFERENCES

Bak, P., C. Tang, and K. Wiesenfeld. 1988. "Self-organized Criticality." *Physics Review* A38.

Berry, B.J.L. 1991. *Long-wave Rhythms in Economic Development and Political Behavior.* Baltimore and London: Johns Hopkins University Press.

Bourdieu, Pierre. 1984. *Distinction: A Social Critique of the Judgment of Taste.* Cambridge, MA: Harvard University Press.

Braudel, Fernand. 1984. *Civilization & Capitalism 15th-18th Century,* Vol. III: *The Perspective of the World.* New York: Harper and Row.

Dosi, G., et. al. 1988. *Technical Change and Economic Theory.* London and New York: Pinter.

Dyke, C. 1988. *The Evolutionary Dynamics of Complex Systems: A Study in Biosociocial Complexity.* Oxford: Oxford University Press.

_____. 1990a. "Strange Attraction, Curious Liaison: Clio Meets Chaos." *The Philosophical Forum* 21(4): 369-392.

_____. 1990b. "Explanations and Strategies in a Nonlinear World." *Systems Research* 7(3): 117-126.

Fox, R. 1988. *Energy and the Evolution of Life.* New York: W.H. Freeman.

Gabisch, G., and H. Lorenz. 1987. *Business Cycle Theory: A Survey of Methods and Concepts.* Lecture Notes in Economics and Mathematical Systems No. 283. New York: Springer-Verlag.

Garfinkel, A. 1981. *Forms of Explanation.* New Haven, CT: Yale University Press.

Goodwin, R.M., M. Kruger, and A. Vercelli. 1983. *Nonlinear Models of Fluctuating Growth.* Lecture Notes in Economics and Mathematical Systems, No. 228. New York: Springer-Verlag.

Hacking, I. 1983. *Representing and Intervening.* Cambridge: Cambridge University Press.

Hall, P., and P. Preston. 1988. *The Carrier Wave: New Information Technology and the Geography of Innovation, 1846-2003.* London: Unwin Hyman.

Haraway, D.J. 1991. *Simians, Cyborgs, and Women: The Reinvention of Nature.* New York: Routledge.

Keller, E.F. 1983. *A Feeling for the Organism: The Life and Work of Barbara McClintock.* New York: W.H. Freeman.

Lane, F.C. 1973. *Venice: A Maritime Republic.* Baltimore, MD: Johns Hopkins.

Lewin, R. 1992. *Complexity at The Edge of Chaos.* New York: Macmillan.

Mokyr, J. 1990. *The Lever of Riches: Technological Creativity and Economic Progress.* Oxford: Oxford Uuniversity Press.

Nelson, R.R., and S. Winter. 1982. *An Evolutionary Theory of Economic Change.* Cambridge, MA: Harvard University Press.

Poincaré, H. [1957] *Les Methodes Nouvelles de la Mechanique Celeste.* New York: Dover reprint.

Schumpeter, J. 1934. *The Theory of Capitalist Development.* Cambridge, MA: Harvard University Press.

————. 1939. *Business Cycles.* New York: McGraw-Hill.

Shinbrot, T., C. Grebogi, E. Ott, and J.A. York. 1993. "Using Small Perturbations to Control Chaos." *Nature* 363(6428, June 3): 411-417.

Swenson, R. 1989. "Emergent Attractors and the Law of Maximum Entropy Production: Foundations to a Theory of General Evolution." *Systems Research* 6(3): 187-197.

Turing, A. 1952. "The Chemical Basis of Morphogenesis." *Philosophical Transactions of the Royal Society, London.* Series B 237.

Vellupillai, K. ed. 1990. *Nonlinear and Multisectoral Macrodynamics: Essays in Honor of Richard Goodwin.* New York: New York University Press.

Waldrop, M.M. 1992. *Complexity: The Emerging Synthesis at the Edge of Chaos.* New York: Simon and Shuster.

THE POLITICAL ECONOMY OF ENVIRONMENTAL PROBLEMS AND POLICIES:

CONSCIOUSNESS, CONFLICT, AND CONTROL CAPACITY

Allan Schnaiberg

ABSTRACT

I present a political-economic analysis of the dialectical conflict, and the role of the modern state in managing it, that exists between the use values of ecosystems (wherein natural resources are directly utilized for subsistence, habitat, or recreation), and the exchange values of ecosystems (wherein natural resources are transformed into commodities that can be marketed.) Modern environmental conflicts are compounded because most use-value interested citizen groups also depend on wages and, thus, are part of the modern treadmill of production, which uses profits from environmental extraction to develop more capital-intensive ways of extracting still more resources. While capital owners and managers try

Advances in Human Ecology, Volume 3, pages 23-64.
Copyright © 1994 by JAI Press Inc.
All rights of reproduction in any form reserved.
ISBN: 1-55938-760-2

to accelerate the treadmill and skew citizen consciouness toward maximizing exchange values, modern states act with volatility but tilt toward permitting expanded extraction. The result of the dialectic is the management of scarcities allocated to producers, consumers, and workers—a synthesis that is reproduced internationally and intranationally, and at local and global ecological scales.

INTRODUCTION

In the past two decades of Western industrial society, there has been more attention paid to the physical-biotic basis of societal functioning than at any previous time in industrial history. By "attention," I refer to verbal, written, and other means of social communcation about the natural environment. Paradoxically, it is by no means clear that there has been net improvement in the functioning of this natural environment (Commoner 1987; World Resources Institute 1992; Worldwatch Institute 1991). This is so despite the historically unprecedented proliferation of policymaking devoted to some form of "environmental protection." During this period, moreover, political attention to such problems has ranged from local concerns to national, international, and, increasingly, to global concerns (e.g., Dowie 1992; Dunlap and Mertig 1992; Gore 1992; Falkenmark 1990). Indeed, within this relatively short period, there have been two United Nations conferences on environmental issues, in Stockholm in 1972 and in Rio de Janeiro in 1992.

This paper seeks to lay out an explanation for this paradox, applying some general paradigms of political economy to the particulars of environmental conflicts. Most of the examples here are drawn from the social-environmental context of the United States, since it is the terrain I know best. However, many of the general arguments will apply, to varying degrees, to other industrial, industrializing, and underdeveloped states in the modern world-system (e.g., Buttel 1985; Lipietz 1987; Redclift 1987; Court 1990; Schnaiberg and Gould 1994). Political economy is one theoretical perspective on social structure and change. It examines economic class structures and their social consequences, including socioeconomic and political dynamics. One crucial focus from political economy is its emphasis on sociopolitical legitimation and social control of economic and related activity. It seeks to trace the roots of both stability and change in sociopolitical conflicts (Mankoff 1972, p. 6). In the case of environmental conflicts, this seems especially appropriate. Analysts have increasingly offered "solutions" to emerging *global* environmental problems such as global warming, ozone depletion, and water scarcity (e.g., Vaahtorantz 1990), often through a program of *sustainable development* (Ayres 1989; Court 1990). However, the view I present in this paper shares a critical stance toward the "new globalism" (Redclift 1987; Davis 1991; Schnaiberg and Gould 1994; Hecht and Cockburn 1992), which is not necessarily new (e.g., Grove 1992) nor solely global (e.g., Newhouse 1992; Buttel and Taylor 1992) in nature.

The most salient *global* social force is the diffusion of liquid capital. From this perspective, I view global problems as the outcome of the interaction between powerful global forces representing the interests of capital-owning classes in industrial societies, and the political, economic, and social forces of classes, sectors, and social groups in every social and economic context where this capital has been applied. Thus, the patterns of conflict depicted in this paper apply to a considerable degree to *every* level of environmental disorganization, from the local to the global (e.g., Brown and Mikkelsen 1990). My emphasis in this paper differs somewhat from the recent view of Buttel and Taylor (1992). They call for environmental sociologists to concentrate on the institutions regulating the global economy itself, and its relation to global environmental change. The guiding assumption of this paper, in contrast, is that many (though not all—e.g., Schnaiberg and Gould 1994) of the dynamics of the global economic and environmental regulatory agencies are shaped by the processes outlined here.

My central goal in this paper is to understand why and how "environmental problems" have been subjected to varying but generally limited political responses in the United States in the twentieth century. Variability and limitation have been largely independent of the scientifically assessed levels of pollution or depletion of ecological systems. Rather, they reflect changes in the power and interests of capitalist producers, social and political movements, and state agencies and actors. Put otherwise, the environment rarely "speaks for itself." It requires social agents to raise political-economic claims about physical-biotic environmental problems, much as is the case with any overtly social problem (e.g., poverty or racism—see Spector and Kitsuse 1977).

The basic conceptual-theoretical paradigm I will use here is as follows. All actors involved in political-economic conflicts around environmental issues have interests in using some parts of ecological systems (Catton and Dunlap 1989). Further, it can be argued that environmental conflicts are about the scarcity of these ecosystem elements, as experienced by groups or social classes. They are thus struggles over decisions to allocate or restrict access by such classes or groups to ecosystems. Moreover, these interests are organized within the structure of modern industrial society that I have elsewhere labeled the treadmill of production (Schnaiberg 1980, ch. 5; Schnaiberg and Gould 1994).[1] This treadmill and its associated class structure is reproduced by a shared commitment of virtually all actors in advanced industrial society to some form of economic expansion, in order to meet their material needs.

The core logic of the treadmill is that ecosystem elements are converted by capitalists through market exchanges into profits. Capitalists reinvest some of these profits in more productive physical capital, which requires still greater ecosystem access to "efficiently" operate this equipment, that is, to generate exchange values and eventually profits by using this equipment in and on ecosystems. This technological change, in turn, raises the capital-intensification of production. Thus, because a growing share of national production is then required to repay capital owners, expanded ecosystem use is necessary. Production must generate enough surplus to support this outlay to capital owners, to provide enough additional exchange values and social surplus to supply an adequate level of wages to maintain consumer demand, and to generate enough tax revenue to cover social expenditures of the state. This need for increasing exchange values typically accelerates the environmental demands of modern treadmills. It is this dominant institutional and cultural commitment to expanding the production of commodities that many contemporary social and ecological theorists see as the root of alienation of humans from natural ecological systems (e.g., Schumacher 1973; Devall 1980; Evernden 1985).

One way of decomposing the treadmill is to examine social classes and their segments within it. At its simplest, we can contrast the major conflicts between capitalist producers and environmentalists, and the role of the state as "mediator" of these conflicts. Producers, whether capitalist or socialist (Goldman 1972; Stretton 1976; Feshbach and Friendly 1991), are largely organized around environmental resources. They attempt to capture the exchange values of such resources through the producers' operation in various economic markets. Because of the routinized calculation of monetary profits, these producers are highly conscious of their material interests in access to such natural resources. Producers mobilize all forms of control capacity (social, political, and economic assets) to capture the exchange values in markets, as well as to influence the modern state, which partly regulates access to ecosystems. Part of the treadmill's bias is that exchange-value benefits are often specific individual goods (e.g, wages, jobs, social security payments), while environmental use-value benefits are diffused collective goods (e.g., clean air, clean water, nature preserves). Individual workers and their families are thus more attentive to their "interests" in the treadmill expansion than in ecosystems, ceteris paribus.

Environmental movement organizations and participants usually have more diffused and diverse mixtures of use-value interests in ecosystems. These range from biological sustenance (from air, water, and agricultural land) to recreational or aesthetic interests in these systems viewed as natural habitats. This interest in use value is usually not directly tied into these movements' activity in economic markets. (One exception is the Nature Conservancy, which purchases tracts of land in the marketplace and converts them into nature preserves rather than resources for production.) However, economic issues such as the levels of taxes for waste or sewage disposal are nonetheless involved in many of these conflicts. By ignoring this distributional issue, environmental movements and environmental agencies become more vulnerable to attacks by potential movement supporters representing the poorer, more disempowered social classes within the United States (van Vliet 1990; Bullard 1990; Schnaiberg 1991; Bryant and Mohai 1992; Betz 1992; Gould 1992). Similar *intersocietal* conflicts against "elitist" environmental movements and their proposals for rainforest protection have emerged from those mobilizing the more disempowered and impoverished groups in Third World societies. Paradoxically, as Rudel and Horowitz (1993) note, it is the allocation of capital from industrial society elites (as well as indigenous elites) that has helped *deforest* tropical rainforests, in the process diminishing the traditional livelihoods of the peasantry. This control over resources exerted by capital controlled by industrial society elites has led to widespread but generally ineffectual opposition (Redclift 1987; Davis 1991; Gore 1992; Rudel and Horowitz 1993; Stonich 1990; Wad, Lavengood, and Scallon 1991). Such interclass and international conflict intensified at the United Nations conferences, from Stockholm in 1972 to Rio in 1992 (Bidwai 1992; Hecht and Cockburn 1992; Begley 1992; Adler and Hager 1992; Little 1992). With the declining economic status of the middle class in the United States, as capital is increasingly allocated outside the U.S. (Barlett and Steele 1992), the burden of environmental protection may also become an issue among middle class voters and their environmental movement organizations (Landy, Roberts, and Thomas 1990). This would parallel the recent upsurge of concern among minorities and the poor (Schnaiberg, Gould and Weinberg 1992; Bullard 1990; Bryant and Mohai 1992).

In contrast to producers, then, environmental movement organizations have diverse, conflicting, and unclear consciousness about environmental protection issues (Gould 1991a; Weinberg 1991b). Their assessment of potential use values from ecosystems are more indeterminate than are many of the market exchange-value estimates done by producers (Meidinger and Schnaiberg 1980). Workers and their labor organizations fall somewhere in the middle of this continuum. They have both exchange-value interests in ecosystem access, as workers in production organizations that are subject to environmental protection regulation; and use-value interests, as citizens living in ecosystems that are being disorganized by these production organizations (Schnaiberg 1983a, 1983b, 1986a,b; Burton 1986; Buttel 1986; Rohrschneider 1991). These groups, who constitute the bulk of the class structure, are thus potential adherents of environmental movement ideologies (Mitchell 1980). But they are always equally capable of being politically mobilized by capitalist classes who employ them in labor markets and who supply them in consumer markets.

Much environmental movement activity has increasingly focused on the political arena, where various actors or agencies attempt to influence the modern state. The state is more than a neutral mediator of competing interests, however. Modern structural theories of the state have moved well beyond the earlier academic consensus around this pluralistic model of mediation (Buttel

1985), although the concept of mediation still exists at the local and national level (e.g., Crowfoot and Wondolleck 1991; Bukro 1992; cf. Schnaiberg 1992c). Three major perspectives on the advanced industrial state have emerged in the past 20 years, each of which has some relevance for this paper.

Instrumentalist views of the state (Miliband 1969) conceptualize it as an agent of the interests of the capitalist class. State actors and agencies reflect the domination by the activities of the members of the dominant class of capitalist producers. A revision of this perspective by Poulantzas (1973a, 1973b) envisioned the state as a reflection of the entire class structure of advanced industrial societies. This structural concept of the state theorized that the major goal of the state apparatus was to reproduce the capital logic of the society, with a broader and longer-term perspective than that imposed by the immediate interests of any segment or fraction of the capitalist class itself. The most recent reformulation of the state, most widely expressed in the work of Skocpol (1980) and her students, offers a more complex and dynamic view of the state. State actors and agencies are conceptualized as having some autonomous interests of their own, and this becomes a factor in determining state actions. As well, this concept of a state-logic argues that the state's policies are more volatile than suggested by the earlier conceptualizations. The embeddedness of the state in national and world-systemic contexts produces a historical and comparative variability across time and states because of the opportunities and constraints that this offers to state actors and to various classes in advanced industrial societies.

My own perspective in this paper is that the state has severe internal conflicts around environmental issues. It has a dual role both as a facilitator of capital accumulation and economic growth, and as a social legitimator of the socioeconomic structure for the citizenry (O'Connor 1973, 1988). The former role commits the state to looking at environmental resources for their exchange values. Conversely, the latter leads the state to view ecosystems' capacities to produce the use values (as habitat and/or biosocial resources) of various constituents, who are among the political constituencies of state actions. These conflicts are often expressed across state agencies, such as the overt and persistent struggles between the Environmental Protection Agency (EPA) and the Department of Commerce (Landy et al. 1990; Yeager 1991). These are the familiar public battles over environmental regulation. Even more complexity is added, however, by the conflicts within state agencies and actors (e.g., Hawkins 1984). State agencies' missions and the careers and powers of state actors take place within the context of a dynamic capitalist society and a world-system with changing competitiveness and alterations of capital and natural resource flows (Lipietz 1987; O'Connor 1988). The final sections of the paper outline the resulting policy shifts over the past five U.S. administrations in the face of such dynamics.

A major unpredictability within the treadmill is the level of material interest and the political expression of such interest by those who are largely dependent on wage income derived from the treadmill. Another major form of dependency is a product of the increasing unemployment and underemployment of working- and middle- class segments, which itself reflects the acceleration of the treadmill through increasing capital intensification of production (Blumberg 1980; Barlett and Steele 1992; Schor 1991). These segments rely on expanding transfer payments from the state (which, in turn, "earns" its revenues by taxing the surplus generated by the treadmill). These groups are numerically the largest components of the modern class system. In their individual work roles, for example, many environmental movement participants often have market exchange-value interests in ecosystems, limiting their political activity. Likewise, the actions of many worker-citizens who are not committed to environmental movement organizations are determined partly by their interests as workers and as taxpayers and partly as ecosystem users (O'Connor 1988; Gould 1991a, 1991b).

Consciousness-raising conflicts, as I note below, often involve competing attempts to mobilize political commitments from these working and middle classes, to support either environmental protection or production expansion. Such classes represent, after all, a clear majority of actors in the pluralist model of the U.S. polity. They are not permanent constituents of any environmental movement organizations (cf. Mitchell 1980). However, they may be either adherents or constituents of environmental movement organizations in any given historical moment, or in any particular environmental conflict (Burton 1986; Morris 1992; Schnaiberg, Gould, and Weinberg 1992). These social classes and segments can thus be seen as one element of the political context within the state-logic theory of Skocpol (1980), and thus are targets of state policies. The political economy of environmental problems emerges from the conflict dynamics of these competing interests in both the politics and markets (Lindblom 1977; O'Connor 1988) of the modern treadmill of production. These dynamics evolve around the nature of the state, as well as the state of nature.

"ENVIRONMENTAL PROBLEMS": FROM THE STATE OF NATURE TO THE NATURE OF THE STATE

To understand the origins of modern environmental problems, we need to appreciate how the environmental interests of actors outlined above relate to the physical-biotic organization of ecological systems. The history of expanding industrial production has provided the data to outline a dialectical conflict between social and ecological organization in advanced industrial societies (Schnaiberg 1980, pp. 423-4; Grove 1992). Dialectical conflicts emerge when social systems have two or more goals which cannot simultaneously be met. Essentially, the dialectical tension in relationships between modern societies and their environments emerges from two axioms: (1) most elements of ecological systems cannot meet both exchange-value needs and use-value needs; and (2) the treadmill of production places a primacy on exchange-value uses of ecosystems, while other ecological uses are a biological and social necessity for all classes. The following propositions delineate the dialectical connections between social and environmental structure.

The Societal-Environmental Dialectic

1. Societal production in industrial societies involves withdrawals from and additions to natural ecosystems, in the process turning ecosystem elements into social resources, producing exchange values and profits in the markets of the treadmill of production;
2. Such withdrawals and additions disorganize the physical-biotic structure of these ecosystems, while producing these exchange values; and
3. Ecosystem disorganization[2] decreases the use values of ecosystems, restricting (among others) social access to recreational habitats, health-sustaining biological supports (air, water, food), and also future levels of social production (exchange values).

This skeletal dialectical model begins to lay the groundwork for a political-economic analysis, but is not itself political-economic. Three possible political-economic syntheses are possible resolutions of this dialectical system. The first is an economic synthesis, which has predominated in U.S. history and that of most other industrial societies. In this arrangement, the state largely fosters capital accumulation and supports primarily the exchange values of ecological systems. Only severe ecosystem disorganization is attended to, and only when it threatens productive systems. State "environmental" policies are localized and short-term.

A second synthesis is one of managed scarcity, where the state attempts some minimal regulation of access to ecosystems by various classes of users. State agencies and actors seek to maintain some balancing of environmental exchange values and use values for competing actors, class segments, and classes (Hawkins 1984). To some extent, this characterizes the modern era of "environmental protection" in the U.S. and elsewhere.

A third synthesis is an ecological one (Schumacher 1973; Evernden 1985). Here, the state attaches a primacy to ecological system protection, emphasizing use values (including the value of preservation of existing species and habitats) over exchange values. This is consonant with the proposals of "deep ecologists" (e.g., Devall 1980) and neo-Marxists who advocate a reorganization of the social relations of production (e.g., Buttel and Larson 1980; O'Connor 1988). Their goal of a sustainable society is, however, rarely supported by modern U.S. state policies (cf. Hays 1969).

The determinants of the syntheses to these dialectical conflicts include the following: (1) social, economic, and political actors' interests in various elements of ecosystems; (2) the power that each group of actors has in pushing its interests in various economic markets and/or political arenas; and (3) emergent institutional structures that reflect these interests and powers (Low 1964, 1972). In short, we need to understand how the motives (consciousness) and power (control capacities) of various social-class segments shape the dynamics of political-economic conflicts and lead to particular syntheses, as classes and class segments seek to control ecosystems for their own interests. Generally, I outline below how the modern treadmill of production produces an enduring systemic bias toward the economic synthesis and against the ecological synthesis. The closing section outlines how this bias eventually is reflected in U.S. state policies around environmental research, environmental protection, and economic expansion, and how variations in the managed-scarcity synthesis are explicable by historical variations in consciousness, conflicts, and economic contexts (O'Connor 1988).

A simple contemporary example will suffice to trace out the dynamics of these syntheses and associated interest structures. Currently, there is much concern about toxic wastes of all kinds, yet despite much rhetoric, there is no ecological final solution for most of these wastes, which range from PCBs (polychlorinated biphenyls) to high-level radioactive waste from nuclear power plants. In Illinois, for example, Outboard Marine Corporation used Waukegan's harbor on Lake Michigan for many years as a dump site for production wastes, including PCBs. After ordering an end to dumping by Outboard Marine, the Environmental Protection Agency attempted to clean up the harbor by dredging the accumulated wastes. But there appeared to be no practical way to dredge without dispersing PCBs farther into the lake and its fish populations. For a long period, the harbor was essentially sealed off and left largely inaccessible to producers and many recreational users, although there is a new and active marina located adjacent to the plantsite (Bukro 1985). (Recent industrial ion-exchange technologies have recently been applied, to reduce the PCB sediment hazards, although the outcomes are unclear at this writing.)

If we analyze this conflict from a political-economic perspective, the following emerges. Outboard Marine managers and their stockholders had an interest in using the harbor as a "sink" for their hazardous wastes (Catton and Dunlap 1989), since this reduced the cost of producing outboard motors. Moreover, as a large and powerful firm in a small city, they avoided political-legal threats for many years, essentially keeping the harbor as an industrial sink. The economic values associated with this industrial production were dominant among the local, regional, and national populations and institutions. When other potential users of the harbor—boaters and fishermen, among others—became aware of fish and water contamination and resulting health hazards arising from contact with the water or fish, they argued for an EPA suit against Outboard Marine, under water pollution legislation provisions.

This consciousness of local groups of the ecological-health problem emerged in part from the general rise in ecological consciousness of the late 1960s and 1970s. The resulting legislation and implementation led to monitoring by EPA and other water control agencies in 1975. The latter regulations were compromises in the political-economic conflict in the United States between capitalist producers and expanding environmental movement organizations, leading to tension within the state organization between economic growth and environmental protection agencies and actors. Outboard Marine mobilized economic development agencies in Waukegan, in Springfield, Illinois, and in Washington, D.C. to substantiate their claims that they would be driven to bankruptcy by cleanup costs, tapping into treadmill exchange value interests and values.

In contrast, environmental and recreational movement organizations attempted to galvanize the Illinois and federal Environmental Protection Agencies around use values. They sought to terminate the dumping (which was successful), and to remove the accumulation (which was not). Stockholders of Outboard Marine had a clear exchange-value interest in fighting the cleanup, and recreational users of the harbor areas had a clear use-value interest in cleanup of the harbor. Other actors were more mixed in motivations: Local political figures stood to lose substantial tax revenue if Outboard Marine closed (Gould 1991a). Employees of the firm had wages and employment hanging in the balance, a frequent issue in "job blackmail" (Kazis and Grossman 1982).

Because of the corporate power of Outboard Marine, dumping accumulated to a point where cleanup became feasible only by a costly damming of the site and by isolating the contaminated sediments to avoid dispersal into Lake Michigan. It was unclear for a prolonged period whether the environmentalist organizations would have the power to induce the state to pay for such a cleanup (Gould 1991a, 1991b). At one point, the EPA administrator approved a $21 million plan under the Superfund provisions, which cycles money from chemical producers into a cleanup fund. However, the Superfund program itself has such a long waiting list that thousands of sites are on it. This lengthy list itself reflected the inadequacy of current management in the U.S. state's managed-scarcity synthesis of pollution problems. Moreover, it was also a reflection of the power of economic actors to avoid higher cleanup cost allotments.

The largely silent Waukegan harbor reflected this standoff between the consciousness and control capacities of these competing actors. Interestingly, there are boating and even recreational fishermen who still use these waters, despite the closing of Waukegan beaches; this illustrates the unpredictability of the consciousness of many use-value interest groups. This quasi-inaccessibility of this natural resource nicely reflects the ambivalence of the state toward expending substantial fiscal resources to clean up a single waste site. It also indicates how rarely a managed-scarcity synthesis clearly allocates ecosystems to use-value interests. Since revenues spent primarily for use-value interests in Waukegan will not predictably generate new taxes, employment, or powerful political support for the government actors/agencies, this state resistance reflects treadmill biases (Evernden 1985).

The length of the list of uncompleted Superfund projects is also a crude indicator of the state's ambivalence about use-value access to ecosystems. EPA wants to "do something" to please use-value interests. But it does not want to extract too many fiscal resources from exchange-value interests to follow through on ecologically meliorative measures. This type of managed-scarcity synthesis essentially officially designates an existing problem of ecological scarcity for use-value interests and limits future access by some exchange-value interests, but does little else (Gould 1992; Weinberg 1991a).

This example illustrates the mixture of ecological and political-economic treadmill constraints on environmental conflicts. Water transport features of Lake Michigan represent an ecological constraint. Species of fish and lake water layers will both decline in social utility for many users if PCBs are more dispersed. Conversely, the political capacity of Outboard Marine to evade costly cleanup charges through the damming procedure represents a political-economic constraint. Large firms regularly and routinely challenge regulatory agencies such as the Environmental Protection Agency. They raise the costs and diminish the efficacy of litigation by both environmental movement organizations and state agencies. Also, because of the institutionalized commitments to economic growth and the legitimacy of state support for capital accumulation to accomplish this, even environmentalists are forced to weigh drags on capital accumulation imposed by reallocating social surplus to environmental cleanups rather than new investments. Crudely put, even these political agents of use-value interests are simultaneously committed to expanding exchange-values from many ecosystems (Evernden 1985; Devall 1980).

Local constituencies are likewise split along lines of competing uses of ecosystems and competing models of distribution of costs to permit access to such environmental amenities. Historical biases of the treadmill were reflected in an historical accumulation of waste and ecological disorganization in Waukegan; this history thus limits other use-value access in Waukegan. Yet, a commercial marina, recently built despite a clear consciousness of the PCB contamination, is now operating in these polluted waters, bringing some exchange-value revenues into the city and permitting some recreational boating uses of the harbor area. Again, this complex pattern of exchange- and use-value accessibility and inaccessibility serves as a safety valve for the state, legitimating rather limited environmental protection. This limited action is explored in the following section.

CONFLICTS OF INTEREST: UNRAVELLING
THE MANAGED-SCARCITY SYNTHESIS

From the above discussion, it seems crucial that we understand the *mechanisms* by which both ecosystems and political systems limit access to ecosystems. An ecological perspective on scarcity emphasizes that societal production involves withdrawals from and/or additions to ecosystems, which produce pollution and/or depletion. These withdrawals/additions create ecological imbalances, altering the composition of living species or nonliving substances, upsetting dynamic equilibria of ecosystems (Schnaiberg 1980, ch. 1).

But from a political-economic perspective, there is an even broader concept of scarcity. Most classes, class segments, and institutions in the modern class structure experience and define scarcity as increased difficulty in attaining their use values or exchange values from ecosystems. At the early stages of the conservation-efficiency movement (Hays 1969) the conflicts were between competing capitalist and precapitalist producers. The goal was sustained-yield production, a reasonably overt and straightforward type of conflict. Much of the conflict was within the capitalist class, with competing exchange-value interests. With the rise of organizations devoted to environmental preservation, a more complex set of conflicts was introduced. But the preservation movement itself was also largely elitist, with conflicts located within the dominant class and largely localized.

The growth of modern environmental movements by the 1970s represented a broader range of challenges to the dominant capitalist producers, generating more complex conflicts around surplus distribution (Schnaiberg 1980, ch. 8; Buttel and Larson 1980; Morris 1992; Schnaiberg, Gould and Weinberg 1992; Dowie 1992; Schnaiberg 1992c). In the example of the previous section, the PCBs dumped by Outboard Marine were a threat to that corporation. But another high-tech firm, ATD (Myers 1984), grew as it developed a new technology designed to extract pollutants like PCBs from Waukegan harbor sediment, concentrating them in preparation for burial or incineration. Likewise, firms like Waste Management have become multibillion dollar enterprises through the rise in environmentalists' consciousness and their control capacity to put waste control on the state's managed-scarcity agenda, coupled with the rapid growth of industrial waste products (Schnaiberg 1992a, 1992b).

Thus, while the major response of capitalist actors has been to resist much new environmental regulation designed to enhance the use values of other classes, another segment of this dominant class has extracted new exchange values from environmental protection activities of the state. Moreover, in keeping with Skocpol's (1980) and other recent conceptions of a somewhat-autonomous state, political support for some types of environmental protection is also designed to preserve corporate access to productive resources for a longer term (sustained yield). As with the early conflicts outlined in the Pinchot era (Hays 1969), this puts the state within Miliband's (1969) model. Essentially, the state substitutes a longer-term view of sustained yield for the short-term calculus underlying political resistance by capitalist managers and stockholders. This view serves the capitalist class in the future, although it may impose burdens on particular contemporary capitalists (O'Connor 1988; Schnaiberg and Weinberg 1992).

Since environmental protection itself produces several types of social scarcity for classes other than capital owners, new conflicts over the implementation of these state policies also emerges. Ecologically based scarcities engender substantial community resistance from NIMBY (not-in-my-backyard) groups. They see modern industrial waste storage and processing sites as increasing the scarcity of these local groups' use values from local ecosystems. On a purely economic level as well, the costs associated with environmental protection introduce new socioeconomic scarcities, regardless of whether environmental protection equipment is funded directly through taxation, issuance of public finance bonds, or through pass-through of corporate costs of pollution abatement. All of these act to reduce the discretionary income of and/or transfer payments by the state to working- and middle-class segments of society (Bullard 1990; Bryant and Mohai 1992). Environmental movement organizations often see themselves as acting to redistribute use values to a broader social constituency (cf. Mitchell 1980; Buttel and Larson 1980; Schnaiberg, Gould, and Weinberg 1992). But many working- and middle-class segments of the society resent and resist the resulting costs and scarcities of environmental protection (Schnaiberg 1983a, 1983b, 1986a,b; Burton 1986; Buttel 1985, 1986; Buttel and Larson 1980).

To understand contemporary political-economic conflicts, then, we need a more elaborated concept of social scarcity. One way of restating the framework of interests posed initially in this paper is in terms of scarcity. As a defining element of the environmental dialectic, I noted above the important fact that ecosystem elements usually have limited capacity to meet the competing demands of political-economic interests (Schnaiberg 1985).

This is a central dilemma for state policymakers, who are increasingly called upon to intervene politically in what have historically been capitalist market transactions (Lindblom 1977; O'Connor 1988). This history of an economic synthesis, moreover, exerts a strong institutional bias in favor of exchange values, as opposed to use values of ecosystems. This is a key element in applying Skocpol's (1980) analysis of state policymaking to environmental regulation. But, she and others pursuing this state logic (e.g., Buttel 1985, 1986; O'Connor 1988) also point to political conditions that can partly offset this bias. Accumulated disruption of ecological use values, disseminated scientific research about this, and the rise of a modern environmental movement industry

(McCarthy and Zald 1977) have all served to provide some of these political conditions. This explains why the U.S. and other advanced societies have moved some distance toward the managed-scarcity synthesis of the environmental dialectic, rather than remaining at the economic synthesis.

Lake Michigan can be used to illustrate the conflict around interests in ecosystems. It provides exchange values for capital owners who use water (1) as a physical or chemical component of their production, (2) as a cooling resource, or (3) as a site for dumping waste products. Conversely, it has use values for residents around the lake, ranging from potable water, a habitat for fish used for consumption or recreational fishing, a site for other recreational activities, to a sink for dumping human and domestic wastes (Catton and Dunlap 1989).

Generally, the greater the range of properties of water required for use, the stricter the requirements are for water quality by industrial or other users. Severely polluted water is acceptable for dumping toxic or other industrial or domestic wastes, but not for the production of many chemical or biological products or for sustaining fish or human life. In terms of its industrial cooling capacity, the crucial elements are the temperature and volume of the water. Waters heated by a nuclear plant may thus be problematic for a nearby steel plant, though acceptable for swimmers. But waters polluted by a municipal sewage treatment plant may still be acceptable for cooling uses, as well as recreation uses such as boating.

In the modern treadmill organization, under the managed-scarcity synthesis, one extreme of the ecological continuum is a highly disorganized ecosystem. It also represents, paradoxically, a potential source of exchange value for various waste treatment firms. Modern examples include waste management conglomerates dealing with toxic and nontoxic wastes, firms involved in removing asbestos from public buildings, and Superfund cleanup organizations removing hazardous wastes from dump sites. Even more paradoxical is the rise of modern recycling as one means of waste treatment, which has enhanced the profitability of many large-scale corporations (Schnaiberg 1992a,b).

All those with occupational interests in these firms also share some exchange-value interests. Such organizations, their professional associates and other employees, and other high-tech firms that design systems to reduce industrial and municipal wastes, have an exchange-value interest in the existence or projection of disorganized ecosystems (O'Connor 1988, pp. 31-32). The presence of these exchange-use interests makes for a more complex consciousness-raising conflict. Public (and social movement) consciousness of ecosystem disorganization is, after all, a necessary element in expanding the markets for their waste treatment services. Likewise, following Skocpol (1979, 1980), state actors charged with environmental protection maintain their professional careers by expanded public fears of ecosystem disorganization, whether real or hypothetical.

At the other ecological extreme, national wilderness areas that restrict productive uses serve to maximize recreational use values of various classes. This approximation to an ecological synthesis severely limits exchange values from these particular ecosystems. But even here, there are producers of camping equipment who derive exchange values from the availability of such recreational areas, as do other recreational service industries. Preservationism is, thus, not purely a use-value interest structure within the modern treadmill. State actors use this diversity of interests in generating support for policies approaching ecological syntheses.

Hence, scarcity is an interactive outcome, reflecting ecological properties of ecosystem elements and social users' criteria for use. A third interactive element is relative cost. For users with either very small volumes of need or with ready availability of monetary resources, the scarcity experienced will be smaller for a given degree of ecosystem disorganization. Because of the inequalities of fiscal resources in highly stratified treadmills of production, this further biases policymaking toward capitalist class segments.

Air pollution, for example, is a major problem for poor innercity residents suffering from respiratory ailments. They continuously require high-quality air to avoid physical deterioration, and yet have limited control over their ambient air quality. Moreover, they lack the financial resources to move to less polluted environments or to buy air purifiers. Also, they lack the political resources to mobilize local governments to reduce air pollution in their areas. Generally, they are reliant on middle-class welfare movement organizations to fight for state allocation of funds sufficient for oxygen bottles and other low-cost alternatives to pollution abatement. Alternatively, they must rely on the "trickle-down" of pollution control benefits from middle-class environmental movement organizations (cf. Mitchell 1980; Schnaiberg 1983a, 1983b).

POLITICAL CONSCIOUSNESS IN THE MANAGED-SCARCITY SYNTHESIS: WASTE MANAGEMENT EXAMPLES

One final extension of a sociopolitical concept of scarcity is required to outline modern political-economic trajectories. Political conflict initially arose from tensions within the historically dominant economic synthesis. Withdrawals from and/or additions to ecosystems from larger-scale production had diminished other users' exchange values and use values from these U.S. ecosystems (Hays 1969; Schnaiberg 1980). Environmental reform legislation emerged within a new managed-scarcity synthesis in the Johnson and Nixon administrations. In turn, these policies were implemented in the Nixon, Ford, and Carter administrations, which led to both anticipated and unanticipated scarcity consequences. (In sharp contrast, the Reagan and Bush administrations struggled to abandon the managed-scarcity thesis and move toward an economic synthesis [e.g, Landy et al. 1990]).

While representing a change in state policy and some relations of production, this managed-scarcity synthesis left intact most of the class structure and institutional arrangements that created and reproduced the treadmill of production (Buttel 1985; O'Connor 1988). To some extent, however, state policies altered both the degree and the costs of access by capitalists to ecosystem elements. This "solution" to the scarcity of environmental use values produced by the economic synthesis itself imposed new scarcities (Schnaiberg, Gould, and Weinberg 1992). This contradiction emerges from the fact that ecosystems cannot satisfy simultaneously all the users competing for the values or functions of a given ecosytem element. Thus, the state-logic of managed-scarcity policymaking entails creating new scarcities within a class structure that had previously been organized within the economic synthesis.

Managed-scarcity syntheses can thus reduce but not eliminate dialectical tensions. Political-economic conflicts emerge with struggles between interest groups competing for access to common ecosystem elements. For example, acid rainfall conflicts emerge from an ecological constraint. The atmosphere can be used as a sink for airborne sulfur dioxide (in the form of sulfuric acid) and other byproducts of combustion (Catton and Dunlap 1989). But there is a concomitant risk that rivers, forests, and even humans will ultimately suffer some loss of functioning because of the deposition of sulfuric acid in rainfall (and other parts of the water cycle). In the 1960s and early 1970s, power companies and other industrial producers used tall smokestacks to avoid conflict with local environmental groups around local air pollution. The consequence of this problem solving was the generation of new long-distance water pollution problems. Gould (1991b) notes the international component of this, as Canadian opposition to U.S.-originated acid rainfall rose largely as a nationalist rather than an environmentalist policy.

As one outcome of this strategy, consciousness patterns were significantly altered. Because environmental groups at some remove from the production sources cannot identify the acid rainfall polluters with any precision, capitalist producers benefit from the long-distance air transport of pollutants in two ways. They avoid political conflict with local environmentalists and state agencies. Likewise, state agencies and actors benefit from a "solution" that mollifies local use-value interests, without imposing high exchange-value costs on local capitalist producers. Moreover, this solution blurs the traces of producers' exchange-value usage of the atmosphere enough so that these more remote producers cannot be politically confronted by environmentalists and state agencies in the destination ecosystem of the pollutants. [The more socially visible national boundary between Canada and the United States and the patterns of rainfall, in contrast, permitted Canadian politicians to oppose the "importing" of U.S.-generated acid rainfall (Gould 1991b).]

Producers' costs of building high stacks for dispersion of pollutants was quite low. Hence, this "solution" only modestly increased their costs of access to atmospheric dumpsites. These costs were much lower than switching to cleaner fuels and electrostatic or other stack cleaning systems which the EPA has imposed on producers in areas of higher air pollution. Conversely, the losers in this solution were the users of ecosystems where acid rainfall is deposited and those state actors responsible for environmental protection there. State policymakers and enforcers were then confronted by frustrated use-value interests, as well as by those capitalist producers whose ecosystem use was curtailed by ecosystem degradation (Landy et al. 1990).

One way of outlining the consciousness-raising and consciousness-lowering dimensions over such managed-scarcity policies is to consider typical political responses of protagonists. Table 1 can be seen as a set of conflict repertoires (Tilly 1986) for environmental movements, their capitalist protagonists, and state agencies. Conflict initially ranges around assertions about problem severity (levels i-ii in Table 1). Ecosystem disorganization is seen as a matter of social survival, the environmentalist extreme (Schnaiberg 1980, ch. 1), or as essentially nonexistent, the producer extreme. While environmentalists use consciousness-raising activity to widen and deepen constituencies and adherents who will share some alarm at ecosystem disorganization, producers engage in consciousness-lowering activity.

A second layer of conflicting claims is about the causes of the problem (levels iii-iv in Table 1). Environmentalists argue that ecosystem disorganization is a specific outcome of production decisions and that changes in production will eliminate the problem. In opposition, producers either disclaim any contribution of production to the problem or minimize their share of the problem. Equally boldly, they may claim that the problem is a generalized outcome of all production, or of industrialization itself ("pollution is a by-product of our way of life"). Earlier and recurrent academic theorizing about environmental degradation as an outcome of population growth, consumer affluence, or "runaway" technology (Schnaiberg 1980, chs. 2-4; Schnaiberg and Gould 1994) has further legitimated some of these self-serving producer counterclaims.

The third tier of conflict repertoires is over *typical* benefit-cost allocations (levels v-vii in Table 1). Environmentalists often minimize consciousness about the amount and allocation of costs (Landy et al. 1990). They also project certain, substantial, and egalitarianly diffused major social benefits from environmental protection. They rarely are concerned with the financial problems of research. Producers play the opposite role, emphasizing the certainty and large scale of environmental protection costs, and the uncertainty, inequality, and modest social returns on environmental investments.

Finally, we have a more recent partial inversion of these alignments, in the fourth tier (levels viii-ix in Table 1). This was earlier present in some form of tentative agreement between protagonists that energy conservation was a social and economic good, although environmentalists often extolled reductions in *usage,* while producers pushed for development of more efficient capital *equipment* (Schnaiberg 1981; Stern and Aronson 1984, chs. 2-4). It is also evident in recent programs of recycling, which involve large-scale *remanufacturing,* using wastes as feedstocks (Schnaiberg, 1992a, 1992b; Schnaiberg and Weinberg 1992). This represents a different socioeconomic choice than more direct *re-use* of consumer and producer wastes. For both these examples of policy conflicts, there was far less conflict, as exchange-value gains by corporations can be viewed as consistent with environmental protection goals.

To illustrate the benefit-cost claims we can turn to the numerous NIMBY voluntary associations (Schnaiberg 1986c) that have been created to eliminate or preclude toxic waste sites in their communities. They raise consciousness about the individual-level threats to human health that such sites entail (in contrast to more diffuse collective environmental protection). Producers, in contrast, broadcast widely the need to find an inexpensive "sink" in which to put their industrial wastes. They stress the loss of jobs in the labor markets and the rising costs of goods in the consumer market in the absence of such sites. Each new chemical that is considered, or each new waste disposal site or process, appears to trigger the use of these repertoires by contending actors. Each party to the conflict attempts to mobilize resources (economic, political, social) for ensuring its own access to ecosystems for its primary use values or exchange values. Recent conflicts over toxic wastes begin with intensive consciousness-raising and consciousness-lowering efforts by environmentalists, waste handlers, and industrial waste generators. Issues center on the predictability, severity, and manageability of the human health impacts of toxic wastes (or all industrial wastes).

Municipal waste disposal conflicts are somewhat less intense, because of the complex sources of municipal wastes (human, domestic, commercial, and industrial), and thus of the complex interest structure. Conversely, radiation hazards of nuclear power accidents represent a clear source and immediate interest structure. Antinuclear conflict was thus often much more aggressively waged by regional and national environmental groups, such as at the Seabrook, New Hampshire plant.

An alternative way of characterizing Table 1 is to consider these claims and counterclaims as competing norms for allocating ecological scarcity. Local toxic waste groups are ultimately interested in maintaining or expanding their use of the local ecosystem for breathing, drinking water, and habitat/space for recreation (Crowfoot and Wondolleck 1991; cf. Schnaiberg 1992c). These are often different patterns of conflict than those over municipal waste disposal, say, because of the fact that human wastes are a major part of the problem. This often induces local environmentalists to soften their attacks (since they are themselves both waste generators and local taxpayers).

Table 1. Managed Scarcity Conflicts: Competing Claims

Environmentalist claim	*Producer counterclaim*
Problem Severity Issues	
i. Ecological disorganization is being produced	There is no ecological disorganization being produced.
ii. There is major ecological disruption "known": we do not need to postpone action for future research.	Some ecological disruption is already occurring, but it is minor; we would need costly ecological and community research to establish any "problem."
Causal Issues	
iii. The disorganization is socially produced, not "naturally occurring."	There is some disorganization, but it is not really socially produced.
iv. There are mechanisms for reducing or eliminating this disorganization without stopping or slowing societal growth	The ecological disorganization is socially produced, but it is an inevitable by-product of societal growth.
Benefit < Cost Issues	
v. There are technologically feasible ways of controlling the disorganization already available or near at hand.	We are currently unable to control this disorganization and will need costly production and ecological research before any production options can be weighed.
vi. We can easily afford to implement the corrective technologies, through implementation of regulatory rules, including fines for producers who violate them.	There are some corrective options possible, but they are costly to use and producers will need some incentives to make them feasible.
vii. Social benefits from environmental protection are far greater than are the relatively modest costs of implementing them.	The costs of correcting these ecological problems really exceed any benefits of melioration.
Cost < Benefit Issues	
viii. Social and ecological benefits of recycling (re-use) are greater than economic costs	Economic and ecological benefits of recycling (remanufacturing) are greater than economic costs.
ix. Social and ecological benefits of energy conservation (reduced use) outweigh economic costs	Economic and ecological benefits of energy conservation (increased efficiency) outweigh economic costs.

At the opposite extreme, national and regional antinuclear movement organizations wage fierce battles around local plants, partly because they are not local consumers or ratepayers for this electric power. Industrial waste handlers seek to preserve or expand their access to land or water sites (or air, in the case of incinerators), since they earn their profits from such transactions. The generators of toxic wastes also seek to preserve various wastesites. Their costs will rise if waste disposal sites are eliminated (i.e., their access to ecosystem sinks will both diminish and become more expensive), potentially reducing their profits because of their diminished competitiveness in markets.

Generally, producers' objectives in these conflicts are to maximize their physical and financial accessibility to ecosystem elements in order to extract maximum exchange value from these transactions. Environmentalist social movement organizations generally seek to maximize their access to ecosystem elements for their use values (often acting in the name of a broader social constituency, of course). From the state-logic of Skocpol (1980) and others, state agencies face different political-economic contexts in dealing with each of the resulting conflicts. They confront the above conflicts of interests. Additionally, though, they operate in a diversity and volatility of local, regional, and national economic conditions, which themselves partly dictate the intensity of claims and counterclaims.

As international competition has intensified, for example, the expenses of waste treatment have become a more important contested terrain. They represent a growing component of production costs and social expenses of all levels of government. State agencies must deal with the fact that both increased capital outlays and higher tax rates are necessary to treat wastes, and these both influence the competitive market struggles in the modern world system. For state environmental agencies, there is a publicly stated desire to maintain social use values, while not impinging overmuch on producers' exchange values (Hawkins 1984). In effect, these agencies seek to maximize a kind of political exchange value in their regulatory behavior (Lowi 1979, 1986). As Hawkins (1984) has noted, whatever the legislative authority for environmental agencies may be, the state operates within the broader political-economic context of capital accumulation represented by the treadmill of production. I turn next to outlining this broader institutionalized structure of the treadmill.

TREADMILL BARRIERS TO ENVIRONMENTALISM: LIMITS OF CONSCIOUSNESS AND CONTROL IN ENERGY POLICYMAKING

Central to the modern treadmill has been the expansion of production away from localized subsistence and into national and international markets (Gore 1992; Buttel and Taylor 1992; Barlett and Steele 1992). At the core of this historical process is the accumulation of social surplus. Capital owners use parts of the surplus generated in each period to invent and produce more economically efficient physical capital. These technological forces of production are more intrusive into ecosystems. However, they simultaneously generate more economic, political, and social power for the capitalist class. These core processes comprise most of the dialectical tensions in the state's environmental policy making (Schnaiberg 1980, ch. 5; Stretton 1976; Buttel 1985; O'Connor 1973, 1988; Buttel and Taylor 1992; Schnaiberg and Gould 1994).

The resultant institutional and class structure of the treadmill is complex and variable, but a general trend is acceleration. Without massive political intervention, the institutional apparatus of the modern treadmill impels investors, managers, workers, and state bureaucrats to demand ever greater ecosystem utilization, to accompany ever greater capitalization of production (Schnaiberg 1980, ch. 5; Commoner 1977). Economic market actors of the treadmill routinely emphasize the exchange values flowing from ecosystem usage. Additionally, state actors must extract, through taxes and other allocations from the treadmill, the funding of transfer payments (O'Connor 1973). Whether these social expenses are in the form of corporate gifts, corporate taxes, or individual taxes, all of these represent allocations of economic surplus from the treadmill (O'Connor 1988).

Thus, one of the expressions of the near-hegemonic power of the institutionalized treadmill and its dominant capitalist class is the perception of most social classes of their dependence on "economic growth" for their future welfare. There have certainly been treadmill critics (e.g., Schumacher 1973; Mishan 1967; Galbraith 1971, Commoner 1977), suggesting that the treadmill is less than perfectly hegemonic (Lipietz 1987; Redclift 1987). But the treadmill's major social institutions diffuse a dominant belief in the necessity of increasing the social surplus through accelerating the treadmill (Schumacher 1973; Schnaiberg 1982).

Two central issues that arise within the treadmill's dominant classes and economic institutions are: (1) how to *generate* more surplus, and (2) how to *allocate* the surplus that has been generated (O'Connor 1988). In modern capitalist systems, we can treat surplus as closely allied to corporate profits, although they are not synonymous. The equivalent in socialist or state-capitalist systems is the level of social profit accruing to a state organization (Stretton 1976; Schumpeter 1950; Feshbach and Friendly 1991). The class structure of the treadmill hegemonically reproduces a need for greater surplus generation. But actual state policies of surplus allocation are quite variable in comparative-historical perspective (Buttel 1985). This results from the ecological reality that ecosystems cannot actualize all exchange-value and use-value interests (O'Connor 1988). This core ecological factor generates many of the dialectical tensions in Skocpol's (1980) state-logic argument.

Under the Carter administration, for example, the state allocated more surplus to public employment. This policy was generally labor-intensive and produced fewer ecological withdrawals and additions per job generated. In the Reagan and Bush administrations, by contrast, the state subsidized high technology, highly capitalized defense industries. Generally, this created substantially higher withdrawals/additions per job created. Owners of the physical capital of the defense industry received much of the funding. However, their capital equipment required much raw material, energy extraction, and waste dumping. Thus, while both state policies are consistent with the macrostructure of the treadmill, their ecological impacts were materially different in degree and type. In contrast, the Clinton administration seems wedded to accelerating the treadmill by expanding production and using some of the resulting surplus to fund both environmental protection and social expenses.

Generally, the treadmill structure of modern societies implies a structural commitment to anti-ecological behavior (Schumacher 1973; Evernden 1985; Devall 1980). Absent some political movements by environmentalists, then, the "solution" to the problem of the treadmill would normally be the economic synthesis. Modern environmentalist movements and state agencies address the surplus issues of numerically and politically dominant treadmill proponents on two levels First, they argue that surplus should be generated with the lowest level of ecosystem withdrawals and additions "possible" per unit surplus generated. Second, because much of this surplus will nonetheless disorganize ecosystems in ways inimical to the use values of citizens, some significant share of the generated surplus should be allocated to protecting these use values as much as "possible." From a political-economic perspective, there is wide lip service paid to these principles even by many treadmill proponents. The most recent version of this lip service is the concept of *sustained development* (Court 1990). Political-economic conflict then occurs only later, in determining what economic action is "feasible" (Mitchell 1980; Morrison 1986; Redclift 1987; Davis 1991; Hecht and Cockburn 1992; Smith 1992), as noted above. The following shifts in consciousness over environmental policymaking have occurred under the past five U.S. administrations:

1. Under the Johnson and Nixon administrations, ecological consciousness-raising took place about the threatened decreases of the use value of ecosystem degradation, which led movements into legislative lobbying and judicial litigation.
2. Under the Nixon, Ford, Reagan, and Bush administrations, political consciousness-raising about the enduring power of the dominant capitalist class emerged, because of their exchange-value interests in ecosystem resources, as these actors fought against legislation and legal sanctions.

3. Under the Nixon, Ford, Carter, Reagan and Bush administrations, economic and political consciousness-raising about the challenge to the existing class structure, posed by implementation of environmental legislation, occured. Such challenges resulted from the higher costs of access to ecosystems, which reduced many exchange values, and some use values of many ecosystems.

4. Finally, under the Clinton administration, there promises to be more complex issues of consciousness-raising, with the dual concerns about economic issues (recession, employment, and competitiveness with new physical technology) *and* global environmental issues (such as ozone depletion and deforestation). The stance of the educated middle class, which was economically squeezed under the Reagan-Bush administrations, seems likely to be a crucial factor in tilting policy closer to a more egalitarian economic synthesis, or toward a more egalitarian planned scarcity synthesis.

Let me illustrate one of these conflict trajectories very briefly, across these recent U.S. adminstrations. During the Ford and Carter administrations, the OPEC embargo on oil and the associated increase in crude oil prices led to many new attacks on the logic of the treadmill. While Schumacher (1973) led a movement to dismantle the treadmill and substitute a more subsistence-like, stable, intermediate technology, a less-radical energy proposal emerged from Lovins (1977) for a soft energy path. Crudely put, Schumacher sought to reorganize the treadmill. Lovins merely sought to alter the treadmill's withdrawals of potential energy sources from ecosystems and additions to ecosystems from the transformation of this potential, into socially usable energy forms. Schumacher sought a change in forces of production in the modern class structure, and also implied a change in the eventual relationships between labor and capitalist classes (Schnaiberg 1982, 1983c). Lovins merely sought a change in the forces of production associated with energy transformations, with little change in capital-labor class relations.

Both these proposals moved far afield from the usual agendas of modern social movements. These movements usually emphasize redistributive goals, that is, allocation of surplus only (Schnaiberg 1982). But environmentalists now moved into the arena of capital accumulation (Friedland, Priven, and Alford 1977; Morrison 1980; cf. Lowi 1986). This historically unprecedented economic-environmental ferment of the Ford-Carter period followed the antipollution challenges of the Johnson and Nixon administrations. What they ultimately produced was a modest change in the ratio of energy consumption per unit GNP (Schnaiberg 1985). This was achieved mostly by the state in the Carter administration's mandating of higher prices for energy and improved energy efficiency in many commercial and residential applications. In short, what emerged was mostly a change within the treadmill, rather than an elimination of the treadmill. Why? The overly simple answer is that both of these proposals posed some threat to the existing class structure of the treadmill of production (O'Connor 1988; Redclift 1987; Davis 1991). Schumacher would have dismantled much of the physical capital that produced surplus, reallocating existing surplus toward meeting basic human needs and protecting natural systems. Similar proposals underly the more recent models of *sustainable development* (Court 1990; Davis 1991). Unless the existing capital-labor class structure were to vanish, these are usually utopian proposals (Schnaiberg 1982, 1983a, 1983c; O'Connor 1988; Schnaiberg, Gould, and Weinberg 1992). Moreover, even if the treadmill passed away and Schumacher's or the Brundtland Commission proposals (Davis 1991) for sustainable development were to be implemented, many of the factors that led historically to the emergence of an industrial class structure and its treadmill would eventually *reemerge*.

Schumacher's or the Brundtland Commission's proposals were not a serious threat to the modern class structure if they were designed to operate in self-selected voluntary communities (Schnaiberg 1982). But, if an entire society embraced an ideology of self-sufficiency and small-scale enterprise, a new form of social relations of production, the existing class structure would be transformed (O'Connor 1988). Historical evidence suggests that emergent inequalities would raise pressures to reproduce variants of the old class structure (Lipietz 1987; Redclift 1987). Unlike Stretton's (1976) detailed class conflict scenarios, though, Schumacher's plan dealt with political conflict within the existing class structure. Hence, we have no model from him outlining how the existing treadmill class structure would collapse, and what its potential for reemergence would be.

Lovins' (1977) plan was less in conflict with the surplus-generating relations of production of the treadmill. But it would have required enormous capital expenditures to redesign our energy systems. He ignored the problems posed for many capitalist producers (and labor groups) in reallocating surplus to new energy facilities. In effect, Lovins' proposals foundered because he confused energy use values with energy exchange values. He dismissed the existing political structure of fossil and nuclear fuel interests as irrational and epiphenomenal, rather than as economically comprehensible and politically potent. Existing energy industry owners did, however, gather new social legitimacy from Lovins and other energy activists. Among other strategies suggested by Lovins' work, they proceeded to market energy conservation to their consumers. This permitted continued profitability from existing physical power plants and reduced their capital needs for rapid expansion of facilities, while simultaneously presenting themselves as environmentally responsible capitalists.

To be sure, many other flowers bloomed during the Carter administration, through a mixture of venture capital and state recycling of tax money (in the form of tax incentives or outright grants). Wind and solar energy incentives blossomed for a short time, including the Solar Energy Research Institute (SERI) and even the National Center for Alternative Technology (NCAT). Shale oil pilot projects went forward in Colorado. Many new high-technology firms innovated various passive and active solar and wind designs, as well as housing retrofitting for energy conservation, ranging from insulation to new heating and cooling appliance designs. But all of these ultimately undergirded the treadmill by relying on market criteria for success or failure beyond the pilot plant stages (Schnaiberg 1982, 1983c). Also, market criteria simply reproduced the class structure of the treadmill.

Most of the state support for alternative energy systems was abandoned in the political marketplace when Reagan's economic policies were implemented. Nuclear energy retained the state's political support, despite its diminished economic attractiveness after the Three Mile Island accident and rising safety costs. Otherwise, conventional treadmill rules for economic survival regained their dominance within most classes. The state merely tinkered with the existing allocation of surplus and generation of future surplus. Much of the state apparatus has since reverted to its usual treadmill role of facilitating capital accumulation and reproducing existing class structure. This energy issue has reemerged in yet a different context in the Clinton administration, with energy reductions being advocated for multiple U.S. goals, including international competitiveness and reductions of U.S. contributions to global warming, as well as national security. Such variable treatment of energy issues thus illustrates once again the persistent limits entailed in a managed-scarcity state synthesis, albeit with considerable variability in historical salience of different limits (cf. Buttel and Taylor 1992).

What does this example imply for the broader environmental conflict? It suggests that the breadth and depth of commitments to the treadmill are repeatedly underestimated by environmental movement participants and their allies in state agencies, which Morrison (1973, 1976, 1986) calls institutionalized movement organizations (cf. Morris 1992; Gould, Weinberg, and Schnaiberg 1993). The near-hegemonic aspect of the treadmill is illustrated in a recent statement by the Executive Director of the Environmental Defense Fund (Krupp 1986):

> If environmentalists worry about the impact of a dam, for example, they had better address the water-supply or power-supply problem the dam was proposed to solve. They must concern themselves with the science and economics of environmental protection. Jobs, the right of stockholders, the needs of agriculture, industry and consumers for adequate water and power—all of these issues must become part of the new environmentalist agenda.

Environmentalists potentially represent a challenge movement (Gamson 1975), threatening capitalists and their allies in the state with new litigative and legislative pressures. Such challenges are heightened when environmental disaffection is occasionally added to the disaffections of those who have smaller or declining shares of social surplus. Major changes in capital flow in the modern world-system (Buttel 1985; Lipietz 1987) have altered opportunity structures in the United States. One consequence is that there are temporarily shared interests and coalitions among the poor, and semi-skilled and skilled blue-collar workers who have become technologically displaced, and even among the managerial-technical staff displaced by mergers, capital flight, and other corporate restructuring (Blumberg 1980; Knapp 1987; Barlett and Steele 1992; Schor 1991). In the Carter administration, such coalitions argued for "lifeline" energy pricing for the poor and increased occupational health enforcement. Under Reagan and Bush, the coalitions seemed to occur more often around toxic health hazards to communities (Schnaiberg 1983b, 1986c, 1987; cf. Burton 1986; Buttel 1986; Landy et al. 1990), and attention was redirected away from many other ecological disruptions produced by an expanded treadmill (Schnaiberg 1992a,b). In the new Clinton administration, there is a less clear picture: displaced middle-class workers could conceivably coalesce with other groups that declined during the Reagan-Bush years (Lardner 1993; Newman 1988, 1993) to demand state support of investment in technologies that would produce more employment *and* more environmental protection. Much of this potential has been deflected by the middle-class emphasis on tax relief, in contrast with working-class and underclass lobbying for jobs and homes (Gould, Weinberg, and Schnaiberg 1993).

Table 2 outlines changing state policies in recent American politics around environmental issues, by each recent U.S. administration. As Table 1 had suggested, there are considerable advantages for treadmill proponents to stop environmentalist consciousness-raising as early in the process as possible. Denial that any ecological disorganization exists is a preferred option. It is generally the least costly option, and it exposes treadmill institutions to the least social and political scrutiny (Friedland et al. 1977). Much of the environmental politics in the Johnson and Nixon administrations were centered around this level of consciousness. In general, environmentalists won this round of conflict. They spearheaded the institutionalization of a historically unprecedented range of voluntary organizations and a new and reorganized set of state agencies, especially the Environmental Protection Agency (Morrison 1973, 1977, 1986).

These 1960s struggles, in turn, led to a new level of institutionalized conflict around environmental consciousness in the Nixon and subsequent administrations. For example, the National Environmental Policy Act of 1969 mandated (in section 102) a form of environmental impact assessment—a new mode of political consciousness-raising. It required all agencies of the state to prepare environmental impact statements whenever their actions had major ecological consequences. Such state actions thus scrutinized included direct

Table 2.   Recent U.S. Environmental Policymaking

| Political Administration | Dimension | |
	Synthesis	Issues
Johnson-Nixon	Managed scarcity	• Costs of pollution
Carter	Managed scarcity (bordering on ecological)	• Costs of pollution control. • Energy conservation. • Soft energy paths. • Resource equity
Reagan-Bush	Manged scarcity (bordering on economic)	• Economic growth with cost-effective pollution controls • New production technologies
Clinton	Manged scarcity (oscillating between economic and ecological poles)	• Environmentally-"benign" technologies. • International pollution control. • Government market incentives

state investment (e.g., dam building), or indirect support of others' investments (e.g., licensing off-shore drilling). This supposed ecological consciousness-raising, though, typically generated a low quality of many environmental impact statements (Schnaiberg 1980, ch. 7; Meidinger and Schnaiberg 1980; Landy et al. 1990).

Subsequent litigation extended NEPA by mandating a social impact assessment (SIA) procedure as well. While many social scientists viewed this as a new opportunity to show the social costs of many ecologically malign projects and programs (O'Connor 1988), SIA has been attenuated in its implementation. Indeed, the original litigants sought just such an attenuation. They argued for the political need to balance the ecological losses of a project against socioeconomic gains (in the immediate case, a power plant).

In my view, this was a successful effort by the dominant capitalist class to reinstate the hegemony of the treadmill into the very heart of legislation naively perceived as anti-treadmill. NEPA's very structure permitted this claim to succeed because it was, itself, a compromise bill that raised environmental concern only in the context of treadmill goals (Buttel 1985; Schnaiberg 1980, chs. 6-7). But SIA litigation was only one of many strategies used by treadmill proponents to counter environmentalist consciousness-raising and more stringent state intervention in the treadmill (e.g., Beneviste 1981; Lundqvist 1980). The routinization of impact assessment, which follows from the application of these strategies, subsequently became transformed into just another transaction cost of modern industries (Schnaiberg 1980, chs. 7, 9). Generally, this outcome follows the following four classes of strategies used by capitalist producers to reduce the state's managed-scarcity intervention in the treadmill:

1. Reduce initial problem consciousness by underreporting withdrawals and additions in environmental impact statements.
2. Reduce implementation of environmental protection policies by slowing the state's environmental agencies in their litigative and administrative activities, as well as in their basic and applied environmental research.
3. Reduce enforcement actions by hampering the research and regulatory monitoring effort of state agencies and environmental movement organizations, through resisting access to production and disposal sites where withdrawals and additions occur, through underreporting violations, and through lobbying against research and regulatory agency funding.
4. Raise public and political resistance to environmental enforcement by generally raising perceptions of economic losses associated with implementation of environmental policies, by threatening to close plants, or by actually relocating capital to other sites or other societies.

Such routinization of impact assessment proceeds through two processes. Each reproduces the existing class structure of the treadmill. First, the historical dominance of treadmill accounting is biased toward economistic data and away from much ecological and other noneconomic social welfare criteria (Schnaiberg 1980, ch. 7; O'Connor 1988). Second, the procedures for NEPA accounting are heavily biased toward existing data sources, reproducing this bias and limiting new ecological research (Schnaiberg 1980, ch. 6). Scientific data-generation processes are structurally unbalanced. The disciplines of economics and management sciences are well financed and continuously reinforce the treadmill. Pro-environmental disciplines such as biology and ecology are much less consistently and adequately funded. Hence, they cannot offer such a continuous and persuasive countermessage. Other scientific disciplines such as chemistry and physics are much more drawn to support of technological change within the treadmill than they are toward expanding a critical impact research program. They further legitimize the modern treadmill (as well as expanding its capacity for surplus generation) and its values. All of these tensions are reflected in the organization of the state's impact assessment processes. The net result of these tendencies is a systematic bias that overstates treadmill economic benefits and understates ecological and social costs of new treadmill projects and programs (Meidinger and Schnaiberg 1980; Schnaiberg, Gould, and Weinberg 1992; Gould, Weinberg, and Schnaiberg 1993).

Not only is there a systematic bias in the data available for scientific assessment, but there is an equally strong bias in the capacity to disseminate such data for political consciousness-raising purposes (Wright 1992). Treadmill representatives are supplied with substantial consciousness-facilitating resources—advertising, public relations, intergovernmental relations, or public service communciations. These outlets all reinforce the perception of the treadmill as a social and an individual good. They do this routinely, powerfully, and often quite creatively (Schnaiberg 1980, chs. 5-6). In contrast, dissident environmentalists operate sporadically, often weakly, and not always very creatively, to document individual stakes in collective environmental protection goods. The social movement organizations within the environmental movement industry depend on volatile voluntary efforts, with only a limited professional staff.

Moreover, the state's environmental regulatory agencies have an unusual structure and mission. Normally, as Friedland et al. (1977) have noted, state agencies have a primary mission of either capital accumulation or social legitimation. The former types of agencies "cloak themselves...[with] the ideology of technical planning and professionalism...[to] discourage any attempts at popular intervention" (Friedland et al. 1977, p. 458). In contrast, the latter agencies operate so that "their policies are far more visible... [in order to] attract the political participation of groups who are excluded from the benefits of economic growth or who may even be its victims" (Friedland et al. pp. 458-459). Environmental agencies (such as the EPA) involved in consciousness-raising and conflict adjudication with treadmill institutions have both types of characteristics. And they have little historical precedent to guide their political and technical staffs (Landy et al. 1990).

Because of the complexities of ecosystem disorganization and the threat of regulation for modern capitalists (Hawkins 1984; Lash et al. 1984; Landy et al. 1990), the EPA and other environmental agencies are continuously adjudicating between economic growth and environmental protection goals. As one consequence of this, they require highly professionalized staff— litigative and political staff at least as much as scientific staff—to protect the agency from capitalist class reactions. Conversely, they desperately need the political support of environmental movement organizations and broader public constituencies for renewing their funding and missions. The balance between the two needs has shifted substantially in recent administrations, as I note in the final section.

The resulting state activity is a mixture of Lowi's (1979, 1986) model of technical-bureaucratic backstage negotiations, along with more public consciousness-raising by the EPA. To some extent, the former represents some degree of collusion with the capitalist class in order to lower public consciousness, to avoid some public pressures on EPA to "do something!" As the earlier statement of the Environmental Defense Fund Director suggests, moreover, even environmental movement organizations feel some of these same political pressures owing to the near-hegemonic structure of the treadmill. Such nongovernmental voluntary associations, let us remember, also require political and fiscal support from various publics, which requires diversion of substantial resources for mobilizing these supporters.

In short, there is substantial resistance to a genuinely balanced "scientific" treatment of environmental (and social) costs and economic benefits of the treadmill (Schnaiberg 1980, chs. 6-7; O'Connor 1988). Imbalances exist in the scientific component (data availability), as well as in the advocacy component (persuasion) of such balancing. Sometimes the imbalance actually favors environmentalists. Threats to life or to some especially valued habitat or specie are vividly registered through skillful use of the media. But these important exceptions do not negate the reliable, routine, and repetitive recommitment to treadmill values evident in media and other socializing institutions. Morrison (1973, 1977, 1986) has forcefully argued, in line with the model of Friedland et al. (1977), that the state agencies are an institutionalized arm of the modern environmentalist movement. But this is a much weaker form of institutionalization than that routinely reproducing treadmill values, consciousness, and organizations. This is amply indicated by the attenuation of political influence of such agencies in the Reagan and Bush years (e.g., Buttel 1985, 1986; Lash et al. 1984; Landy et al. 1990; Mintzmyer 1992).

A thought experiment serves to point out this asymmetry. Imagine a conference on the future of the United States which had no representatives of major capital interests. Generally, this is unimaginable. But the selfsame conference could still take place, even today, with no representatives of environmental entities, either of movements or state agencies. One does not have to be a neo-Marxist to appreciate that the nature of the treadmill economy is at the very base of modern industrial societies like the United States (Schumpeter 1950). Virtually all actors, including dissidents, acknowledge this despite their dissidence. The treadmill is currently the source of all social surplus, and this surplus ultimately supports the state. Thus, social movement organizations that challenge (Gamson 1975) the existing principles allocating this surplus have a formidable task of offsetting such political and sociocultural momentum.

Paradoxically, only if the treadmill could be dismantled could its consciousness-influencing powers be diminished along the dimensions noted above. But environmentalists who project a nontreadmill future consistently ignore the fact that they must coexist with the treadmill's class structure until that future is reached (Schnaiberg 1982, 1983c). This coexistence is viewed by utopian environmentalists (Evernden 1985; Devall 1980) rather like the biblical allegory of the lamb lying down with the lion. The Realpolitik is that the lion sleeps much better.

Interestingly, in the world of Realpolitik, the power of the treadmill is often expressed by its proponents as threats to dismantle capital stock. Workers and citizens alike are often confronted with treadmill actors threatening to move their productive capital elsewhere when confronted with new environmental protection demands (Schnaiberg 1986b, 1987). This potential loss of treadmill participation, whether expressed in terms of job blackmail threats (Kazis and Grossman 1976) or of rustbelt tax base and employment losses (Bluestone and Harrison 1982) drives many labor and community groups to withdraw support from some environmental causes. With the increasing globalization of capital flows, moreover, this fear is intensified, as the U.S. state has far less influence over the allocation of capital by U.S. capitalists, with their capacity to invest abroad (Lipietz 1987).

The conservative interpretation is that workers are revealing a political preference for the treadmill (Rorhschneider 1991). My own view is that there are few viable options for all but a handful of workers with monopolies of skills or control over unique resource locations (Barlett and Steele 1992; Schor 1991). Interestingly, even these last privileged status groups benefit from the surplus allocated by the treadmill in numerous ways. Treadmill income, for example, permits consumption of expensive handicrafts or custom services (e.g., wilderness guide activity) performed for tourists or wealthy patrons. Little economic activity in the modern world-system is in fact unconnected to that global structure (Buttel and Taylor 1992). Also, much of that global system rests upon the treadmill of production in the industrial world (Stretton 1976; Lipietz 1987).

THE FUTURE OF ENVIRONMENTAL POLICYMAKING: FROM LINEAR SCIENTIFIC CONSCIOUSNESS TO DIALECTICAL POLITICAL-ECONOMIC CONFLICT

New scientific and political consciousness about environmental costs of these global treadmill systems has unquestionably emerged in the U.S. state within the past two decades. But even within the scientific community, there are historical political-economic factors affecting the demands for and supply of environmental awareness, which are largely independent of the changes in ecosystem disorganization (Schnaiberg 1975, 1980, ch. 6, 1986a, Wright 1992). The same is true throughout environmental movement organizations and in their various attentive publics (O'Connor 1988). While ecological changes are never totally irrelevant to environmental conflicts, they also never determine policy outcomes. This reflects a modern variant of Karl Marx's principles of political action:

> men make [environmental] history, but they do not make it just as they please: they do not make it under circumstances chosen by themselves, but under [ecological and political-economic] circumstances directly encountered, given, and transmitted from the past. (adapted from Feuer 1959, p. 320).

Ecosystem disorganization must be perceived, defined, evaluated, and disseminated by various social entities with use-value interests. Therefore, any societal changes that either directly or indirectly alter the resources of such actors also influence their capacity to blow an environmental whistle. In turn, such use-value groups exist within the exchange-value interest structure of the treadmill. Increasingly, social scientists are coming to view all scientists as social actors, reflecting structural and personal conditions in their work (e.g., Latour and Woolgar 1986). Scientists are structurally classified as scientific laborers (Schnaiberg 1980, ch. 6). They are thus reactive to many types of market changes. Resources for basic environmental impact research, both among impact scientists in universities and applied scientists in regulatory agencies such as the EPA (Schnaiberg 1986a), have been highly volatile in the past 25 years, and especially under Reagan and Bush administrations (e.g., Mintzmyer 1992). So, too, have been resources of the environmental movement industry.

Under the Reagan and Bush administrations, good scientific theories and estimates of environmental disorganization processes have been withdrawn from the agendas of scientists and political advocates alike, and placed into a scientific-political inventory (Schnaiberg 1986a). In this state of limbo, they awaited more favorable political-economic conditions (e.g., resources for research, attentive audiences). While the new Clinton administration, with its environmental Vice President, Al Gore, Jr. (Gore 1992) was anticipated by environmentalists to infuse new energy into environmental policymaking, the treadmill pressures on the new administration to provide deficit reduction, new employment, and new investment incentives are likely to offset this environmental protection orientation (Schnaiberg and Gould 1994, ch. 10). There *are* changes in international collaboration on global warming and species protection under the new administration, however, and new approaches to an "energy tax." These political variations are broadly consistent with the arguments of Skocpol (1980) about the state-logic of policymaking, in which contextual factors play an important role in shaping the trajectories and policy outcomes.

Nowhere was this type of strategic retreat clearer than in the case of the EPA under its Administrator Ann Gorsuch (Landy et al. 1990). Her Reaganomics-based ideology stifled EPA's scientists from exploring many environmental problems (Szasz 1986). A similar scenario occurred in James Watt's tenure as secretary of the U.S. Department of the Interior, which undermined ecological consciousness within that agency (Claybrook 1984; Lash et al. 1984; Burton 1986). While organized environmental and other movements stimulated the removal of these two administrators, the damage to environmental science and regulation of that period was largely irrevocable. Recent evidence by former administrators under the Bush administration (e.g., Mintzmyer 1992) suggest a continuity of prior pressures. (It is still too early at this writing to evaluate the Clinton nominees and their priorities.)

The battlegrounds were shifted by Reagan's economic synthesizers from the political frontstage to the executive backstage (Lash et al. 1984; Lowi 1979, 1986). Congressional struggles over legislation were replaced by battles over appropriations and detailed regulatory procedures. Federal administrative pressures on regional offices to defer regulatory sanctions rose as part of the same processes (Lash et al. 1984; Claybrook 1984; Commoner 1987). Agencies such as the EPA consequently faced additional problems in recruiting and retaining competent scientists and lawyers. These professionals' usual constraints (Schnaiberg 1980, chs. 6-7, 1986a) were now exacerbated by new intraagency barriers imposed by Reagan's program for an economic synthesis. All of these historical patterns challenge Morrison's (1977, 1986) assertions about the institutionalization of environmentalism in state agencies (Buttel 1985, 1986). At the very least, they raise questions about the degree of such institutionalization, or at least the policy-effectiveness of these state agencies (cf. Dunlap 1987; Weinberg 1992).

But direct restraints on scientific consciousness-raisers and their state and movement allies constitute only one factor influencing recent volatility in environmental policymaking. The declining competitiveness of the U.S. economy in the modern world-system has imposed substantial chastening of labor of all types. Skilled and unskilled blue-collar jobs in manufacturing have been transferred from many U.S. communities to foreign-based plants, themselves often built with capital in flight from the United States (Blumberg 1980; Bluestone and Harrison 1982; Lipietz 1987). College-educated groups, the backbone of environmental movement organizations (Mitchell 1980), have also been negatively impacted, as has the middle class in general (Knapp 1987; Schnaiberg and Goldenberg 1989; Schor 1991; Barlett and Steele 1992; Newman 1988, 1993; Lardner 1993).

These publics were mobilized in unprecedented ways by environmental movements in the Johnson-Nixon years to support the new legislation of managed scarcity (Morrison 1973, 1986). But both scientific and other labor segments have increasingly struggled with personal economic troubles (Mills 1959). There has been recent growth in concern about environmental problems, and some movement expansion in response to Reagan's anti-environmental policies. But this was not translated into stricter control of treadmill acceleration in most of the Carter, Reagan, and Bush years (Dunlap 1987; Lash et al. 1984; Landy et al. 1990). Capital owners have often become more resistant to environmental regulation or enforcement. They face new cost competition from overseas, and thus are even more motivated to fight "unproductive" investment in pollution control (Lipietz 1987). The fiscal crisis of the state (O'Connor 1973), most recently evidenced in the United States by sharply rising budget deficits, further restricts state support for environmental research. Ironically, the sharp rise in such deficits in the Reagan and Bush years are largely a result of the diminished effectiveness of their economic syntheses, and not of increased environmental protection (Lipietz 1987; O'Connor 1988). With the emphasis of the new Clinton administration on a form of global competitiveness "with a human face" (Reich 1991) and an "environmental face" (Gore 1992), it is unclear what these tensions will produce in implemented policies (Lardner 1993).

Economic strains on environmental scientists and other labor segments interact in complex ways within the treadmill (O'Connor 1988). For example, environmental professionals may gravitate away from public employment in environmental protection when there are (1) good industry positions utilizing their technical-environmental skills, and/or (2) unstable opportunities in the state's environmental protection agencies. Under some conditions, though, more of a skilled scientific group is attracted to public service when private-sector opportunities diminish sufficiently. The question then emerges: will there be sufficient public service employment when there is lowered surplus generated by the treadmill's private sector? Only a strong political coalition around use values and the exchange-value interests of labor can reallocate surplus in this way, namely, to simultaneously protect the environment and provide socially useful employment of skilled human capital (O'Connor 1988).

Trajectories of managed-scarcity conflicts are illustrated by the issue of acid rainfall. Acid rainfall and associated global warming processes have likely been growing since air pollution regulation of the late 1960s was implemented (Gore 1992), due to increased levels of sulfuric acid and carbon dioxide. But both the ecological additions (and subsequent withdrawals of species) and the political-economic context have been changing (Morrison 1986; Buttel and Taylor 1992). Ecological impacts of acid rainfall grew sufficiently to retain the environmental movement's attention. But there was also more resistance in the 1970s and 1980s by major trade assocations and the capitalist class in general. They feared projected increases in production costs necessitated by future control over combustion processes. Their resistance was sufficient to prevent both major state research efforts and the legislation of new managed-scarcity regulations (e.g., Lash et al. 1984; Buttel 1985).

It is possible, perhaps, to envision the ongoing political-economic conflicts around every stage of managed scarcity, from initial consciousness to policy implementation, as a kind of political seesaw, reflective of the dialectical shifts in Skocpol's (1980) state-logic. Challenges from environmental use-value groups rise and fall, depending on changes in their consciousness, mobilization, and resources. These changes reflect actual ecological disorganization, and the capacity of scientific laborers to identify and publicize these changes. Responses and counter challenges from the capitalist groups also vary according to their resources and the demands on their budgets from competitors, consumers, and state regulators (O'Connor 1988).

From the perspective of many state officials—elected and bureaucratic— an ideal balance exists when enough surplus is being generated to permit a sufficient allocation to both capital owners (for economic growth) and environmental constituents (to enhance environmental entitlements). This requires delicate political juggling and a great deal of luck. In recent periods, surplus generation appears to have been more problematic because of changes in world competition (O'Connor 1988; Lipietz 1987). Thus, the state tilted away from environmentalist support, moving closer to the economic synthesis (Gore 1992). Ironically, movement toward this synthesis seemed to contribute to the further decline of the middle and much of the working class (Blumberg 1980; Knapp 1987; Barlett and Steele 1992; Newman 1993; Phillips 1989, 1993). These classes are distracted by personal troubles (Mills 1959), and the capitalist class urged them to see environmental issues as responsible for their economic issues (O'Connor 1988). State transfer payments rose, in part to deal with the problems of unemployment and underemployment. Moreover, under Reagan's and Bush's fiscal policies, state indebtedness rose still more sharply, attenuating allocations for environmental research and enforcement, as well as for other social expenses. In turn, this historical legacy of huge state deficits and indebtedness has further reduced the Clinton administration's potential to act in socially and environmentall benign ways, using standard treadmill logic.

Yet, we must remember that this is a dialectical and not a linear process. Reaganism revitalized many movement organizations by slashing much environmental enforcement. Reagan thereby generated new movement and public fears about health hazards (Burton 1986). His supply-side economic policies also reactivitated the movement fears characteristic of the Johnson-Kennedy period, about loss of habitat and sustenance (Schnaiberg 1980, ch. 1), especially illustrated by growing toxic waste conflicts (Dowie 1992; Morris 1992). Likewise, the prospects of a more socially sensitive Clinton administration has spurred new interests in coalitions of environmentalists and social welfare movements. This is perhaps symbolized by the 1993 election of Reverend Dr. Benjamin Chavis, Jr., as head of the National Association for the Advancement of Colored People: He coined the term environmental racism in his work for the United Church of Christ in the 1980s.

In contrast to the utopian beliefs of deep ecologists (Devall 1980), appropriate technologists (Schumacher 1973), or radical theorists (e.g., Ophuls 1977) of the 1965-1980 period, then, the culmination of environmental consciousness-raising produced more volatility within the treadmill. It did not lead to a transition to an ecological synthesis that would have dismantled it (Buttel and Larson 1980; Buttel 1986; O'Connor 1988). The radical environmentalism that Lowi (1986) characterized as "cost-oblivious" was eventually displaced in the Carter-Reagan period by environmental liberalism, which he labels as "cost-conscious," and there were strong pressures in the Reagan and Bush years to revert back to the economic synthesis (Lash et al. 1984; Dunlap 1987; Landy et al. 1990; Yeager 1991), and a modified managed-scarcity approach in the Clinton administration (Reich 1991). In like manner, the more recent rise of a "model" of sustainable development (Redclift 1987; Davis 1991; Court 1990) seems likely to follow a similar path of accomodation to existing capital interests (Schnaiberg and Gould 1994).

Lowi (1986) and Buttel (1985, 1986) see the future paths of environmental conflict as more intense in relatively decentralized states like the United States, in contrast with countries such as Sweden, Canada, and West Germany. I concur with these projections. However, I am far less certain about the future historical changes in either the state attentiveness or ecological outcomes of future policymaking. Consciousness and control capacity within the class structure of the treadmill have, as noted above, fluctuated substantially in the past two decades of U.S. history. But they have produced only limited managed-scarcity policies.

This is understandable when we face the fact that environmental conflicts are redistributive conflicts about access to ecosystems and the allocation of different types of social scarcity (Burton 1986; Buttel 1985, 1986). Environmental conflict operates within a class structure that is highly resistant to fundamental changes in the social relationships of production (O'Connor 1988). In part this explains the lower effectiveness of U.S. environmental protection, because the U.S. state is less autonomous than Sweden, for example (Buttel 1986), and thus less free to confront the dominant capitalist class. Whereas environmentalists see society as embedded within the biosphere, national and international ecosystems are simultaneously embedded in an equally enduring political-economic system. Consciousness- and control-conflicts among different ecosystem users reflect their search for the support of other social class segmments in their efforts to sway state agencies and actors. Thus, variability in the managed-scarcity synthesis is likely to be large and unpredictable in the foreseeable future (Meidinger and Schnaiberg 1980; Schnaiberg 1986c; O'Connor 1988; Schnaiberg, Gould, and Weinberg 1992; Schnaiberg and Gould 1994).

NOTES

1. Although my usage of the concepts of exchange value and use value borrows heavily from Marxist frameworks, I deviate substantially from many theoretical principles and concepts of neo-Marxism. For a more explicitly neoMarxist analysis, which only partly concurs with my formulation, see the recent essay of James O'Connor (1988). Other perspectives somewhat more consistent with my own here are those of Buttel and Larson (1980) and Buttel (1985). The latter coincides more with the limited expectations of social redistribution through modern environmental protest posited in this paper than does Buttel, which preceeded the regressive policies of the Reagan administration. O'Connor, in contrast, sees more progressive possibilities in modern environmentalism as one possible outcome of the conflicts it adds to the conjunction of broader crises of capitalism. I shared more of this view some ten years ago, before Reagan and Bush took office (Schnaiberg 1980, chs. 8-9); my optimism has diminished substantially in the intervening years (e.g., Schnaiberg 1983a, 1983c), with the strains imposed both by the constraints imposed

by OPEC and the flight of American capital away from the United States (e.g., Bluestone and Harrison 1982; Blumberg 1980; Lipietz 1987; Barlett and Steele 1992; Phillips 1989, 1993; Newman 1988, 1993).

2. Despite an eloquent argument to label this as environmental "degradation" (Lee Freese, personal communication 1989), I prefer the term disorganization. In this, I choose to emphasize the social rather than the ecological factors, and reflect human interests in the environment rather than the interests of other species (cf. Evernden 1985). There are costs to this, but I believe that a political-economic perspective must perforce examine competing social forces operating in the modern state. Other nonhuman species are thus represented in this paper only by the social movements that represent them in political discourses. "Degradation" is, from my perspective here, a sociopolitical consciousness-raising term, and it ignores the political-economic implications when consciousness is suppressed (e.g., Hays 1969).

ACKNOWLEDGMENTS

The comments of Fred Buttel, Riley Dunlap, Lee Freese, Kenneth Gould, and Adam Weinberg are gratefully acknowledged.

REFERENCES

Adler, J., and M. Hager. 1992. "Earth at the Summit." *Newsweek* (June 1): 20-22.

Ayres, R.U. 1989. "Industrial Metabolism and Global Change: Reconciling the Sociosphere and the Biosphere—Global Change, Industrial Metabolism, Sustainable Development, Vulnerability." *International Social Science Journal* 41(3): 363-374.

Barlett, D.L., and J.B. Steele. 1992. *America: What Went Wrong?* Kansas City: Andrews and McNeel.

Begley, S. 1992. "Is it Apocalpse Now?" *Newsweek* June 1: 36-42.

Beneviste, G. 1981. *Regulation and Planning: The Case of Environmental Politics.* Berkeley: University of California Press.

Betz, C.1992. "Call to Detroit Summer '92." Letter. *Greens Clearinghouse,* May 1.

Bidwai, P. 1992. "North vs. South on Pollution." *The Nation* (June 22): 853-854.

Bluestone, B., and B. Harrison 1982. *The Deindustrialization of America: Plant Closings, Community Abandonment, and the Dismantling of Basic Industry.* New York: Basic Books.

Blumberg, P. 1980. *Inequality in an Age of Decline.* New York: Oxford University Press.

Brown, P., and E.J. Mikkelsen. 1990. *No Safe Place: Toxic Waste, Leukemia, and Community Action.* Berkeley: University of California Press.

Bryant, B., and P. Mohai, eds. 1992. *Race and the Incidence of Environmental Hazards: A Time for Discourse.* Boulder, CO: Westview.

Bukro, C. 1985. "EPA May Forego PCB Clean-Up at Waukegan Harbor." *Chicago Tribune,* April 14.

———. 1991. "From Coercion to Cooperation." In "Ecology—Special Report 1991." *Chicago Tribune* (November 17): 6-8.

Bullard, R.D. 1990. *Dumping in Dixie: Race, Class and Environmental Quality.* Boulder, CO: Westview.

Burton, D.J. 1986. "Contradictions and Changes in Labour Response to Distributional Implications of Environmental-resource Policies." Pp. 287-314 in *Distributional Conflicts in Environmental-Resource Policy,* edited by A. Schnaiberg, N. Watts, and K. Zimmermann. Aldershot, England: Gower.

Buttel, F.H. 1985. "Environmental Quality and the State: Some Political-Sociological Observations on Environmental Regulation." Pp. 167-188 in *Research in Political Sociology*, Vol. 1, edited by R.G. Braungart and M.M. Braungart. Greenwich, CT: JAI Press.

_____. 1986. "Economic Stagnation, Scarcity, and Changing Commitments to Distributional Policies in Environmental-Resource Issues." Pp. 221-238 in *Distributional Conflicts in Environmental-Resource Policy*, edited by A. Schnaiberg, N. Watts, and K. Zimmermann. Aldershot, England: Gower.

Buttel, F.H., and O.W. Larson, III. 1980. "Whither Environmentalism? The Future Political Path of the Environmental Movement." *Natural Resources Journal* 20(April): 323-344.

Buttel, F.H., and P.J. Taylor 1992. "Environmental Sociology and Global Environmental Change: A Critical Assessment." *Society and Natural Resources* 5(3): 211-230.

Catton, W.R., and R.E. Dunlap 1989. "Competing Functions of the Environment: Living Space, Supply Depot, and Waste Repository." Paper presented at the Conference on Environmental Constraints and Opportunities in the Social Organization of Space, International Sociological Association, University of Udine, Italy, June.

Claybrook, J. 1984. *Retreat from Safety: Reagan's Attack on American Health*. New York: Pantheon.

Commoner, B. 1977. *The Poverty of Power: Energy and the Economic Crisis*. New York: Bantam.

_____. 1987. "A Reporter at Large: The Environment." *The New Yorker* (June 15): 46-71.

Court, T. de la. 1990. *Beyond Brundtland: Green Development in the 1990s*. London: Zed Books.

Crowfoot, J.E., and J.M. Wondolleck 1991. *Environmental Disputes: Community Involvement in Conflict Resolution*. Washington, DC: Island Press.

Davis, D.E. 1991. "Uncommon Futures: The Rhetoric and Reality of Sustainable Development." *Environment, Technology and Society* 63: 2-4.

Devall, B. 1980. "The Deep Ecology Movement." *Natural Resources Journal* 20(April): 299-322.

Dowie, M. 1992. "The New Face of Environmentalism: As Big Environmental Organizations Dodder, the Movement's Energy Shifts to the Grass Roots." *Utne Reader* (July/August): 104-111.

Dunlap, R.E. 1987. "Polls, Pollution and Politics Revisited: Public Opinion on the Environment in the Reagan Era." *Environment* 29(6): 7-11, 32-37.

Dunlap, R.E., and A.G. Mertig, eds. 1992. *American Environmentalism: The U.S. Environmental Movement, 1970-1990*. Washington, DC: Crane Russak.

Evernden, N. 1985. *The Natural Alien*. Toronto: University of Toronto Press.

Falkenmark, M. 1990. "Global Water Issues Confronting Humanity." *Journal of Peace Research* 27(2): 177-190.

Feshbach, M., and A. Friendly, Jr. 1991. *Ecocide in the USSR: Health and Nature Under Siege*. New York: Basic Books.

Feuer, L.S., ed. 1959. *Basic Writings on Politics and Philosophy: Karl Marx and Friedrich Engels*. Garden City, NY: Anchor Books.

Friedland, R., F.F. Piven, and R.R. Alford. 1977. "Political Conflict, Urban Structure, and the Fiscal Crisis." *International Journal of Urban and Regional Research* 1(3): 447-471.

Galbraith, J.K. 1971. *The New Industrial State*. 2nd ed. New York: New American Library.

Gamson, W.A. 1975. *The Strategy of Social Protest*. Homewood, IL: Dorsey.

Goldman, M.I. 1972. *The Spoils of Progress: Environmental Pollution in the Soviet Union*. Cambridge, MA: MIT Press.

Gore, (Senator) A. 1992. *Earth in the Balance: Ecology and the Human Spirit*. Boston: Houghton Mifflin.

Gould, K.A. 1991a. "The Sweet Smell of Money: Economic Dependency and Local Environmental Political Mobilization." *Society and Natural Resources* 4: 133-150.

_____. 1991b. "Money, Management, and Manipulation: Environmental Mobilization in the Great Lakes." Unpublished Ph.D. dissertation, Department of Sociology, Northwestern University, June.

_____. 1992. "Putting the [W]R.A.P.s on Public Participation: Remedial Action Planning and Working-Class Power in the Great Lakes." *Sociological Practice Review* 3(3): 133-139.

Gould, K.A., A.S. Weinberg, and A. Schnaiberg. 1993. "Legitimating Impotence: Pyyrhic Victories in the Modern Environmental Movement." Pp. 207-246 in "Social Equity and Environmental Activism: Utopias, Dystopias and Incrementalism," edited by A. Schnaiberg. *Qualitative Sociology* 16(3, September-October).

Grove, R.H. 1992. "Origins of Western Environmentalism." *Scientific American* (July): 42-47.

Hawkins, K. 1984. *Environment and Enforcement: Regulation and the Social Definition of Pollution.* Oxford: Clarendon Press.

Hays, S.P. 1969. *Conservation and the Gospel of Efficiency: The Progressive Conservation Movement, 1890-1920.* New York: Atheneum.

Hecht, S., and A. Cockburn 1992. "Rhetoric and Reality in Rio." *The Nation* (June 22): 848-853.

Kazis, R., and R. Grossman 1982. *Fear at Work: Job Blackmail, Labor and the Environment.* New York: Pilgrim.

Knapp, T. 1987. "The Declining Middle Class: Causes and Consequences." Paper presented at meetings of the Society for the Study of Social Problems, Chicago, August.

Krupp, F.D. 1986. "The Third Stage of Environmentalism." *EDF Letter* XVII(August): 4.

Landy, M.K., M.J. Roberts, and S.R. Thomas 1990. *The Environmental Protection Agency: Asking the Wrong Questions.* New York: Oxford University Press.

Lardner, J. 1993. "The Declining Middle." *The New Yorker* May 3: 108-114.

Lash, J., et al. 1984. *A Season of Spoils: The Story of the Reagan Administration's Attack on the Environment.* New York: Pantheon.

Latour, B., and S. Woolgar 1986. *Laboratory Life: The Construction of Scientific Facts.* Princeton, NJ: Princeton University Press.

Lindblom, C.E. 1977. *Politics and Markets: The World's Political-Economic Systems.* New York: Basic Books.

Lipietz, A. 1987. *Mirages and Miracles: The Crises of Global Fordism.* Trans. by David Macey. London: Verso.

Little, P. 1992. "The Rio Summit Falls to Earth as U.S. Snubs Global Treaties." *In These Times* (June 24-July 7): 8-9.

Lovins, A. 1977. *Soft Energy Paths: Toward a Durable Peace.* New York: Harper Colophon.

Lowi, T. 1964. "American Business, Public Policy, Case-studies, and Political Theory." *World Politics* 16(4): 677-715.

_____. 1972. "Four Systems of Policy, Politics, and Choice." *Public Administration Review* 32(4): 298-310.

_____. 1979. *The End of Liberalism.* 2nd ed. New York: W.W. Norton.

_____. 1986. "The Welfare State, the New Regulation, and the Rule of Law." Pp.109-149 in *Distributional Conflicts in Environmental-Resource Policy*, edited by A. Schnaiberg, N. Watts, and K. Zimmermann. Aldershot, England: Gower.

Lundqvist, L.J. 1980. *The Hare and the Tortoise: Clean Air Policies in the U.S. and Sweden.* Ann Arbor: University of Michigan Press.

McCarthy, J.D., and M.N. Zald 1977. "Resource Mobilization and Social Movements: A Partial Theory." *American Journal of Sociology* 82(6): 1212-1241.

Mankoff, M. 1972. *The Poverty of Progress: The Political Economy of American Social Problems.* New York: Holt, Rinehart and Winston.

Meidinger, E., and A. Schnaiberg 1980. "Social Impact Assessment as Evaluation Research: Claimants and Claims." *Evaluation Review* 4(4): 507-535.

Miliband, R. 1969. *The State in Capitalist Society.* New York: Basic Books.

Mills, C. Wright. 1959. *The Sociological Imagination.* New York: Oxford University Press.

Mintzmyer, L.L. 1992. "An Environmental Vision Thing." *Harper's Magazine* (October): 20-24.

Mishan, E.J. 1967. *The Costs of Economic Growth.* New York: Frederick A. Praeger.

Mitchell, R.C. 1980. "How 'Soft', 'Deep', or 'Left'? Present Constituencies in the Environmental Movement." *Natural Resources Journal* 20(April): 345-358.

Morris, D. 1992. "The Four Stages of Environmentalism." *Utne Reader* (March/April): 157, 159.

Morrison, D.E. 1973. "The Environmental Movement: Conflict Dynamics." *Journal of Voluntary Action Research* 2(2): 74-85.

————. 1977. "Growth, Environment, Equity and Scarcity." *Social Science Quarterly* 57(2): 292-306.

————. 1980. "The Soft, Cutting Edge of Environmentalism: Why and How the Appropriate Tchnology Notion is Changing the Movement." *Natural Resources Journal* 20(April): 275-298.

————. 1986. "How and Why Environmental Consciousness Has Trickled Down." Pp. 187-220 in *Distributional Conflicts in Environmental-Resource Policy,* edited by A. Schnaiberg, N. Watts, and K. Zimmermann. Aldershot, England: Gower.

Myers, L. 1984. "Environmental Innovators Feed on Technology's Mess." *Chicago Tribune,* July 15.

Newhouse, J. 1992. "The Diplomatic Round: Earth Summit." *The New Yorker* (June 1): 64-78.

Newman, K. 1988. *Falling from Grace: The Experience of Downward Mobility in the American Middle Class.* New York: Free Press.

————. 1993. *Declining Fortunes: The Withering of the American Dream.* New York: Basic Books.

O'Connor, J. 1973. *The Fiscal Crisis of the State.* New York: St. Martin's Press.

————. 1988. "Capitalism, Nature,Socialism: A Theoretical Introduction." *Capitalism, Nature, Socialism* 1(Fall): 11-38.

Ophuls, W. 1977. *Ecology and the Politics of Scarcity: Prologue to a Political Theory of the Steady State.* San Francisco: W.H. Freeman.

Phillips, K. 1989. *The Politics of Rich and Poor: Wealth and the American Electorate in the Reagan Aftermath.* New York: Random House.

————. 1993. *Boiling Point: Democrats, Republicans, and the Decline of Middle-Class Prosperity.* New York: Random House.

Poulantzas, N. 1973a. "The Problem of the Capitalist State." Pp. 238-253 in *Ideology in Social Science,* edited by R. Blackburn. New York: Vintage Books.

————. 1973b. *Political Power and Social Classes.* London: New Left Books.

Reich, R.B. 1991. *The Wealth of Nations: Preparing Ourselves for 21st Century Capitalism.* New York: Alfred A. Knopf.

Redclift, M. 1987. *Sustainable Development: Exploring the Contradictions.* New York: Methuen.

Rohrschneider, R. 1991. "Public Opinion Toward Environmental Groups in Western Europe: One Movement or Two?" *Social Science Quarterly* 72: 251-266.

Rudel, T.K., and B. Horowitz 1993. *Tropical Deforestation: Small Farmers and Land Clearing in the Ecuadorian Amazon.* New York: Columbia University Press.

Schnaiberg, A. 1975. "Social Syntheses of the Societal-Environmental Dialectic: The Role of Distributional Impacts." *Social Science Quarterly* 56(June): 5-20.

————. 1980. *The Environment: From Surplus to Scarcity.* New York: Oxford University Press.

————. 1981. "Conservation, Energy Policy, and Political Backlash." Paper presented at International Society of Political Psychology, Mannheim, West Germany, June.

————. 1982. "Did You Ever Meet a Payroll? Contradictions in the Appropriate Technology Movement." *Humboldt Journal of Social Relations* 9(2): 38-62.

_____. 1983a. "Redistributive Goals Versus Distributive Politics: Social Equity Limits in Environmental and Appropriate Technology Movements." *Sociological Inquiry* 53(2/3): 200-219.

_____. 1983b. "Saving the Environment: From Whom, For Whom, and By Whom?" Preprint, International Institute for Environment and Society, Wissenschaftszentrum-Berlin.

_____. 1983c. "Soft Energy and Hard Labor? Structural Restraints on the Transition to Appropriate Technology." Pp. 217-234 in *Technology and Social Change in Rural Areas*, edited by G.F. Summers. Boulder, CO: Westview Press.

_____. 1985. "Gas Today or Food Tomorrow? Social Choices and Energy Policies." *Progress, Museum of Science and Industry* 36(5): 10-15.

_____. 1986a. "The Role of Experts and Mediators in the Channeling of Distributional Conflicts." Pp. 348-362 in *Distributional Conflicts in Environmental-Resource Policy*, edited by A. Schnaiberg, N. Watts, and K. Zimmermann. Aldershot, England: Gower.

_____. 1986b. "Future Trajectories of Resource Distributional Conflicts: Trends and Projections." Pp. 435-444 in *Distributional Conflicts in Environmental-Resource Policy*, edited by A. Schnaiberg, N. Watts, and K. Zimmermann. Aldershot, England: Gower.

_____. 1986c. "Reflections on Resistance to Rural Industrialization: Newcomers' Culture of Environmentalism." Pp. 229-258 in *Differential Social Impacts of Rural Resource Development*, edited by P.D. Elkind-Savatsky. Boulder, CO: Westview.

_____. 1987. "Economics of Environmental Regulation: The Impact of Environmental Protest Dynamics." Paper presented at the Annual Meetings of the American Association for the Advancement of Science, Chicago, February.

_____. 1991. "The Political Economy of Consumption: Ecological Policy Limits." Paper presented at the Annual Meetings of the American Association for the Adancement of Science, Washington, DC, February.

_____. 1992a. "Recycling vs. Remanufacturing: Redistributive Realities." Working paper WP-92-15, Center for Urban Affairs and Policy Research, Northwestern University, Spring.

_____. 1992b. "The Recycling Shell Game: Multinational Economic Organization vs. Local Political Ineffectuality." Working paper WP-92-16, Center for Urban Affairs and Policy Research, Northwestern University, Spring.

_____. 1992c. "Oppositions." *Science* 255(March 20): 1586-1587.

Schnaiberg, A., and S. Goldenberg. 1989. "From Empty Nest to Crowded Nest: The Dynamics of Incompletely-Launched Young Adults." *Social Problems* 36(3): 251-269.

Schnaiberg, A., and K.A. Gould. 1994. *Environment and Society: The Enduring Conflict*. New York: St. Martin's Press.

Schnaiberg, A., K.A. Gould, and A.S. Weinberg. 1992."Losing the Environmental Battle But Winning the Legitimacy War: A Revisionist Analysis of 'the Environmental Movement.'" Paper presented at the Annual Meetings of the American Sociological Association, Pittsburgh, August.

Schnaiberg, A., and A.S. Weinberg. 1992. "Lubricating Conflict: The Example of Recycling Oil." *Environment, Technology, and Society* 69: 9.

Schor, J. 1991. *The Overworked American: The Unexpected Decline of Leisure*. New York: Basic Books.

Schumacher, E.F. 1973. *Small Is Beautiful: Economics as if People Mattered*. New York: Harper and Row.

Schumpeter, J.A. 1950. *Capitalism, Socialism, and Democracy*. 3rd ed. New York: Harper and Brothers.

Skocpol, T. 1979. *States and Social Revolutions*. New York: Cambridge University Press.

_____. 1980. "Political Response to Capitalist Crisis: Neo-Marxist Theories of the State and the Case of the New Deal." *Politics and Society* 10(2): 155-201.

Smith, E.T. 1992. "Growth vs. Environment: In Rio Next Month, A Push for Sustainable Development." *Business Week* (May 11): 66-75.

Spector, M., and J.I. Kitsuse. 1977. *Constructing Social Problems*. Menlo Park, CA: Cummings Publishing.

Stonich, S. 1990. "The Dynamics of Social Processes and Environmental Destruction: A Central American Case Study." *Population and Development Review* 15(2): 269-296.

Stern, P.C., and E. Aronson, eds. 1984. *Energy Use: The Human Dimension*. New York: W.H. Freeman.

Stretton, H. 1976. *Capitalism, Socialism, and the Environment*. Cambridge: Cambridge University Press.

Szasz, A. 1986. "The Process and Significance of Political Scandals: A Comparison of Watergate and the 'Sewergate' Episode at the Environmental Protection Agency." *Social Problems* 33(3): 202-217.

Tilly, C. 1986. *The Contentious French: Four Centuries of Popular Struggle*. Cambridge, MA: Belknap Press of Harvard University Press.

Vaahtorantz, T. 1990. "Atmospheric Pollution as a Global Policy Problem." *Journal of Peace Research* 27(2): 169-76.

van Vliet, W. 1990. "Human Settlements in the U.S.: Questions of Even and Sustainable Development." Paper presented at a colloquium on Human Settlements and Sustainable Development , University of Toronto, Canada, June.

Wad, A., T. Lavengood, and M. Scallon. 1991. "International Cooperation for Environmentally Sustainable Industrial Development (ESID)." Draft paper, Center for the Interdisciplinary Study of Science and Technology, Northwestern University, Evanston, IL, May.

Weinberg, A.S. 1991a. "Community Right To Know and the Environment." Paper presented at the American Sociological Association Meetings, Cincinnati, Ohio, August.

_____. 1991b. "Defining the Success of a Social Movement." Paper presented at the Midwest Sociological Association Meetings, Kansas City, April.

_____. 1992. "Where is the Community in Community Right To Know?" Paper presented at the North American Symposium on Society and Resource Management, Madison, WI, May.

World Resources Institute. 1992. *The Environmental Almanac*. Washington, DC: World Resources Institute.

Worldwatch Institute. 1991. *State of the World: 1991*. Washington, DC: Worldwatch Institute.

Wright, W. 1992. *Wild Knowledge: Science, Language and Social Life in a Fragile Environment*. Minneapolis: University of Minnesota Press.

Yeager, P.C. 1991. *The Limits of Law: The Public Regulation of Private Pollution*. Cambridge and New York: Cambridge University Press.

THE ASSEMBLING OF HUMAN
POPULATIONS:
TOWARD A SYNTHESIS OF ECOLOGICAL AND
GEOPOLITICAL THEORIES

Jonathan H. Turner

ABSTRACT

Assembling is defined as those processes influencing the number of actors in a population, their distribution in space, and their control of territory. It is argued that this dimension of the social universe has been somewhat undertheorized in sociology. An effort is made to model representative theories in human ecology, urban ecology, and geopolitics with an eye to what they can offer a more general theory. Then, these representative models are combined into a more general model and set of principles on the dynamics of assembling. This theory emphasizes that the underlying forces behind assembling are the level of production and the concentration of power.

Advances in Human Ecology, Volume 3, pages 65-91.
ISBN: 1-55938-760-2

ASSEMBLING AS A FUNDAMENTAL
DOMAIN OF SOCIAL REALITY

Some of the most important dimensions of social organization are the number of individuals to be organized, the distribution of these individuals in space and over time, and the amount of space used to organize individuals. These dimensions of social reality have been an important domain of theorizing in specialized theories. For example, there is a large literature on the processes involved in the formation and collapse of empires; there has been an enormous amount of theorizing and research on the processes involved in the development of urban communities; there has been some theorizing and much research on the processes influencing population growth and decline; and there has been considerable theoretical concern on the effects of density of individuals on social processes. Yet, despite a substantial number of specialized theoretical efforts, assembling processes have not been explored as generic and basic social processes about which a general theory can be developed. There are several reasons for this situation. First, variables such as population size, extent of territory, patterns of migrations, and related processes are so heavily influenced by historical and contextual events that it is difficult to see them as obeying certain general laws. Second, these kinds of variables are often ceded over to disciplines such as demography and geography, which are out of sociology's theoretical mainstream. And third, these variables are more typically viewed as background conditions or parameters for the "real theory."

This last consideration is crucial to understanding the inadvertent neglect of space, population size, and distribution as a domain of theorizing. At a macro level, for instance, emphasis has been on social differentiation, integration, and conflict, with population size and distribution viewed as background conditions. At the meso level, urban sociology explicitly incorporates the processes of size and density of settlements, but in more recent decades these often take a back seat to other social processes such as centralization/decentralization of power, corporate domination and exploitation of space, patterns of migration, and resource flows in a system of megacities and urban areas. At a micro level of theorizing, the density of actors and the physical structure of the setting are important theoretical concerns, but they are typically seen as either starter variables or background conditions for theorizing and research on the flow of interaction. Thus, while concern with space, numbers of individuals, and densities of individuals are easy to find in sociological theory, they have not been considered as fundamental a domain of theorizing as other social processes.

The goal of this paper is to overcome this situation by initiating an effort to build theory at the macro level on what will be termed *assembling processes*. The term assembling is a reasonable label for this domain of reality because it connotes the gathering together of varying numbers of people in different configurations of space and over varying lengths of time. At a macrostructural level, then, assembling refers to those forces that produce a set of interrelated phenomena, including the absolute size of a population, its distribution in a territory, its density of settlement, its movements, and its control of territories and regions. In theorizing about these processes, two forces—the mobilization of power and the level of production—will be seen as the underpinnings of assembling dynamics. For these two forces ultimately determine how large a population can become, how much territory it can occupy, how concentrated or dispersed a population is, and how long a population will hold together as an identifiable whole.

This effort at developing a general theory of assembling is, of course, tentative and confined to producing theory at the macro level. But, this is an appropriate place to begin theorizing because assembling at the meso and micro levels would appear to be determined by the dynamics of assembling at a more macro level. At least this is a reasonable assumption with which to begin theorizing. In seeking to develop a general theory of assembling, it is desirable to consult a broad range of representative approaches. These approaches draw upon the foundation laid by such early theorists as Herbert Spencer (1874-1896, vol. 1, pp. 449-600, vol. 2, pp. 568-602), Émile Durkheim ([1893] 1933), Karl Marx ([1845-1846] 1947), and early Chicago School urban ecologists (e.g., Hurd 1903; Park 1916; Burgess 1925; Park and Burgess 1925; Wirth 1928; Zorbaugh 1926; McKenzie 1933; Park 1936; Hoyt 1939; Harris and Ullman 1945), but these intellectual roots of theorizing on assembling will not be explored here. Instead, three contemporary approaches will be examined. One is general human ecological theory; another is the ecological framework within contemporary "urban sociology" as well as the critics of urban ecology who, in the end, produce an ecological theory; and, finally, geopolitical theorizing. Taken together, representative formulations within this broad range of theories provide a base for constructing a robust macrostructural theory of assembling.

GENERAL ECOLOGICAL THEORIZING ON ASSEMBLING

The most persistent general theorist in human ecology has been Amos Hawley (1944, 1950, 1973, 1978, 1981, 1986) whose ideas on assembling are modeled in Figure 1. For Hawley, the level of technology determines directly and indirectly those processes affecting the assemblage of a population. In particular, communication and transportation technologies establish the mobility costs of moving materials, people, and information; and these costs ultimately set limits on how large a population can be and how much territory it can occupy (hence, the negative arrows from mobility costs and transportation/communication technologies). Conversely, the size of a population and its territory escalate mobility costs, thereby increasing the

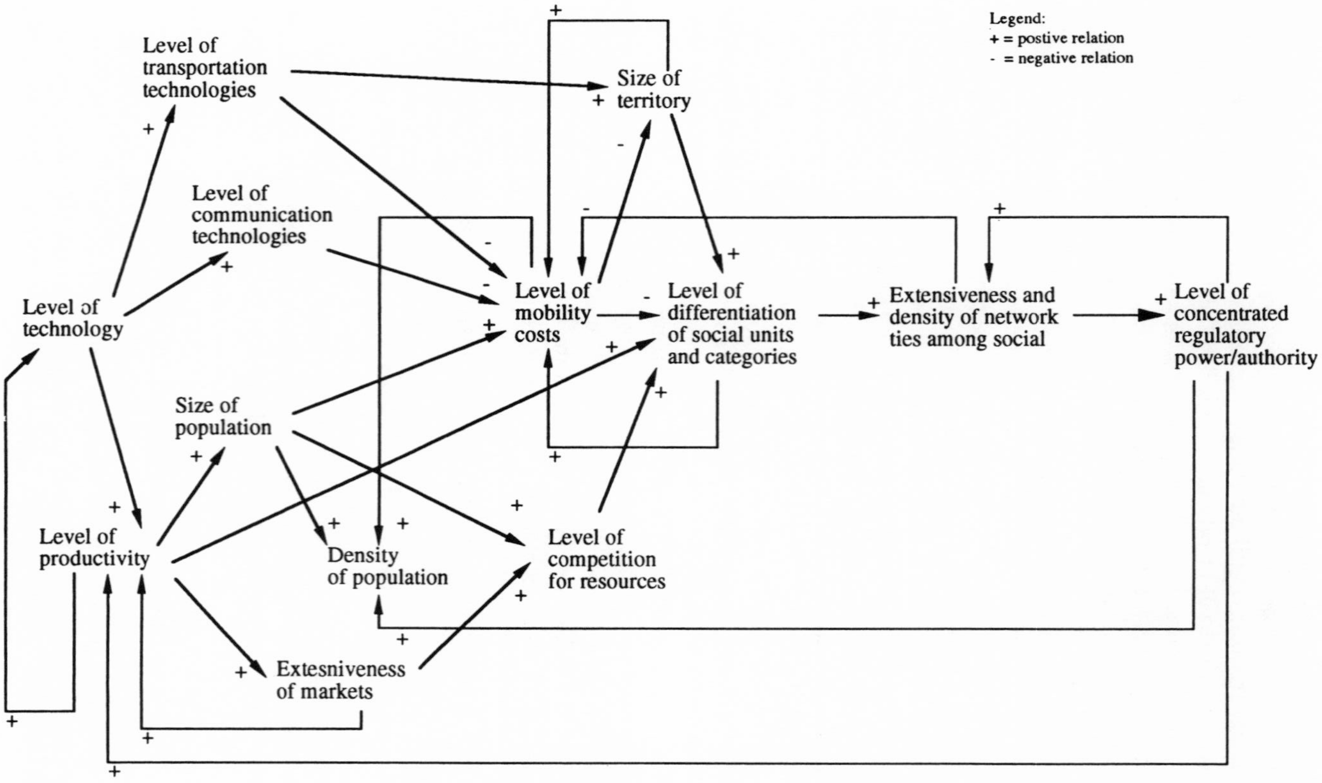

Figure 1. Hawley's Ecological Model of Assembling

Legend:
+ = postive relation
- = negative relation

Level of
concentrated
regulatory
power/authority

Extensiveness and
density of network
ties among social

Level of
differentiation
of social units
and categories

Size of
territory

Level of
mobility
costs

Level of
competition
for resources

Density
of population

Level of
transportation
technologies

Level of
communication
technologies

Size of
population

Extesniveness
of markets

Level of
technology

Level of
productivity

68

logistical loads on further growth and expansion of territory. Mounting mobility costs also work against differentiation of organizational units (what Hawley terms "corporate units") and social categories (Hawley's "categoric units"); therefore, if mobility costs can be lowered with new technologies, then a major barrier to differentiation is lifted.

Technologies also determine the level of production, and vice versa, which in turn causes the expansion of markets for distribution of goods and services. Markets not only have direct reverse causal effects on productivity but they also indirectly encourage the development of new technologies in the productive sector, thereby lowering mobility costs and encouraging social differentiation. Markets also increase the level of competition for resources, with such competition then initiating selection pressures for further social differentiation (up to the limits imposed by mobility costs). In addition to its indirect effects on differentiation through markets and competition, expanded production causes social differentiation directly by virtue of the fact that such expansion is only possible with an increase in the number and size of organizational units.

Production and markets operate, in Hawley's terms, as "key functions" because they mediate exchanges with the external environment of a population and flows of resources to system units; as a result, they concentrate population and organizational units in space, thereby increasing population densities that in turn escalate competition and differentiation into diverse social niches. Additionally, high levels of production allow for the support of a larger population, and when this potential is realized, further differentiation is possible (i.e., there are more people who can be differentiated) and encouraged (through the effects of population size on competition).

In Hawley's model, power is related to differentiation and the formation of networks among differentiated social units. Differentiation raises mobility costs, and one mechanism for reducing these is to create networks among social units—for example, alliances, confederations, coalitions, mergers, oligopolies, and so forth. Such networks concentrate power which, in turn, is used to forge additional networks so that regulation and control are facilitated. As power is consolidated in the mutually escalating cycle, it is used to increase production and, as a result, it determines indirectly the size of territories and populations as well as their density in space. Also, as another type of "key function," power concentrates organizational units in space and, hence, increases population densities.

Thus, Hawley's model provides a number of useful leads for a theory of assembling. It recognizes that concentrated power pulls organizational units together and increases densities of settlement. It emphasizes that population size as it influences competition affects not only differentiation of a population but its density of settlement. It makes production the force behind assembling, in several senses: First, increases in production are causally connected to the development of technologies (as both a cause and effect of new technologies) which, in turn, lower mobility costs, allowing for larger populations and expanded territories. Second, expanded production sets into motion a series of processes—markets, competition, and differentiation of new types of organizational units or "corporate units"—that have reverse causal effects on the size and distribution of the population. These effects are various: Expanded production ultimately increases the size and number of organizational units which, in turn, enable the population to grow; such corporate units often develop patterns of network linkage (alliances, associations, coalitions, internal contacts, cartels, etc.) that reduce mobility costs (especially with respect to information, but also material flows), while facilitating the concentration of power (by virtue of creating networks of elites); the concentration of power works to expand production through capital formation which lowers mobility costs, but if power is used to expand territories through conquest and war, then it eventually becomes a drag on production, while increasing mobility costs as territories are expanded and as diverse subpopulations are incorporated.

URBAN ECOLOGICAL THEORIZING ON ASSEMBLING

As Hawley was "upsizing" the early Chicago urban ecology model to a more macro level, while selectively borrowing from the macro models of Spencer and Durkheim, the urban ecology "school" continued to develop theory at a meso level. Figure 2 represents a composite of these meso efforts in "urban sociology." In rendering this model, I have not tried to conceptualize the dynamics of intra-urban areas in the same detail as much modern urban ecology (see, for example, Kasarda 1972; Hawley 1971, 1981; Frisbie 1980; Berry and Kasarda 1977). Rather, I have restated somewhat the processes that influence the concentration of the population (i.e., the density of people within spatially bounded areas), the level and rate of geographical expansion (i.e., the movement of individuals outward from concentrated core areas), and the overall level of agglomeration (i.e., the extent to which the population as a whole is located within densely settled spatial areas, many of which are contiguous and connected). Much urban sociology, and urban ecology in particular, seeks to specify the dynamics of these processes in fine-grained detail. In contrast, my goal is to represent the ideas of urban ecology as they inform us about macro issues—i.e., assembling varying numbers of individuals in varying amounts of space.

What, then, does the model tell us? The key variable in most modern urban ecological models is communication and transportation technologies. As these technologies develop, they are used to expand the material infrastructure for transportation (roadways, canals, ports, railroads, airports, etc.) and

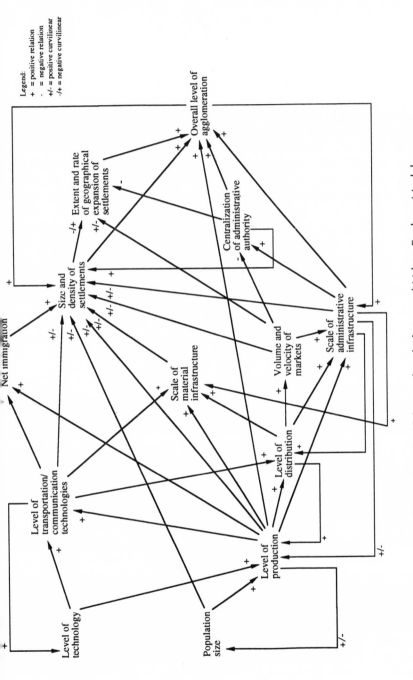

Figure 2. The Elaborated and Abstracted Urban Ecology Model

Legend:
+ = positive relation
- = negative relation
+/- = positive curvilinear
-/+ = negative curvilinear

Net immigration

Overall level of agglomeration

Extent and rate of geographical expansion of settlements

Centralization of administrative authority

Size and density of settlements

Scale of administrative infrastructure

Volume and velocity of markets

Scale of material infrastructure

Level of transportation/ communication technologies

Level of distribution

Level of technology

Level of production

Population size

71

communication (which historically overlap with those for transportation, except in recent history with the advent of the material means for the "information age"). The density of a population is, to some degree, related to the capacity to move people and information, which is connected to the ability or willingness of productive units to generate a material infrastructure. This connection is often left implicit in urban ecology models, but I see technology (or knowledge about how to construct and use transportation and communication systems) and its manifestation in a material infrastructure as different variables which can vary independently (a population can have knowledge, but not implement it for a variety of reasons, most of which revolve around the level of production and the administrative infrastructure to organize material development). Production, distribution, and markets also create organizational burdens which increase the administrative infrastructure of a population (courts, laws, agencies, and other organizational units involved in coordination of activities). In turn, the administrative structure determines the scale of the material infrastructure. More recent ecological models stress the centralization of this administrative structure in both governmental authority systems as well as nongovernmental units. This process is conceptualized as concentrations of administrative authority and control.

The assembling processes enumerated in the model in Figure 2 are concentration of the population, its extension of space, and its overall level of concentration in areas of high density (what I term overall level of agglomeration). Let me now examine the effects of the material infrastructure (as it is influenced by technologies, population size, production, and administrative capacities) and the administrative infrastructure (as it is influenced by the level of production and distribution) on these three general assembling processes. The density of a population reveals, I believe, a curvilinear relationship with the level of production, material infrastructure, and administrative infrastructure (hence, the $+/-$ designation on the causal arrows). Initial increases in production pull individuals to centers of capital concentration, but as production expands under ever higher levels of technology, greater distributive capacities (i.e., higher volume/velocity of markets), extended administrative systems, and increasingly efficient transportation/communication infrastructures, it operates to decrease density by facilitating the movement of a population out from dense urban centers, or by allowing for the creation of new population centers away from older ones. Yet, the decrease in density is only relative to the very high levels of density generated during initial increases in productive capacity, as it directly pulls individuals to urban areas and as it sets into motion expanded material and administrative infrastructures which also pull individuals to urban areas. The concentration of administrative authority (e.g., city governments and other regulatory agencies) also works to concentrate population by limiting the extension of boundaries and by encouraging land-use patterns that concentrate capital (usually under the political influence of elites in the productive sector), but eventually this concentrated power is insufficient to overcome the effects of market dynamics (which encourage "urban sprawl" as competition increases) and population size and density, per se (which eventually make it necessary for the population to spill outward, especially as production and administrative structures consume the core areas of urban space). Moreover, higher technology processes, expanded administrative functions, and escalating market velocity generate pressures for more horizontal space, forcing the outward movement of populations and the extension of geographical boundaries. Such movement must often overcome efforts of concentrated administrative authority to control spatial boundaries, but eventually, new centers of concentrated authority emerge in urban centers around older core areas. As these processes accelerate and as transportation and communication technologies assume very high values, entirely new urban centers revolving around both production and administrative functions are created, often far removed from early concentrations of a population.

The specific pattern of these processes has consumed much of the conceptual energy of urban sociology. Much of what occurs, I suspect, is contingent on the specific conditions under which the forces of production, the volume and velocity of markets, and the development of material and administrative infrastructures increase; as a result, it has been difficult to theorize about the precise details of this process. There are, however, some interesting generalizations that have emerged from efforts to account for the patterns of urban settlement. Whereas these may apply only to more recent urban processes, they may have more generic and general relevance. Thus, let me briefly mention some of these principles.

One principle (Clark 1951) posits that the density of settlement in an urban area declines exponentially as the distance from the center of this area increases. This principle follows from the assumptions of ecological theory as it was first formulated by the early "Chicago School": costs for land decrease in locations removed from the market competition inherent in the high-density urban core; those economic, administrative, and domestic units that can afford the higher prices of the densely settled core are able to make maximum utilization of this core space, whereas those units which cannot do so are willing to acquire less expensive land from the core and assume the additional transportation and communication costs (Berry and Kasarda 1977, pp. 95-97). Yet, as Frisbie and Kasarda (1988, p. 634) note, "recent technological and organizational changes have tended to attenuate the bond between centrality and accessibility." The most significant of these technological and organizational changes revolve around the movement of the material and administrative infrastructures to more outlying regions, coupled with the dramatic changes in communication technologies of the last decades that reduce the costs of the shifts in settlement patterns (Kasarda 1972; Castells 1985). These changes have created a more polycentric system across an urban region (Kasarda 1980); also, in the eyes of some investigators (e.g., Gottdiener 1985), this represents a true decentering of the administrative and material infrastructures.

Related principles seek to explain the *system* of densely settled areas that follows from this size-distance hypothesis. One principle argues that there is a pattern to the relative sizes of cities (Zipf 1949; Hawley 1971, 1981; Stephan 1979a, 1979b). The number of intermediate cities is a positive and proportionate function of the number and size of large cities in a society or region. This pattern, however, appears not to hold true in small societies where one or two large or "primary" cities appear to be sufficient to provide services without a proportionate number of intermediate cities to mediate between large urban centers and smaller rural towns. Thus, this "gradient principle" might be restated as follows: The larger the territorial expanse of a population, the greater the likelihood that there will be a larger number of intermediate size urban areas that link large cities to small rural areas; conversely, the smaller the territorial expanse of a population, the more likely will the number of intermediate size cities decrease.

This principle follows from another which states that the rates of interaction of populations are an inverse function of their distance (Stephan 1979a, 1979b). Hence, societies with large cities that are proximate to very small urban centers do not need intermediate cities for rural areas to be integrated into larger urban places. A related idea from ecological theory (Frisbie and Kasarda 1988, p. 643) is that the volume of resource flows among urban areas determines the degree to which they constitute an integrated system and, in all likelihood, the extent to which there is a hierarchical structure (economic and political dominance) to this system of cities.

All of these principles are relevant to the variable that I have labeled, for lack of a better term, "overall agglomeration" in the model in Figure 2. What I am trying to capture with this term is the fact that populations reveal different levels of density in their settlement within urban areas of varying size. A highly agglomerated population is one where a large proportion of the population resides in a densely settled spatial area; the more these spatial areas are contiguous and / or functionally interdependent, the more agglomerated is this population. Thus, there can be a degree of deconcentration of a population into suburban areas, or even to new urban settlements, but this population would still reveal a high degree of agglomeration because the population still resides in relatively dense spaces that are, to a high degree, spatially contiguous and functionally interdependent in terms of the flow of resources.

Many of the particulars of urban sociology seek to explain the development and the precise form of settlement for a highly agglomerated population (e.g., Hall 1984, 1988; Klassen, Molle, and Paelinck 1981). For my more macro purposes, however, the key variable is the general level of agglomeration, with this level being a joint function of the variables enumerated in the model in

Figure 2: density of population in spatial areas, scale of administrative infrastructure, concentration of administrative authority, net immigration (which, in most cases, is into densely settled areas), scale of material infrastructure (as this is influenced by production and technologies, especially with respect to communication and transportation), and degree as well as rate of geographical expansion. What I argue, then, is that increased production, growth of the material and administrative infrastructures, and expansion of markets cause increased density of settlement and, over time, geographical expansion in the form of contiguous urban settlements *and* larger numbers of smaller, noncontiguous, but still dense, settlements. Very high levels of communication and transportation technologies as well as very high levels of production and market distribution accelerate geographical expansion as well as the development of larger numbers of noncontiguous areas of dense settlement which are, nonetheless, integrated into larger and more densely settled urban cores (this latter process can extend to the world-system level, as is evident today as different populations are, to a degree, agglomerated by virtue of their functional interdependence, that is, resource flows, with large urban centers in different parts of the world).

These rough generalizations will, I believe, apply to more than the "modern world" and account for processes in less developed regions of the world today, and of the distant past. That is, populations of the past or present with low productivity, little material or administrative infrastructure, and low volume markets (the situation in most parts of the world until relatively recent history) will be: (1) smaller and less densely settled in space; (2) less likely to expand geographical space outward from existing urban cores (assuming they have them); and (3) less agglomerated into a variety of dense urban centers. Populations with moderate levels of productivity, some material and administrative infrastructures, and viable markets revealing some volume and velocity (and this is the case for most of the "nonmodern world" today and most of the preindustrial world three hundred years ago) will evidence dramatic increase in the size and density of a few urban cores, some degree of expansion from these cores, and potentially, an increase in the number of noncontiguous urban centers, and only relatively low levels of agglomeration.

These kinds of generalizations may be timebound, especially since it is difficult to know what the extremely high loadings for population size, production, markets, and transportation/communication technologies will bring about in the future. The model in Figure 2 argues that, despite local and historically unique variations in the precise patterns, increase in the size, density, extension of urban space, and agglomeration will ensue.

Urban ecology has been heavily criticized by a variety of approaches, the most notable being those perspectives derived from Marxian concepts. The basic argument of these approaches (e.g., Gottdiener 1985; Castells 1977, 1978, 1985, 1988; Feagin 1983; Molotch 1976; Logan and Molotch 1987) is that urban ecological theory does not devote sufficient attention to the dynamics of capitalism and state power.

As one of the most prominent of these critical theorists, Manuel Castells is an appropriate candidate for review (Castells 1977, 1978, 1985, 1988). Yet, as with most urban sociologists, Castells focuses on the contemporary profile of urban regions, producing generalizations from current urban trends; as a result, he does not offer a general theory so much as a running commentary on the effects of very high levels of technology in capitalist systems on patterns of spatial distribution. For this reason, it is difficult to extract and abstract a more general model from his work (and that of most urban sociologists as well) that can be applied across a much longer time span. Nonetheless, Figure 3 represents a more abstract model of his approach (that Castells would not, in all probability, deem appropriate). In constructing this model, the terminology is altered somewhat so as to encompass more than spatial patterns in capitalist, industrial, and postindustrial societies. When this kind of exercise is done, much of the critical and empirical "punch" of Castells' work is missing, but more fundamentally for my purposes, most of the underlying theoretical ideas converge with those of other ecological theories.

The basic intent of Castells' work is to explain patterns of distribution (i.e., concentration/dispersal) and differentiation (intra- and inter-urban) of populations in space. The master explanatory variable is "high productive technologies" which are seen to alter (1) other technologies, such as those for communication and transportation, (2) the nature of production and, hence, the relation between capital and labor, and (3) the ratio of service to manufacturing activity. These effects of high technology are accelerated by (4) the expanding functions of government, especially around welfare and warfare administrative activities, and (5) the international division of labor in the emerging world capitalist system. All of these processes, as they interact with each other, produce a variety of urban patterns, including: a decline of labor-intensive manufacturing at the core of urban areas; an expansion of the service sector, some of which remains at the urban core (e.g., services for concentrated corporate headquarters, export-import), with the rest following the movement of the population to the suburbs; a polarization of labor markets (between low- and high-wage activities) in urban areas; an uneven development of regions with respect to capital investment by government and economic interests; a functional division of economic activity (manufacturing and varying service activities) within and between urban areas; and an increasing degree of functional interdependence, greatly facilitated by communication technologies, among varied and differentiated urban regions and sectors.

The model in Figure 3 tries to state these processes more generically and abstractly. Ever higher levels of technology increase the level of production and capacities for communication/transportation. Various paths emanate from these forces and intersect with other processes to generate a variety of

Figure 3. Castelles' Ecological Model of Assembling

77

outcomes for the distribution and differentiation of populations in space. One crucial path is the expanded administrative activity of the state, as fueled by external threat, population growth, and new communication/transportation technologies; another stems from expanded production and distribution, which also encourage an increase in administrative activity. The expansion of administrative infrastructure—both governmental and economic—initially encourages concentration of populations; but as this infrastructure grows under very high levels of productive, communication, and transportation technologies (Castells' point of departure), it encourages the outward expansion of settlements (deconcentration) and the creation of new settlements, while increasing the functional differentiation of spatial areas (with respect to types of production, administration, and servicing). These differentiating processes are punctuated by the increase in polarization of labor markets, as the substitution of capital for labor increases. The result is that differentiation tends to be intra-urban, especially when fueled by polarization of labor markets in already densely settled areas. In contrast, when expansion of settlements under the impact of the increasing size and scale of the administrative infrastructure occurs, differentiation of urban regions around various economic and governmental activities is likely to ensue.

These differentiating processes are not my concern here, where the focus is on assembling, but the general model is very much like those in human ecology when addressing population size, density, and dispersal questions: Production increases population size and density, but as a service sector develops, especially under the impact of expanded markets and governmental regulation, the extension of settlements ensues, although initial increases in the size and scale of the administrative infrastructure will increase the density of urban areas. (Only when this administrative infrastructure is dramatically expanded, under new technologies, will it cause deconcentration.) Such expansion of urban areas is followed by creation of new urban areas, but the overall level of urban living—what I termed agglomeration in Figure 2—still remains high.

GEOPOLITICAL THEORIZING ON ASSEMBLING

From a macroscopic perspective, assembling almost always involves interpopulation dynamics influencing the cultural/ethnic diversity of a population, its size, and its expanse of territory. Thus, to complete a macrostructural picture of assembling processes, it is useful to include theories of geopolitics revolving around conflict and conquest of one population by another. Among the various theories that could be examined, Randall Collins' (1986) analysis of geopolitics is the most relevant to a macrostructural theory of assembling.

Much like Spencer's early theorizing on "militant societies," Collins (1986, pp. 167-212) views internal system processes and external geopolitical activities as interconnected. Geopolitical empires are created by war, but success in war depends upon the level of productivity, population size, resource levels, capacity to mobilize and legitimate concentrations of power, and most significantly, extent of "marchland advantage" (i.e., the degree to which a population is "protected" from "enemies" by natural barriers and, as a result, can fight wars on only one front, or on a small proportion of its borders).

In Figure 4, I have modeled the dynamic relations among the variables in Collins' theory. High levels of coercive power can only be mobilized by high productivity and surplus wealth, which are related to levels of technology, resource advantages, and population size. The mobilization of coercive power can be sustained by success in conflict, which legitimates the use of power and which, at times, provides additional resources and wealth (through plunder and exploitation). But, much as Spencer recognized over one hundred years ago, success in warfare extends the territorial space of an empire which, eventually, works against further expansion of territory. For as the extent of territory increases, several countervailing forces are set into motion: (1) the level of ethnic diversity increases (as conquered peoples are added to the population) and creates problems of potential revolt which increase the logistical loads revolving around control, cooptation, and coordination of diverse and restive subpopulations; (2) the level of logistical loads also increases as a result of having to move materials (supplies, weapons), people (administrators, soldiers), and information (orders, directives, guidelines) across larger territories, farther and farther removed from centers of power and administration; (3) the marchland advantage is eventually lost as an empire expands and must confront enemies on more than one front and, inevitably, another empire (creating the possibility of a showdown war); (4) the technological advantage will also be lost as enemies copy those technologies (both economic and military) that enabled one population to subjugate and control another.

Under these escalating conditions, territorial expansion reaches the point of overextension, as logistical loads increase and previous marchland and technological advantages are lost. Thus, there is a built-in corrective to assembling processes across space; at some point, it becomes difficult to conquer and control additional populations and territories. For this basic reason, Collins argues that empires have historically reached a maximum size of about 4-6 million square miles and, then, begun to disassemble as their point of overextension was reached. The reverse causal chains in the model can also indicate why empires often collapse or begin to implode back on themselves at the point of overextension. Once there is little chance of success in external wars, several chains of events unfold: The capacity to hold territory and control populations decreases; the ability to extract wealth to finance power and its

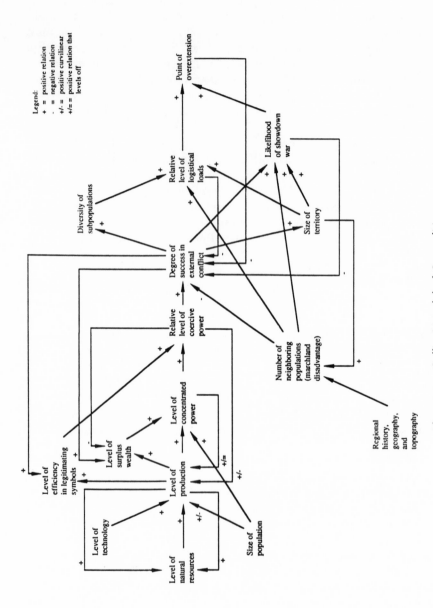

Figure 4. Collins' Model of Geopolitics

mobilization into coercive force declines; the legitimacy of centers of power is eroded as success in the geopolitical sphere declines, setting the stage for coups or revolts; and, given that mobilization of coercive capacities skews production to military needs, while discouraging technological innovation in the domestic sphere and usurping capital from the domestic economy, the economy becomes incapable of expanding production and generating increases in the economic surplus wealth upon which coercion and its legitimation depend. The result is that the empire disassembles slowly or, if it loses a showdown war, the process is accelerated. Moreover, I might add that once disassembly of a geopolitical empire has occurred, it is virtually impossible for it to reemerge, primarily because the forces that produced it—technological advantage, high production, legitimated power, resource and marchland advantages, and coercive capacities—have been reduced and, in the case of show-down war, destroyed and plundered.

There is, then, a kind of rhythm to assembling processes: Populations expand their territory, collapsing at the point of overextension, only to have the geopolitical vacuum reassembled by another expanding empire which, inevitably, will collapse. Since empires have difficulty reconstructing themselves, I would add to Collins' theory the hypothesis that the long-term trend in the world has been for assembling of large territorial empires to stagnate and decline, with warfare increasingly fought over geopolitical boundaries among smaller territorial units in various regional arenas.

The dynamics of the model presented in Figure 4 also help to explain specific patterns and configurations of territorial assemblage. Those empires that had to traverse oceans and other significant ecological barriers or, in the modern world, that must rely upon air technologies to traverse long distances, are the least stable over time, primarily because their logistical loads are so high. Movement of materials, people, and information becomes very costly the greater the distance from a home base, especially if natural barriers as well as distances require heavy reliance of air and sea transportation technologies. Moreover, while high levels of technology facilitate the movement of materials and people over long distances, the costs of these technologies are very high, thereby increasing logistical loads ever further. Assemblage of populations in large territories is thus considerably easier if the land masses are contiguous and allow the movement of materials and people on the ground and if there are few natural barriers to escalate logistical problems.

Thus, in Collins' theory, the patterns of assembling territories tend to revolve around several basic considerations: (1) resource, marchland, and coercive power advantages of some populations over others; (2) distance from the home base, or capital region, with increasing distance placing an ever greater logistical burden on a population; (3) points of potential contact between two expanding empires; and (4) previous assembly and disassembly of populations that once engaged in territorial expansion. So, while there is certainly much that is historically unique to geopolitical processes, there are basic underlying processes which are subject to theorizing and which can, therefore, become part of a general theory of assembling.

TOWARD A GENERAL THEORY OF ASSEMBLING

We are now in a position to pull these representative theories together into a general macrostructural model of assembling processes, where our central concerns are to explain a population's size, its extent of territory, and its patterns of settlement. Figure 5 extracts and extends the key ideas from the models presented in Figures 1-4 and arrays them in a way that captures, I hope, the general contours of assembling.

Population Size and Production

As is portrayed in the model, the size of a population is fundamental to understanding macrostructural processes. A growing population causes the level of production and degree of concentrated power to escalate. For, as the number of individuals to be supported grows, production increases or, if production cannot be increased, the population begins to dissolve. As production expands, it encourages further population growth. Expanding production also facilitates the development of new technologies (information and knowledge about how to manipulate the environment) and the expansion of capital (i.e., tools and implements used in production) as well as the level of wealth which can be used to buy capital. And, once technological innovation, capital formation, and expanded production are initiated, they have mutually reinforcing effects, up to the point where various reverse causal processes, most of which stem from power and inequality, dampen capital formation and technological innovation. These initial changes in the economy, as indirectly stimulated by population growth, create the principal condition allowing for the concentration of power: the existence of an economic surplus which can be extracted and used to consolidate power and privilege (Lenski 1966). Aside from this indirect effect of population growth, population size directly influences the concentration of power by presenting problems of coordination and control which can only be resolved by regulating authority.

The relationship between population size, on the one hand, and production and power, on the other, is curvilinear. At some point, continued population growth works as a drag on productivity by forcing political authority to expend surplus wealth on social control; as these social control activities increase, the usurpation of wealth to concentrate power decreases the level of capital available to economic units and dampens incentives for technological

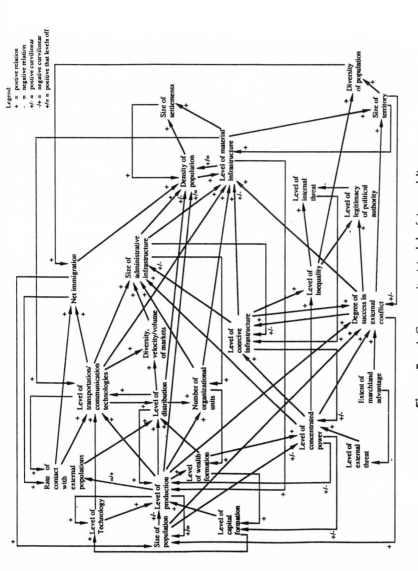

Figure 5. A Composite Model of Assembling

innovation (note the path of reverse causal arrows in the model in Figure 5 from concentrated power to technology and capital formation).

Thus, expanded production sets into motion a series of political dynamics which, in turn, have feedback consequences for production, while setting the conditions for various assembling processes. Let me explore some of these political processes in more detail.

Production and Power

Production increases the level of material surplus or what I have labeled "wealth formation," which is then usurped by those with power to create a system of inequality. Power and inequality generate a self-sustaining, if not self-escalating, cycle: power becomes concentrated to usurp wealth and privilege; as this process continues, those in disadvantaged positions become resentful; such resentment poses internal threats which lead to further concentration of power, which is employed to usurp more wealth in order to finance mechanisms of social control; with increased control, more usurpation of wealth and privilege can occur. Throughout most of human history since hunting/gathering, this escalating cycle has stagnated populations for long periods of time by decreasing capital and repressing technological development; often this cycle has burst populations apart through internal revolt. Such was particularly likely to have been the case in agrarian systems, where a hereditary nobility and elites would usurp virtually all surplus, thereby increasing inequalities to the point of internal revolts. A few hundred years ago in western Europe, this cycle was partially broken with movements toward political democratization under the effects of new commercial and market arrangements for the application of new sources of energy to production. The result was some decline in the concentration of power and in the level of inequality (hence the $+/-$ reverse causal chain between inequality and concentrated power), although there are always pressures for power to reconcentrate itself and for inequality to increase unless checked by popular mobilizations of the masses. As this dynamic has unfolded in the histories of human populations, it has influenced assembling in a variety of ways. First, concentrated power and inequality require an administrative infrastructure to coordinate and channel the use of power which, in turn, increases population density by aggregating individuals in organizational units (e.g., the state bureaucracy). Such density feeds back to encourage more diversity, velocity, and volume in distributive processes in order to provide the goods and services to support administrators and their activities (such distributive processes feed further back and escalate production, as is indicated in the model). Second, concentrated power requires a coercive infrastructure for creating and distributing the physical implements of coercion (weapons, storage facilities, etc.) and for organizing the individuals who use these implements (armies, police, and their administration, authority, and maintenance). As these infrastructures grow, they tend to become concentrated in space and, as a result, increase population densities among not only those directly involved in coercive activity but also those in the expanding state bureaucracy that the coercive infrastructure serves. Third, concentrations of power, coupled with an expanding coercive base, encourage the development of a material infrastructure: roads, shipping, ports, buildings, productive facilities for weapons, and other material facilities, all of which increase population densities.

These infrastructural developments bear complicated relations to each other. The development of an administrative infrastructure—for example, "the state" in agrarian and industrial social systems—provides an initial organizational base for a coercive infrastructure, and initial efforts at developing a capacity for coercion encourage the development of administrative structures (hence, the initially positive relationship between the two). But over time, as the coercive system expands, it enters into an increasingly zero-sum situation with noncoercive facets of administration, creating conflicts of interest and infighting which consume time and resources (hence, the negative portion of the curvilinear relation from coercive to administrative structures, and vice versa). Thus, as a general principle, the relationship between coercive and administrative infrastructural development is positively curvilinear, initially increasing and then decreasing. In turn, as the coercive infrastructure increases, it works to reduce the level of production via a variety of reverse causal chains delineated in the model in Figure 5. The relationship between coercion and material infrastructure is similarly curvilinear, initially increasing the physical facilities for housing people and goods as well as moving them about but eventually distorting these toward military ends and thereby reducing their availability for domestic productive and distributive activities. For, as the costs of coercive activity escalate, the capacity of the centers of coercive power to provide capital, administrative or entrepreneurial encouragement, and incentives for technological innovation to those productive activities that expand the material infrastructure (through a variety of direct and indirect causal paths outlined in the model in Figure 5), begins to decrease. Moreover, the capacity to generate further increases in the level of wealth and economic surplus that can be used to finance all state activities begins to decline. As a result, the rate of assembling may stagnate or decrease; if internal threats escalate as a consequence of increased inequality and cause revolt/revolution, then dissolution and disassembly may occur and reduce, for a time, population densities as people flee the turmoil of urban areas.

Geopolitical processes have a variety of effects on these dynamics. External threat—whether real, imagined, or manufactured—accelerates the concentration of power and the construction of a coercive infrastructure; in so doing, it intensifies the processes discussed above. The degree of success in external war will, as Collins emphasized, be a joint and multiplicative function (via the various causal paths mapped in the model) of population size, production (and indirectly technology), wealth, power, and coercive capacity *relative to* the levels of these variables in surrounding populations. The greater the relative advantage in these variables, the greater will be the success in war and, as a consequence, the larger will be the size of the territory controlled by a population and the more diverse will be the population within this territory. War and conquest also encourage material infrastructure, especially systems of transportation; coupled with the disruptions of war, net immigration will increase, generally producing an increase in the size of geographical units— towns and cities—and their level of density. However, across an entire region, conquest can lower overall population density if conquered populations are not settled in urban areas; but, over time, conquest and expansion of the material infrastructure, coupled with disruption of people's lives and routines (through plunder and exploitation), will increase migration to densely settled areas in search of new opportunities and options, thereby increasing overall population density and, usually, the size of settlement units. In turn, the size, diversity, and scale of densely settled areas encourage migration directly by providing a physical place for immigrants and, equally important, those forces that stimulate distributive processes (e.g., markets and organizational units servicing markets) which encourage migration by providing a sense of (often illusionary) opportunities. These attractions are highlighted by previous migrations which have generated diverse subcultures which can absorb new immigrants. It is because of these self-reinforcing dynamics that conquest and initial urbanization, once set into motion, can become self-perpetuating processes (via the various causal chains delineated in Figure 5).

Such are some of the political consequences initiated by increased production. Now, let me turn to some of the distributive forces that are also set into motion by expanded production and that have important effects on assembling.

Production and Distribution

Increased production requires expanded distribution unless, of course, consumption simply cannot absorb new goods and services. This relationship is exponential in that distributive structures only expand moderately with initial increases in production (due to the inability to consume all goods and services), but as distributive processes expand, they begin to create new sources of demand and to provide the facilities (money, credit, retail systems, etc.) to escalate consumption. In so doing, they encourage dramatic increases in production. For example, with industrialization and postindustrialization, markets successively differentiate many times over, and vast servicing industries develop to facilitate the flow of goods and services. New organizational units are one consequence of expanded distribution, and these feed back to encourage additional production. Together, the expansion of distribution and servicing units begins to decrease the ratio of goods to services produced in the economy, although only with postindustrial economies is this shift in the ratio dramatic. The expansion of distributive processes directly increases population densities by concentrating individuals directly engaged in buying and selling; these distribution functions increase the numbers and densities of those involved in servicing the expanded market. This additional concentration of individuals is escalated by organizational units that interact with the expanding administrative infrastructure of concentrated power to aggregate increased numbers of individuals. Conversely, the existence of an administrative infrastructure (e.g., laws, taxing agencies, courts, etc.) facilitates an increase in the number and size of market- and production-related organizational units, further escalating the concentration of the population. As these entrepreneurial forces feed back to production, they become self-perpetuating and self-escalating, while setting into motion not only the political forces discussed above (and the effects these have on assembling) but also improvements in transportation and communication facilities (for moving goods and services about) which, in turn, increase migration to densely settled areas. Moreover, expansion of these facilities indirectly increases population densities by their effects on increasing the size and concentration of the administrative infrastructure (for financing, organizing, and regulating communication and transportation) as well as the material infrastructure (for providing the physical means and modes for moving information and materials about). Thus, in general, the density of a population is a multiplicative function of the expansion of: (1) distributive processes as these increase the number of organizational units and the burdens on the administrative infrastructure; and (2) the development of communication and transportation technologies as these encourage migration and increase the scale of the administrative and material infrastructure.

CONCLUSIONS

The model presented in Figure 5 is obviously complex,[1] but it seeks to map the basic forces organizing a large portion of social life. Thus, it needs to be robust, but we can ask: Is there a way to simplify the dynamics addressed in the model? It is at this point, when models are getting highly complex, that propositions become a useful alternative. In propositions, it is possible to simplify analytical models by accentuating some causal relations over others, while at the same time generating testable hypotheses.

Below, I have extracted from the model in Figure 5 a series of abstract principles. To the extent that we can theorize about spatial dynamics, Propositions I, II, III, and IV state the basic forces determining, respectively, the *size of a population,* the overall *density of its settlement,* the *size of its settlements* as well as *their level of agglomeration,* and the *size of the territories* enclosing a population and its settlements.

I.   The size of a population is a positive and additive function of:
   A.   The level of production which, in turn, is a positive curvilinear function of:
      1.   Population size, while being a positive and additive function of:
      2.   The level of technology,
      3.   The level of capital formation,
      4.   The number of organizational units, and
      5.   The level of distribution.
   B.   The rate of net immigration which, in turn, is a positive and additive function of:
      1.   The level of transportation and communication technologies,
      2.   The rate and extent of contact with external populations,
      3.   The differentiation as well as volume and velocity of markets,
      4.   The diversity of the population, and
      5.   The size of population settlements.
   C.   The degree of success in external conflict which, in turn, is a function of the conditions listed under IV-A.

II.   The density of population settlements is a positive
   A.   *S*-function of the level of production which, in turn, is a function of the conditions listed under I-A above.
   B.   *S*-function of the level of material infrastructure which, in turn, is:
      1.   A positive curvilinear function of the size of the coercive infrastructure, and
      2.   A positive function of the size of the administrative infrastructure.
   C.   Curvilinear function of the level of distribution which, in turn, is a positive and additive function of:
      1.   The level of production,
      2.   The level of wealth formation,
      3.   The level of differentiation as well as volume and velocity of markets,
      4.   The number of organizational units,
      5.   The rate and extent of contact with external populations, and

6. The level of transportation/communication technologies.
D. Curvilinear function of the rate of net immigration which, in turn, is a function of the conditions listed under I-B.
E. *S*-function of the size of settlements which, in turn, is a function of the conditions listed under III.

III. The size of settlements and their level of agglomeration are a positive and additive function of:
A. The density of settlements which, in turn, is a function of the conditions listed under II-A, B, C, D, and E.
B. The level of material infrastructure which, in turn, is a function of the conditions listed under II-B.

IV. The size of territory controlled by a population is a positive and additive function of:
A. The degree of success in external conflict with other populations which, in turn, is a positive and additive function of:
1. The level of coercive infrastructure relative to that of potential enemies,
2. The level of production relative to that of potential enemies,
3. The size of the population relative to that of potential enemies, and
4. The degree to which marchland advantage exists and can be sustained.
B. The level of material infrastructure which, in turn, is a function of the conditions listed under II-B above.

NOTES

1. Moreover, it is clear that the model contains too many positive loops, resulting in a view of assembling as inexorable and as constantly escalating. Clearly, further consideration will need to be given to endogenous and exogenous forces that dampen these effects. Here is where existing empirical research can help finetune the model.
2. There are many more "technical" explanations for population growth within the field of demography. I have not included these here, but they could be easily incorporated into subpropositions.

REFERENCES

Berry, B.J.L., and J.D. Kasarda. 1977. *Contemporary Urban Ecology.* New York: Macmillan.
Burgess, E.W. 1925. "The Growth of the City: An Introduction to a Research Project." Pp. 47-62 in *The City,* edited by R. Park, E. Burgess, and R. J. McKenzie. Chicago: University of Chicago Press.

Castells, M. 1977. *The Urban Question: A Marxist Approach.* Cambridge, MA: MIT Press.
————. 1978. *City, Class and Power.* New York: Macmillan.
————. 1985. "High Technology, Economic Restructuring and the Urban Regional Process in the United States." Pp. 11-24 in *High Technology, Space, and Society,* edited by M. Castells. Newbury Park, CA: Sage.
————. 1988. "High Technology and Urban Dynamics in the United States." Pp. 85-110 in *The Metropolis Era: A World of Giant Cities,* edited by M. Dogan and J.D. Kasarda. Newbury Park, CA: Sage.
Clark, C. 1951. "Urban Population Densities." *Journal of the Royal Statistical Society,* Series A, 114: 490-496.
Collins, R. 1986. *Weberian Sociological Theory.* Cambridge: Cambridge University Press.
Durkheim, É. [1893] 1933. *The Division of Labor in Society.* New York: Free Press.
Feagin, J.R. 1983. *The Urban Real Estate Game.* Englewood Cliffs, NJ: Prentice-Hall.
Frisbie, P.W. 1980. "Theory and Research in Urban Ecology." Pp. 203-19 in *Sociological Theory and Research: A Critical Approach,* edited by H.M. Blalock, Jr. New York: Free Press.
Frisbie, P.W., and J.D. Kasarda. 1988. "Spatial Processes." Pp. 629-66 in *Handbook of Sociology,* edited by N.J. Smelser. Newbury Park, CA: Sage.
Gottdiener, M. 1985. *The Social Production of Urban Space.* Austin: University of Texas Press.
Hall, P. 1984. *The World of Cities.* 3rd ed. London: Weidenfeld and Nicolson.
————. 1988. "Urban Growth and Decline in Western Europe." Pp. 111-27 in *The Metropolis Era: A World of Giant Cities.* Newbury Park, CA: Sage.
Harris, C., and E. Ullman. 1945. "The Nature of Cities." *The Annals of the American Academy of Political and Social Sciences* 242: 7-17.
Hawley, A.H. 1944. "Ecology and Human Ecology." *Social Forces* 27: 398-405.
————. 1950. *Human Ecology.* New York: Ronald Press.
————. 1971, 1981. *Urban Society: An Ecological Approach.* New York: Ronald Press.
————. 1973. "Ecology and Population." *Science* (March): 1196-1201.
————. 1978. "Cumulative Change in Theory and History." *American Sociological Review* 43: 787-797.
————. 1981. "Human Ecology: Persistence and Change." *The American Behavioral Scientist* 24: 423-444.
————. 1986. *Human Ecology: A Theoretical Essay.* Chicago: University of Chicago Press.
Hoyt, H. 1939. *The Structure and Growth of Residential Neighborhoods in American Cities.* Washington, DC: U.S. Government Printing Office.
Hurd, R.M. 1903. *Principles of City Growth.* New York: The Record and Guide.
Kasarda, J.D. 1972. "The Theory of Ecological Expansion: An Empirical Test." *Social Forces* 51: 165-175.
————. 1980. "The Implications of Contemporary Redistribution Trends for Urban Policy." *Social Science Quarterly* 61: 373-400.
Klassen, L.H., W.T.H. Molle, and J.H.P. Paelinck, eds. 1981. *Dynamics of Urban Development.* New York: St. Martins Press.
Lenski, G. 1966. *Power and Privilege.* New York: McGraw-Hill.
Logan, J.R., and H.L. Molotch. 1987. *Urban Fortunes: The Political Economy of Place.* Berkeley: University of California Press.
Marx, K. [1845-1846] 1947. *The German Ideology.* New York: International.
McKenzie, R. 1933. *The Metropolitan Community.* New York: McGraw-Hill.
Molotch, H. 1976. "The City as a Growth Machine: Toward a Political Economy of Place." *American Journal of Sociology* 82: 309-333.
Park, R.E. 1916. "The City: Suggestions for the Investigation of Human Behavior in an Urban Environment." *American Journal of Sociology* 20: 577-612.
————. 1936. "Human Ecology." *American Journal of Sociology* 42: 1-15.

Park, R.E., and E.W. Burgess. 1925. *The City*. Chicago: University of Chicago Press.

Spencer, H. [1874-1896] 1898. *The Principles of Sociology*. 3 volumes. New York: D. Appleton.

Stephan, E.G. 1979a. "Variation in County Size: A Theory of Segmental Growth." *American Sociological Review* 36(June): 451-461.

_____. 1979b. "Derivation of Some Socio-Demographic Regularities from the Theory of Time-Minimization." *Social Forces* 57: 812-823.

Wirth, L. 1928. *The Ghetto*. Chicago: University of Chicago Press.

Zipf, G. 1949. *Human Behavior and the Principle of Least Effort*. Reading, MA: Addison-Wesley.

Zorbaugh, H.W. 1926. "The Natural Areas of the City." *Publications of the American Sociological Society* 20: 188-197.

A CULTURE SCALE PERSPECTIVE ON HUMAN ECOLOGY AND DEVELOPMENT

John H. Bodley

ABSTRACT

This paper argues that achieving truly sustainable development, social equity, and ecological balance in the world will require a conscious reordering of the primary cultural processes that drive culture change. Cultural processes, and especially those contributing to the concentration of political and economic power, have produced a world in which cultures that were formerly organized exclusively on a small scale of cultural complexity are now arranged in an unstable and inequitable multiscale hierarchy. Emphasizing culture scale and the processes that produce them means taking the very broadest view of human ecology to encompass all cultures throughout the world, from the orgins of humanity to the present, within a necessarily simple explanatory framework. The emphasis is on *culture* rather than *society* in order to include all the human variables most relevant to human ecology: demography, technology, economy, society, polity, and ideology. I suggest that the bewildering diversity of the world's 5,000 or so known ethno-linguistic groups can usefully be reduced to just three scales of cultural complexity: small, large, and global, representing tribal, state, and market-based societies, respectively. These three cultural scales were produced by three distinctive cultural processes: sapienization, politicization, and commercialization, each surpassing the previous in importance as an agent of

Advances in Human Ecology, Volume 3, pages 93-112.
ISBN: 1-55938-760-2

cultural change. I describe the culture scale approach, show how it can help explain the development of cultures, and apply insights derived from this approach to the solution of contemporary human ecological problems.

INTRODUCTION

The restoration of ecological balance, social equity, and human well-being in the world will require making the sapienization process dominant over the processes of politicization and commercialization. Sapienization is the process in which small human populations organized in small-scale cultures adapt to local ecosystems and neighboring peoples in order to satisfy their basic human needs on a sustained basis. Politicization refers to the institutionalization of centralized political authority and the emergence of social classes, both of which were the foundation of the state and conquest empires. Commercialization refers to the complex process by which the market economy has become the dominant cultural force in the world. Interpreting contemporary world problems in reference to these three processes demands a holistic, truly interdisciplinary approach. It forces us to question the importance of overpopulation, resource depletion, technology, and pollution, as *primary* causes of environmental problems. Looking at culture scale and culture process may help to identify the more fundamental basis of our problems.

It is commonplace to observe that the way in which human groups relate to their physical environments is shaped by culture. It is also apparent that as culture has developed over the past 100,000 years, the human impact on the environment has profoundly changed such that people are now capable of culturally altering the entire course of biological evolution on the planet. No one would dispute that population growth, industrial technology, and high rates of consumption of energy and materials are conspicuous immediate "causes" of the contemporary global environmental crisis. However, what is not as obvious is how best to conceptualize the underlying cultural features and processes that have created these problems and thus have the most significance for human ecology. I propose that the concept of *culture scale* can help pinpoint some of the most critical aspects of culture that shape human ecology. The culture scale concept can also help identify cultural solutions to global environmental problems. In a general sense, culture scale refers to the size and complexity of human groups and focuses attention on the distinctive ways in which they are culturally organized.

Culture scale is not particulary novel as a general concept in anthropology, although the term *scale* has not been commonly applied to culture until recently. Historically, anthropologists have used a variety of evolutionary stages to discuss the development of different scales of culture. Especially noteworthy in this regard are the familiar technological stages *paleolithic* and *neolithic* widely used by archaeologists, or the quaintly ethnocentric stages of *Savagery, Barbarism,* and *Civilization* used by Morgan (1877) and Childe (1936). More recently *Band, Tribe, Chiefdom,* and *State* (Service 1962) have been widely used as developmental stages. These approaches to culture scale issues have often proved useful for specific theoretical debates, but their application to contemporary human ecological problems has been limited because they do not make the distinctions that are ecologically the most important. One of the most obvious problems with the earliest evolutionary approaches was the implied assumption of superiority and inevitability. Cultures of more complex scale at later stages in the developmental sequence were assumed to be more advanced, progressive, and adaptive, while smaller-scale cultures at earlier stages were considered to be backward and inferior. This Social Darwinist viewpoint supported the political realities of colonial expansion in which the systematic conquest of tribal peoples and preindustrial states was justified as "survival of the fittest." The assumption that cultures frozen at earlier evolutionary stages would inevitably be superseded precluded serious consideration of government policies that would have permitted the coexistence of states and tribes as autonomous entities. It also made it difficult to imagine that solutions to present ecological problems might be contained in the cultural processes that produced earlier "stages" of culture.

A further problem of early cultural evolutionary theory was its bias toward technological and material determinants of evolutionary progress and its failure to adequately identify the most important causes of cultural change. For example, Morgan used technological inventions such as farming and metal-working as indicators of particular stages, but did not really explain how or why they come about. Anthropologists now recognize that the main events in human development did not occur as sudden inventions; rather, they were gradual processes carried on independently in many parts of the world. Standard evolutionary approaches also tend to portray "civilization" as the end point of evolutionary progress, with industrial civilization as a variation defined by its "advanced" technology. This obscures the emergence of the global market economy as the primary cultural process that produced a global culture and a global human ecological crisis within the past 500 years.

CULTURE SCALE AND CULTURE PROCESS

Grouping cultures by scale of organizational complexity into three broad categories—*small, large,* and *global*—will not only simplify the diversity of the world's cultures, but it will also help avoid the assumptions of cultural superiority and inevitability which are so often a part of evolutionary stage thinking. Significant differences in demography, technology, economy, society, polity, and ideology that are directly relevant to human ecology characterize cultures at each scale. See Tables 1 and 2.

Table 1.   The Scale of World Cultures

	Small	Large	Global
Population	500-100 Low-density	10,000 or more High-density	1 million or more Urban
Technology	Foraging Gardening Herding	Intensive Agriculture	Industrial Fossil fuel Monocrop
Economy	Subsistence Display Reciprocal exchange	Tribute tax Wealth Specialists	Markets Corporations Capitalist
Society	Egalitarian Kin-based Age grades	Ranked Class-based Castes	Class-based literate
Polity	Acephalus Bigman Descent groups	Chiefdoms Kingdoms Empires	Nation states Supranational
Ideology	Animism Shamanism Ancestor cults	High gods Divine kings	Patriotism Monotheism Progress

Source: Bodley (1994).

Table 2.   Culture Scale and Culture Process

Culture Scale	Culture Process	Food Objective	Cost/Benefit
Small	Sapienization	Nutrition	Stability Equality
Large	Politicization	Taxable Surplus	Instability Inequality
Global	Commercialization	Profit making Commodity	Inequality Instability Poverty

Source: Bodley (1994).

These three culture scales represent fundamentally different conditions of human existence that were produced in sequence as *Homo sapiens* became a successful culture-bearing species (small scale), institutionalized political power (large scale), and developed a global market economy (global scale). Each culture scale displays a unique constellation of cultural features that set it apart. Larger-scale cultures do not represent simply a quantitative change, because although they will be characterized by a larger population, they will also be organized differently. The difference is also qualitative. Larger-scale cultures have different institutions, more elaborate divisions of labor, and more complex structures. Cultures of different scale can coexist and interact, and individuals may move between them. Before the emergence of the global culture, larger-scale cultures, because they were relatively more powerful, regularly dominated and incorporated small-scale cultures, modifying them in the process but not completely eliminating their preexisting patterns. In this process of incorporation and modification, the conquered tribal peoples were converted into ethnic peasants. However, when comparisons are made with the situation of tribals within the global system, it is important to remember that ancient empires did not dominate the entire world. They expanded to the limits of their political power. As recently as 500 years ago, well over half the land area of the world was still controlled by autonomous tribal peoples living in small-scale cultures. It is likely that this balance between the world's small- and large-scale cultures would have remained relatively constant in the absence of a global-scale culture.

While absolute population size is a distinctive indicator of culture scale, it is not by itself a primary determinant of culture scale. Imbalances between population and resources must have been a critical part of both the sedentarization process that resulted in the aggregation of human populations into villages and the domestication process in which people steadily increased their control over the reproduction of "wild" plants and animals. These processes, in turn, must have disrupted previous balances and contributed to small increases in population growth. However, I assume that in general, human population size is culturally regulated and that populations are likely to increase only when there is some cultural incentive. It is likely that the larger populations and higher densities that resulted from sedentarization and domestication provided the conditions that made political centralization and large-scale culture possible, but they did not by themselves cause large-scale cultures to appear.

The first real incentive for increasing population above replacement levels did not arise until the politicization process began. Central political authorities had a vested interest in a growing population because that was the only way to raise larger armies, and bring in more tribute, and thereby increase their personal power. Increasing demands by the state for soldiers and tribute made larger families a rational choice for individual households. Later, the commercialization process favored rapid population growth in many ways. Conquest of tribals disrupted cultural checks on fertility while antibiotics reduced mortality. Newly induced massive poverty conditions and the need for vast numbers of people to operate at the margins of the market economy and the bottom of the social hierarchy in the "developing world" often encouraged larger families as survival insurance. Many industrial states also adopted pronatalist policies to generate larger workforces and larger consumer markets.

Anthropologists define culture as the learned ways of life and thought shared by a given society. A culture includes the people, their patterned ways of life and thought, and their products. Sapienization is the complex cultural and biological process that produced fully modern *Homo sapiens* and small-scale culture sometime during the paleolithic some 50,000 years ago, or perhaps as long as 100,000 years ago. Since culture is heavily dependent on symbolic meanings which are most productively conveyed by spoken language, it is likely that human speech, *Homo sapiens,* and small-scale culture developed simultanously. Small-scale cultures can be considered primary cultures because they were the earliest form of culture. They also have persisted the longest and could easily be considered the most successful cultures, because the primary problem they confronted was how to maintain a stable human population within a stable ecosystem.

Small-scale cultures were based on domestic units or households, composed of related nuclear families, which were loosely organized for daily security and sociability into cooperative camps or villages of 25 to 200 people. These multihousehold groups were virtually autonomous, but the cultural system existed and was reproduced at the multigroup level, because people needed connections with people in other groups in order to jointly manage resources and to secure mates and emergency assistance. This multigroup level can be identified by a common language and shared culture. It may be called a "tribe" and its members "tribals," but it must be understood that such a "tribe" had no centralized political leadership and rarely acted jointly. Individual households normally produced their own food, shelter, and other essentials, but shared their labor and resources with other households. Since decision making concerning production and distribution occurred primarily at the household level, there was little need for supra-household leadership. Indeed, in the absence of stored food surpluses, there was no basis for the development of coercive political authority as long as individual households could withhold their support at will from would-be tyrants. People worked to meet their own immediate needs, not to satisfy a chief's need for prestige or power.

Small-scale cultures were the only form of culture in the world until approximately 7,500 years ago. Technologically, this was a "Stone Age" world. However, scale or organizational complexity is the defining characteristic of small-scale culture, and people who live in small-scale cultures today should not be considered relics of a past Stone Age. As soon as larger-scale cultures appeared, the world was changed and smaller-scale cultures were forced to adapt to their new cultural neighbors. It is important to stress that from a culture scale perspective, "paleolithic-like" foraging cultures and "neolithic-like" village farmers are both small-scale cultures because they have no centralized political authority. Thus, political organization is a more important feature than the technological details of their subsistence technology. It is perfectly possible for people in small-scale cultures to drive cars, farm with tractors, and hunt with guns, as long as their primary objective is satisfying basic human needs within a local community that is relatively egalitarian and internally distrubutes goods and services on the basis of reciprocity or sharing.The physical and cultural environment of the world changed with the emergence of a culture scale hierarchy. However, as a product of sapienization, small-scale culture coevolved with humans and is therefore highly adapted to specific natural environments, coexistence with other small-scale cultures, and the satisfaction of basic human needs.

Large-scale cultures, whether organized as chiefdoms, states, or empires, were created by *politicization,* a process in which certain individuals became permanent political leaders over more than a single village. This must have occurred under specific environmental conditions that prevented independent villages from escaping political domination. Small-scale cultures normally survived by constantly limiting the political power and wealth of ambitious individuals, but when this proved impossible, hierarchy and inequality emerged. War, as an instrument of political conquest, was one of the primary paths to large-scale culture. Many small-scale cultures were forced to transform themselves into large-scale cultures in self-defense.

Chiefdoms were historically the first multi-community political units, and were thus the first large-scale cultures (Carneiro 1981). This occurred only within the past 7,500 years. The term chiefdom refers to a hierarchy of villages and districts under a paramount chief. Many theorists emphasize that chiefs were redistributors of economic surplus, but the essential feature of chiefdoms was their political organization. Surplus, defined as production above the maintenance requirements of individual households, must be extracted by political power and is used for political purposes, as Harris (1959) has observed. Small-scale cultures were characterized by politically autonomous villages or mobile bands. They had no surplus because there were no leaders to force households to produce beyond their own needs.

The great divide between small- and large-scale culture was the surrender of tribal village autonomy in order to create a second level of political authority. Adding a third administrative level to form a state, and a fourth to form an empire, would then follow logically as the politicization process proceeded to concentrate more power in fewer hands.

The primary economic function of large-scale cultures is the extraction by political elites of a food surplus in the form of tribute and taxes used to maintain non-food-producing specialist classes. This politically motivated economic objective of food production is a powerful force which takes precedence over the domestic function of food production in small-scale cultures. The costs and benefits of intensified food production under large-scale cultures are necessarily unequally distributed. Furthermore, production intensification and political and economic inequality introduce significant degrees of instability, causing chiefdoms, states, and empires to rise and fall.

The world today is dominated by a relative handful of powerful industrial nations interconnected by a complex web of market exchanges and political alliances. This is a relatively new scale of organization, a global culture, that has emerged only within the past 200 years. Its consequences have been enormous and complex. This global system has systematically absorbed large- and small-scale cultures and is itself so homogeneous that it could be treated as a single culture. Industrialization has enriched, impoverished, and destabilized the world. The global system was created by a *commercialization* process that reversed the relationship between political and economic organization. Political organization is now in the service of ever more powerful economic interests. The global economy is primarily dedicated to the production of profit for the stockholders of corporations. When the costs and benefits of global-scale culture are considered, poverty must be added to inequality and instability, because the global system contains economically stratified nations, which are themselves highly stratified internally. It is the dominance of the commercial market economy that best distinguishes global culture. The unique features of this system represent a total contrast to the subsistence-based, reciprocal production and exchange system that operates in small-scale cultures.

"BALANCE WITH NATURE" AND SMALL-SCALE CULTURE

The archaeological record demonstrates that small-scale cultures maintained a relative balance with the natural resource base. This is shown by the extremely low rate of population growth and the low intensity of subsistence technology that prevailed when the world was dominated by small-scale cultures. During the first 35,000 years of human existence people lived exclusively in small-scale, self-sufficient societies based on mobile foraging. Sedentary village life, which began a mere 15,000 years ago when the world population stood at less than eight million, was rapidly followed by the domestication of plants and animals. However, it was another 10,000 years before the appearance of large-scale, stratified societies living in cities and organized into political states. People in small-scale cultures had no cultural incentive for increasing the density or total size of their populations and no reason for producing food beyond their immediate domestic needs. Indeed, these cultures were organized to prevent overexploitation of resources, runaway growth, and the concentration of political power.

I stress that the "balance" between small-scale cultures and their resources is relative. This is not the "green primitivism" that Ellen (1986) warns against. I am not suggesting that tribals ever achieved perfect harmony with an unchanging nature. Since ecosystems themselves are constantly changing, such balance would be an illusion. Tribals do know a great deal about their environment and often have religious injunctions agains overexploitation, but they kill animals and cut

down trees, sometimes more than they need. For example, I witnessed a foraging party of Amazonian Indians chop down a tree to save themselves the bother of climbing for the fruit. Over the millenia, grazing, slash-and-burn cultivation, and grassland burning by tribals, modified ecosystems over vast areas. Paleolithic hunters may have contributed to the extinction of many pleistocene animals at the end of the last Ice Age. Acknowleding all this, there remains a critical difference between small-scale cultures, where domestic needs dictate how resources are used, and global-scale cultures where class inequalities, governments, and commercial profit-seeking drive resource exploitation.

This assessment of the relative environmental balance of small-scale culture is supported by the distinction drawn by anthropologist John W. Bennett (1976) between two idealized cultural types representing societies that are either in equilibrium or disequilibrium with the environment. According to Bennett, *equilibrium societies* harvest natural resources on a sustained yield basis and are locally self-sufficient. They are small-scale cultures, whereas *disequilibrium societies* are defined as out of balance with their resources and ecosystems and are typified by global-scale cultures. Bennett's equilibrium/disequilibrium typology closely resembles the distinction drawn simultaneously by conservation ecologist Raymond Dasmann (1976) between "*Ecosystem*" and "*Biosphere*" peoples. Ecosystem peoples are members of small-scale cultures that draw their resources from local ecosystems. Dasmann argues that this makes them more likely to practice sustainable resource management. Biosphere peoples operate as members of the global culture and, therefore, extract resources from throughout the globe. In the short run, this allows them to disregard the damage to local ecosystems that this might cause because they can simply shift their extraction activites to another ecosystem.

In order to avoid any accusation that he was romanticizing the "noble savage," Bennett stressed that all peoples have the same "behavioral propensities," are involved in similar technical processes, and have the ability to "modify and pollute Nature" (1976, pp. 12, 139-140). In general, this is correct, as I suggested above, but by using an evolutionary stage perspective, Bennett may have too quickly disregarded small-scale cultures as "only pauses in the overall historical tendency toward exponential increases in environmental use and impact." He specifically warns against:

the "ethnological fallacy" of locating desirable remedies for our own environmental ills in the specialized systems of tribal societies (Bennett 1976, p. 12).

However, when the focus shifts from evolution to scale, it is obvious that quantitative differences between cultures can also be critical qualitative differences. Small-scale cultures may indeed point to important remedies that can help solve present problems in a multicultural world. Bennett (1976, p. 148) recognizes that cultural conditions and institutions can reduce the tendency toward overexploitation, and he even asks whether certain features of equilibrium and disequilibrium cultures might be combined to produce a stable, high-technology, nonpolluting, high-living-standard society. This is a reasonable question, but it may be too technologically centered and does not place enough emphasis on genuine cultural diversity based on qualitative differences in cultural scale.

DISEQUILIBRIUM IN LARGE-SCALE CULTURES

In striking contrast to the relative stability of small-scale cultures, history demonstrates that states are unstable entities, prone to frequent episodes of expansion and collapse. In the process, they accelerate economic production, putting increased pressure on the environment. Because large-scale cultures are created by political processes, they are more likely to break down for political reasons than directly from ecological crises. States tend to break down more readily than tribes because they are more complex systems containing more pieces and more things to go wrong. However, this is not just a quantitative matter. States require specialized organs to maintain their integrity, while small-scale cultures can sustain and reproduce themselves from tiny segments because they are relatively homogeneous. Tribes cannot break down because there is no tribal political structure to collapse. Villages and bands undergo continuous reorganization and can be dissolved at any time with no particular impact on the larger society and culture. In contrast, large regional states break down into local kingdoms or city states, which in turn may further split into chiefdoms or autonomous villages and bands.

States are especially vulnerable to collapse because they contain social classes based on major inequities in wealth and power. States create special interest groups and give them a reason to risk bringing the whole system down in order to improve their own position. A limitation on the number of political offices generates perpetual rivalries. Inequalities of wealth and power may be the most critical defining feature of states and the single most important cause of their breakdown. The creation of wealth requires revenue, but revenue extraction by taxation is a doubly risky state function. State authorities will seek as much revenue as possible, but if they take too much, the peasantry may rebel. Too high a rate of revenue extraction also forces people to intensify their subsistence activities, which increases the pressure on natural ecosystems.

Unequal concentrations of wealth, whether in the form of luxury goods, stored food, or labor-intensive construction projects, appear to be functional prerequisites for state organization, but by their presence they also cause dangerous instability. Warehoused food is required to support non-food-producing specialists and as a strategic reserve to sustain dense populations that might be threatened by fluctuations in production. Luxury goods are necessary status markers and rewards for political service. Storehouses are prime targets for looters from both within and without a particular state, and their defense requires expensive walls and standing armies. The unequal distribution of luxury goods also makes police forces and court systems necessary.

Creating and defending state wealth was a primary reason for costly military campaigns against neighboring states. The maintenance of a full-time officer corps, palace guards, and frontier garrisons were permanent military expenses, while specific campaigns in which large numbers of peasant soldiers were mobilized could be extremely costly. Military expenditures may have been the largest category in many state budgets and created constant pressure for potentially destabilizing increases in revenue extraction.

The primary problem for the ruler of a state is how to increase the production of food staples which can be taxed to finance growth in the non-food-producing sector of the population. There are two immediate ways to increase agricultural productivity: by increasing the number of peasant farmers and / or by increasing the amount of land farmed, but either approach will ultimately require technological changes because of diminishing returns on labor. Danish agricultural economist Ester Boserup (1965) has argued that intensification of food production typically follows a predictable sequence of diminishing returns, involving shortened fallow periods, increased effort per unit of land, and technological change. People must work harder for a smaller return for their effort in order to increase the total production per unit of land. Along the way, critical natural resources may deteriorate.

Tainter (1988) argues that environmental imbalance is only one example of the more general problem of diminishing returns that affects virtually all state functions and most human endeavors. Technological or organizational changes that increase or maintain cultural complexity will eventually experience diminishing returns and "collapse" will occur when the cost of maintaining cultural complexity becomes prohibitively expensive.

DISEQUILIBRIUM IN THE GLOBAL SYSTEM

The world's dominant culture is often conceptualized as industrial civilization, implying that it was a "natural" technological invention simply waiting to be discovered. The industrial revolution must be seen as something more than a shift to fossil fuels and assembly line factory production which began in Western Europe and North America at the end of the eighteenth century. This change in production technology and energy base was called for by the commercialization process. It was commercialization that transformed the world, drawing small- and large-scale cultures into a single global system. In the process, world population increased nearly sixfold, from some 800 million people in 1750 to 5.4 billion in 1992, while per capita rates of resource consumption and standards of wealth soared to unprecedented levels for many in the industrial centers and declined for the majority elsewhere.

The modern capitalist economy is radically different from all previous systems of production and exchange and it is the distinctive features of capitalism that created the commercialization process and the global political economy. The concept of "political economy" emphasizes the fact that economics cannot be separated from politics. This shifts attention from the technological and ecological foundations of "economic" activity to a consideration of cultural factors such as political organization and ideology that ultimately determine the ways in which humans exploit the earth. Capitalist economic organization uses social inequality to promote wealth accumulation and political expansionism on a scale unequaled in human history.

It is significant that Adam Smith, Karl Marx, and modern economists all agree that the commercialized capitalist economy is a unique historical development based on social inequality and profit seeking. Economists Heilbroner and Thurow (1987, pp. 13-17) consider capitalism to be "utterly alien" in comparison to the "tradition and command" systems that preceded it. In their view, there were no "factors of production" in precapitalist societies, because "labor, land, and capital were not commodities for sale." Instead, these factors:

> are the creations of a process of historic change, a change that divorced labor from social life, that created real estate out of ancestral land, and that made treasure into capital. Capitalism is the outcome of a revolutionary change—a change in laws, attitudes, and social relationships as deep and far-reaching as any in history (1987, pp. 15-16).

This view of the capitalist economy accurately highlights the cultural features that generate economic and sociocultural expansion on an unprecedented scale. The disembodied capitalist economy is no longer merely at the service of political rulers, it is a system of creating endlessly increasing profits for a new wealthy elite, and is itself now supported by political power. Under capitalism, production and distribution are separated from the satisfaction of basic human needs, and social inequality promotes further economic growth. Capitalism created a distinctive world system that brought together diverse societies into what has now become a global hierarchy of wealthy and poor nations.

Wallerstein (1990) lists six destabilizing realities that characterize the modern world-system under capitalism: (1) a hierarchical division of labor; (2) periodic expansion and incorporation; (3) continuous accumulation; (4) continuous progress; (5) polarization of individuals and groups; and (6) the impossibility of perpetual growth. A key feature of Wallerstein's model is his distinction between the wealthy capitalist "core" nations, such as Europe, North America, and now Japan, where capital accumulates, and the poor nations in the "periphery," where labor and raw materials are extracted by unequal economic exchange. This core/periphery system projects the elite/commoner inequities of ancient civilizations onto the global stage. These characteristics imply critical contradictions in the system and have generated particular ideologies that tend to obscure the realities and help keep the system functioning.

According to Wallerstein, the global division of labor integrates the world into a single production system based on exploitation and inequalities that paradoxically are supported by ideologies that stress universal values of peace and world order. Racist ideologies are also used to justify the disadvantaged position of peripheral groups with the argument that economic rewards are apportioned differentially according to the intrinsic merit and ability of different groups.

Since 1450, the world-system has gone through cycles of expansion marked by the steady incorporation of external cultural groups into the periphery. This trend has been supported by an ideology calling for all peoples to be assimilated into a universal Western culture, on the assumption that other cultures were simply incapable of "advance." A universalist counter-theme arguing for cultural diversity could also be used to justify an exploitative division of labor, in which newly incorporated groups would be encouraged to retain their ethnic identities while working at specific poorly paid jobs and perhaps living in ghettos. Continuous capital accumulation requires workers to accept increases in workload in exchange for reductions in pay. This is made easier when workers also accept a "work ethic" ideology, extolling the virtues of hard work and competitiveness to overcome inequality.

According to Wallerstein, capitalism tends to polarize people by steadily widening the gap between rich and poor. However, such a reality is destabilizing and is therefore vigorously denied by the world system's "central myth of the rising standard of living." Wallerstein argues that elites in the wealthiest countries try to persuade the poor that wealth inequality is decreasing. Such myths minimize the impoverishing effects of population increase, increased workloads, and environmental impacts, which might show a declining standard of living. Elites also exhort the poor to greater "development" efforts, while implying that failure to achieve development must be due to racial or cultural inferiority. The most serious contradiction of the capitalist world-system is its failure to acknowledge that the system as constituted can not expand forever.

SHORTCOMINGS OF THE DOMINANT ECONOMIC DEVELOPMENT PARADIGM

In 1988, near the end of the Third United Nations Development Decade, there were more impoverished people in the world than ever before. While global averages showed some improvements, the UN goal of an adequate standard of living for everyone had clearly not been realized. Obviously, poverty is not a problem of technological "underdevelopment" or "ignorance;" it is an amplification of the inherent inequities in the social hierarchies of large-scale cultures. These inequities are intensified by the operation of the global market economy. If eliminating poverty were the sole objective of technologically focused development programs, an impartial observer in 1988 might have concluded that the wrong course was being followed, but by then development efforts had come to serve many other interests.

Development as it has been practiced throughout most of the twentieth century has systematically undermined the self-maintenance abilities of small-scale peasant communities leaving them highly vulnerable to outside exploitation. While the primary ideological justification for externally planned development was that it would ultimately raise rural living standards, the outcome of decades of development suggests that a fundamental reassessment of the entire issue is called for. The barriers to progress are more likely to lie beyond, rather than within, local communities.

The formal structures through which technical assistance and development finance reach the developing world consist of many complex bureaucracies linked in a ponderous network. Priorities are set by relatively few key organizations at the top that make decisions that affect the smallest details of life for millions of people living in remote villages throughout the impoverished world. Development decisions pass through so many hands before actually being implemented that the entire enterprise is extremely costly and often proves counterproductive.

The consistency with which global poverty has been treated as a technological problem is in part because development policies are formulated and financed by professional elites who are far removed from the daily realities of poverty. Development is much more than a humanitarian concern. It has become a thoroughly institutionalized and highly complex industry with important political and economic functions for the wealthy donors, which may be quite unrelated to the needs of the poor.

ECOLOGICAL BALANCE IN A MULTICULTURAL WORLD

DeWalt (1988) argues that what is needed is an alternative development paradigm to set new goals. He proposes a list of principles which, if adopted by the major development agencies, would transform the way development is presently being practiced to make it both achievable and sustainable throughout the world. Specifically, he proposes that development must emphasize:

1. Long-Term community goals;
2. Nature/culture balance;
3. Local regions and ecosystems;
4. Local resource self-sufficiency;
5. Basic human needs;
6. Decentralization, local autonomy;
7. Local cultural integrity;
8. Justice and equity;
9. Reduction of resource competition; and
10. Gradual change and diversity.

This kind of development would, in effect, return power to small- and large-scale cultures, while reducing the role of the global market economy and the international political hierarchy. DeWalt notes that the goals that he outlines are not new. Many international development agencies already acknowledge the validity of many of the above precepts as individual goals, but they have had difficulty actually implementing them as a comprehensive development strategy.

SMALL-SCALE CULTURES, SMALL NATIONS, AND GLOBAL EQUITY

Many scholars have concluded that the most promising solution to global problems would build on the adaptive advantages of small-scale cultures. The basic principle, alluded to above in DeWalt's 10 precepts, would be to create a global system with economic and political power concentrated at the lowest levels in cultural units of the smallest feasible scale. This would reverse the present trend toward centralization, scaling down the problem-causing "macro-framework" while maximizing democracy, independence, and diversity at all levels. A pioneer proposal for such a world was presented by economist Leopold Kohr in 1957 in his obscure book *The Breakdown of Nations*. Kohr argued that size or *scale* was the key to understanding and solving most of the world's problems. As he states (1978, p. 79):

> a small-state world would not only solve the problems of social brutality and war: it would solve the equally terrible problems of oppression and tyranny. It would solve all problems arising from power.

In Kohr's view, nations generate "social misery" and tend to break down when they became too large and uncontrollable. He felt that a world composed of small nations of relatively equal power would be safer and more humane. Taking the ethno-linguistic map of Europe as an example, he argued, like

Bernard Nietschmann (1988), that small nations already exist as ethnic groups. They have simply been submerged by the larger, more artificial political units that composed the old empires or were created during the 20th-century decolonization process. Anticipating the modern struggle of indigenous peoples and other ethnic "nations" for political autonomy, Kohr proposed that large countries and empires break themselves down into more manageable sized nations, by offering local "nationalities" equal voting power within a federal system, which would then dissolve itself after a transitional period. This is precisely the course that the Soviet Union undertook in 1991-1992 after granting autonomy to the other Warsaw Pact nations.

Kohr's proposal was premature, and his book was largely ignored at the time because it ran counter to the dominant economic development and national integration trends of the late 1950s as the Cold War was intensifying. His work did inspire the economist E. F. Schumacher to explore the advantages of small-scale solutions to economic problems in his important book, *Small is Beautiful* (1973).

American anthropologist Sol Tax, working independently, came up with a similar culture scale solution to global problems with his 1977 proposal that the world be divided into 10,000 relatively self-sufficient, politically autonomous "localities" averaging 500,000 people. This world of five billion people would be connected by an egalitarian global communication network (Tax 1977, p. 229). Even in the late 1970s, when world affairs were still dominated by the seemingly static great power blocks of the Cold War, such a devolution of power seemed inconceivably idealistic. However, political events in eastern Europe in the 1990s have demonstrated the continued importance of small ethnic "nations" and have shown that large political and economic structures can scale down relatively peacefully (although events in Yugoslavia also show that this process will not be easy and may require military intervention by neutral international authority). Perhaps the most difficult problem is the reality that ethnic groups are so frequently intermixed within a common territory.

A more detailed application of the small nation alternative to solving environmental problems was developed in 1972 by a group of British ecologists, who borrowed ideas directly from small-scale cultures. Their *Blueprint for Survival* (Goldsmith et al., 1972) spelled out in some detail how Britain could transform itself into a stable and sustainable society that would "give the fullest possible satisfaction to its members." They proposed a series of measures to be carried out over a 200-year period that would reduce and then stabilize the population at 50% of its size at that time. The tax system would be restructured to phase out unsustainable technologies and reward energy and materials-conserving alternatives. For example, biological controls and organic fertilizers would gradually replace agricultural chemicals. They wanted to decentralize the political and economic system by creating maximally self-sufficient and self-regulating local communities of 5,000 people, grouped into regions of 500,000 with national representation. The local communities were consciously modeled after anthropological descriptions of tribal societies. They would be composed of "neighborhoods" of 500 people that would reproduce face-to-face tribal relationships. The *Blueprint* planners argued that small-scale societies would offer personal satisfactions that would compensate for the reduction in consumption that stability would require. At the same time, such an arrangement would reduce the importance of individual self-reliance as a driving force behind capitalist accumulation. Furthermore, the *Blueprint* planners argued that decentralization, self-sufficiency, and self-regulation would greatly reduce the need for, and the costs of, transportation, urbanization, and political bureaucracy.

The *Blueprint for Survival* thus envisioned a world composed of "small-scale states" combining the best elements of large- and small-scale cultures. Such a solution would imply not that the global system and industrial technology would disappear but that the world would certainly be structured around different goals. A global system of decentralized nation-states would not only be able to respond more effectively to environmental problems, it would also create ideal conditions for cultural diversity, equality, and democracy.

The devolution of political and economic power would promote the kind of "food self-reliance" that researchers at the Institute for Food and Development Policy advocate as a solution to world hunger and poverty. Lappe, Collins, and Fowler (1978, pp. 458-474) argue that control over agricultural resources needs to be returned to democratically based communities, to give rural peoples greater economic power. Genuine democracy would also promote greater equality at both community and national levels and would allow the initiative for development to come directly from the people it was designed to benefit. Lappe and Collins are not opposed to international trade but argue that placing food self-reliance, or local self-sufficiency, as a first priority would mean that trade would be more responsive to local needs and would not undermine local markets. Locally based food systems would also be more concerned with the direct nutritional value of food than with its commercial value.

It is significant that moving political power downward to small-scale social units is precisely what the leaders of political groups organized by existing small-scale cultures are demanding. This is exemplified by the policy positions they have presented before international forums such as the United Nations Special Working Group on Indigenous Peoples, which was first convened in 1982. Planners who are dominated by evolutionary stage thinking might see this as a regressive move "back to the Stone Age." However, the issue is not any particular technology by itself; rather, it is how cultures are organized. Contemporary indigenous communities may optimize small-scale cultural features while still operating within a market economy. They make wide use of many types of industrial technology, often using them effectively to protect and extend their independence.

The restructuring envisioned by decentralization really means restoring a more stable balance between the three broad levels of culture scale. This is not a rejection of market-based exchanges, international trade, or state political structures as such. Each organizational level can contribute to human well-being, and a truly stable world probably requires the presence of all three levels. The goal is to create a world that enhances the best aspects of each level. Some form of international organization for conflict resolution, coordination of exchange, and protection of the biosphere will certainly be needed. Before the global system became the dominant level, small-scale cultures continued to thrive and trade with states. Politically independent small-scale cultures often occupied buffer zones between rival states. States can be made more stable if their internal inequalities can be reduced, and they may become effective organizations for managing regional resources and reducing conflict between small-scale cultures. Given democratically chosen political hierarchies, it is also possible for states to minimize the inequalities and inhumanities that historically have been so common.

The most important adjustment in a sustainable world will be establishing social equality and justice in the absence of long-term economic growth. Using the language of capitalist economics, anthropologist Robert Textor (1991) suggests that it may be possible to use a peace dividend created by the end of the Cold War to deal with the problems of injustice and inequity which he refers to as the social deficit. As was noted above, perpetual growth has always been a fundamental ideological assumption of market economies and many fear that no growth would mean stagnation and would condemn the impoverished to perpetual poverty. However, "stationary-state" economist Herman E. Daly (1971) and the *Limits to Growth* study (Meadows et al. 1972, p. 179) point out that *distribution*, rather than production and growth, will become the most important global issue when production and population are both stabilized at constant levels. Zero growth would mean that social equality would become the highest-priority development goal. When this happens, it will be obvious that small-scale cultures are already highly developed. It would be well to recall that even the evolutionary anthropologist Leslie White, who measured culture advance by increasing energy use, called small-scale mobile foraging cultures "the most satisfying kind of social environment that man has ever lived in" and elaborated (1959, pp. 277-278):

[T]heir social systems...were unquestionably more congenial to the human primate's nature, and more compatible with his psychic needs and aspirations than any other of the cultures subsequent to the Agricultural Revolution, including our own society today.

Developments in the global culture's ideological system, beginning with the 1948 Universal Declaration of Human Rights and its expansion to include group cultural rights, demonstrates that global institutions can help restore equity and sustainability in a world that has become dangerously imbalanced by the dominance of its commercially driven political economy and energy-intensive technology. Small-scale cultures may yet point the way to a more secure world, because a world that can be made safe for small-scale cultures will also be safe for large- and global-scale cultures.

CONCLUSIONS

A very broad view of cultural development suggests that politicization and commercialization, as culture processes, have reduced the effectiveness with which cultures can satisfy basic human needs and have increased the magnitude of environmental problems. Small-scale cultures, which were produced by sapienization, emphasized the satisfaction of human needs and stability and were sustainable with only minor changes over very long periods of time. Large- and global-scale cultures are characterized by chronic instability and inequality, suggesting that the processes of politicization and commercialization will need to be more effectively controlled and subordinated to the satisfaction of basic human needs if development is to become truly sustainable.

Sustainable development requires that small-scale cultures must be granted sovereign powers within the global system as maximally autonomous and self-sufficient local communities, whose human rights will take precedence over the political demands of state governments and the economic demands of the global market. Sustainable development is not fundamentally a technological problem; it is a human rights and culture scale issue. What must be developed is the *ideology* of the global system, such that the rights of small-scale human communities to health, security, and a decent environment can be conceptualized and guaranteed internationally. When this occurs, human ecological security will also be possible for larger-scale cultural systems.

ACKNOWLEDGMENTS

Some of the ideas presented here, and especially the culture scale approach, were first presented publicly in a paper titled "Indigenous Peoples vs. the State: A Culture Scale Approach," which the author presented at the "Indigenous Peoples in Remote Regions: A Global Perspective" conference held at the University of Victoria, British Columbia in July 1991. With the publisher's permission, I have borrowed freely from my 1994 textbook *Tribes, States and the Global System: An Introduction to Cultural Anthropology,* published by Mayfield Publishing Company, Mountain View, California. The present paper condenses many of the major themes of that book and recasts them to focus on problems of human ecology.

REFERENCES

Bennett, J.W. 1976. *The Ecological Transition: Cultural Anthropology and Human Adaptation.* New York: Pergamon.

Bodley, J.H. 1994. *Cultural Anthropology: Tribes, States, Global Systems.* Mountain View, CA: Mayfield.

Boserup, E. 1965. *The Conditions of Economic Growth.* Chicago: Aldine.

Carniero, R.L. 1981. "The Chiefdom: Precursor of the State." Pp. 37-39 in *The transition to Statehood in the New World,* edited by G.D. Jones and R.R. Kautz. Cambridge: Cambridge University Press.

Childe, V.G. 1936. *Man Makes Himself.* London: Watts.

Daly, H.E. 1971. "Toward a Stationary-State Economy." Pp. 236-237 in *The Patient Earth,* edited by J. Harte and R. Socolow. New York: Holt, Rinehart, & Winston.

Dasmann, R. 1976. "Future Primitive: Ecosystem People Versus Biosphere People." *CoEvolution Quarterly* 11(Fall): 26-31.

DeWalt, B.R. 1988. "The Cultural Ecology of Development: Ten Precepts for Survival." *Agriculture and Human Values* 5(1/2): 112-123.

Ellen, R.F. 1986. "What Black Elk Left Unsaid: On the Illusory Images of Green Primitivism." *Anthropology Today* 2(6): 8-12.

Goldsmith, E. et al. 1972. *Blueprint for Survival.* Boston: Houghton Mifflin.

Harris, M. 1959. "The Economy Has No Surplus." *American Anthropologist* 61: 185-199.

Heilbroner, R., and L.C. Thurow. 1987. *Economics Explained.* Englewood Cliffs, NJ: Prentice-Hall.

Kohr, L. 1978. *The Breakdown of Nations.* New York: Dutton. (Originally published 1957.)

Lappe, F.M., J. Collins, and C. Fowler. 1978. *Food First: Beyond the Myth of Scarcity.* New York: Ballantine.

Meadows, D.H., D.L. Meadows, J. Randers, and W.W. Behrens, III. 1972. *The Limits to Growth.* New York: Universe.

Morgan, L.H. 1877. *Ancient Society.* New York: Holt.

Nietschmann, B. 1988. "Third World Colonial Expansion: Indonesia, Disguised Invasion of Indigenous Nations." Pp. 191-207 in *Tribal Peoples and Development Issues: A Global Overview,* edited by J.H. Bodley. Mountain View, CA: Mayfield.

Schumacher, E.F. 1973. *Small is Beautiful: Economics as if People Mattered.* New York: Harper & Row.

Service, E. 1962. *Primitive Social Organization.* New York: Random House.

Tainter, J.A. 1988. *The Collapse of Complex Societies.* Cambridge: Cambridge University Press.

Tax, S. 1977. "Anthropology for the World of the Future: Thirteen Professions and Three Proposals." *Current Anthropology* 36(3): 225-234.

Textor, B.B. 1991. "Toward Conceptualiziang the 'Peace Dividend' Anthropologically." *Human Peace* 9(1-3): 1-6.

Wallerstein, I. 1990. "Culture as the Ideological Battleground of the Modern World-System." *Theory, Culture and Society* 7: 31-55.

White, L. 1959. *The Evolution of Culture.* New York: McGraw-Hill.

THE ECOLOGY OF MACROSTRUCTURE

Jonathan H. Turner

ABSTRACT

Since the work of Herbert Spencer and Émile Durkheim, selection as a mechanism of social differentiation has been a prominent feature of ecological theories, especially with respect to urban and organizational processes. In these approaches, Darwinian metaphors are introduced—for example, resource niches, niche density, competition, and selection among social units—to account for patterns of differentiation, or "social speciation." Less noticed have been more organicist selection arguments which also emanate from Spencer's and Durkheim's works. In these arguments, the potential for systemic disintegration is viewed as creating selection pressures for the creation of new and differentiated structural forms; while these kinds of arguments are often mixed in problematic notions of functional needs and requisites, they are nonetheless an implicit theme in much macrosociology. In this paper, the works of Spencer, Durkheim, and several prominent ecological theorists are examined with an eye to developing a general ecological model of macrostructural differentiation that incorporates both types of selection arguments.

Advances in Human Ecology, Volume 3, pages 113-137.
Copyright © 1994 by JAI Press Inc.
All rights of reproduction in any form reserved.
ISBN: 1-55938-760-2

INTRODUCTION

Several lines of sociological theorizing emerged from 19th century analogies to biological processes. Two of the most prominent and persistent have been (1) functionalism, where organismic analogies have produced an emphasis on those processes determining the differentiation and integration of systemic wholes; and (2) human ecology, where Darwinian analogies[1] have led to a concern with competition, selection, and differentiation of social units. Although these two traditions remain distinctive, their initial founders— Herbert Spencer (1874-1898) and Émile Durkheim ([1893] 1933)—used both in developing their macrostructural theories. More recent work by Hawley (1986) has once again blended these two traditions. But in this 100 year period since the seminal analyses of Spencer and Durkheim, functional-organicist theorizing has maintained its emphasis on the integrative forces holding differentiating populations together (e.g., Parsons 1966; Alexander 1985; Alexander and Colomy 1990; Colomy 1990). In contrast, both urban ecology (Park and Burgess 1925; Burgess 1925; Mckenzie 1933; Park 1936; Hawley 1971, 1981; Berry and Kasarda 1977; Kasarda 1972; Castells 1985, 1988; Frisbie 1980; Frisbie and Kasarda 1988)—and organizational ecology (Hannan and Freeman 1977, 1984, 1986, 1987, 1988, 1989; McPherson 1981, 1983a, 1983b, 1988, 1990; Bidwell and Kasarda 1985, 1987) have sustained a focus on competition and selection as a driving force behind differentiation of the structures organizing a population. In this paper, I explore how theories on the ecology of organizations can be reconciled with the more macrolevel theories of Herbert Spencer, Émile Durkheim, and Amos Hawley. I have chosen organizational ecology because its focus—that is, the differentiation of subpopulations of organizations—should have implications for macrostructural theories of societal differentiation; and I have selected the macrolevel analyses of Spencer, Durkheim, and Hawley because they provide the necessary conceptual leads for connecting ecological and organismic theories. Obviously, this will not be a comprehensive approach, but it will initiate a way to theorize about the ecology of macrostructural differentiation.

THE EARLY CONVERGENCE OF ECOLOGICAL AND ORGANISMIC ANALYSES

Spencer's Demographic-geopolitical Model

Even though the Darwinian sounding phrase "survival of the fittest" can be found in early philosophical works by Spencer ([1851] 1888), his sociology (Spencer [1874-1896] 1898) is mostly devoid of such metaphors. Instead, as is modeled in Figure 1,[2] Spencer's approach is demographic and geopolitical, revealing a highly robust model on the ecology of macrostructure. Several potential leads in developing an even more robust theory are suggested by Spencer's approach. (1) The differentiation of distinctive types of organizational units is a positive function of population size, as the latter escalates the logistical loads for maintaining a population in an environment; and this differentiation will occur with respect to (a) the production of goods and services, (b) the distribution of such goods and services, and (c) the regulation, coordination, and control of internal activities through concentrations of power. (2) If logistical loads are exceeded, dissolution of the population occurs. (3) Segmentation rather than differentiation occurs in response to initial increases in population size and logistical loads, but as a population continues to grow, logistical loads increase and cause either differentiation or disintegration. (4) The differentiation of organizational units has effects on the creation of various types of social categories (class, ethnic, regional, occupational, etc.). (5) The differentiation of centers of power, coupled with the concentration of such power under the influence of external and/or internal threats, escalates the level of inequality which, in turn, produces more differentiation of social categories. (6) Concentrated power under conditions of external threat often leads to success in war and conquest which, in turn, increases the size and diversity of a population (and thereby escalates logistical loads directly or via effects on internal threat). (7) Differentiation is the result of several intersecting and, at times, countervailing processes: The number of distinctive strata and categories is increased with the differentiation of productive and distributive organizational units, whereas ever higher degrees of concentrated power and inequality will initially increase the number of strata (and associated social categories) but eventually polarize a population into a smaller number of strata (the "haves" and "have nots") and corresponding social categories. Each of these conceptual leads will prove, I believe, useful in developing a more general model on the ecology of macrostructure, but by themselves they lacked an explicitly Darwinian focus—a focus that Émile Durkheim was to supply.

Durkheim's Ecological Model

Unlike Spencer's model, which is demographic and geopolitical, Durkheim's ([1893] 1933) macrostructural theory is clearly ecological because structural differentiation is viewed as a function of the competition and selection processes (delineated in the middle portion of the model in Figure 2). As with Spencer's model, there are important conceptual leads for a more general theory on the ecology of macrostructure. (1) Differentiation occurs when material and moral densities are high, because concentration in physical or moral "space" reduces the capacity for segmentation and forces competition for resources and, hence, selection. (2) Communication and transportation technologies are a force behind sociocultural differentiation, via their direct effects on increasing

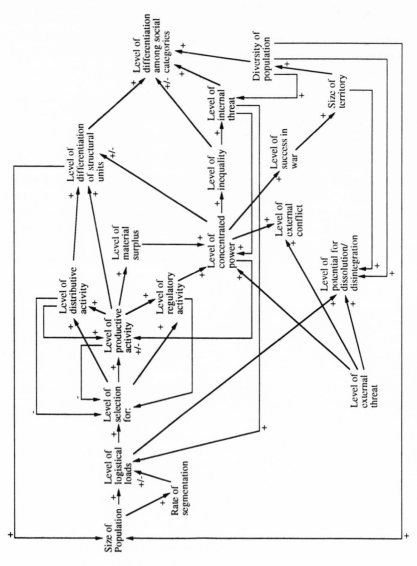

Figure 1. Spencer's Demographic-geopolitical Model of Differentiation

material and moral density which, in turn, fuel competition for resources and selection. (3) Differentiation of positions and subgroupings is causally related to both a corresponding differentiation of symbol systems with respect to (a) regulation (by specifying, normatively, relations within and between differentiated units), and (b) evaluation (by generalizing values and thereby providing common moral force for diverse structural units). (4) As Durkheim hoped in his "Preface" to the second edition of *The Division of Labor* ([1902] 1933), organizational units engaged in common domains of activity will form networks (a) mediated by sets of regulatory symbols, and (b) unified by applications of generalized evaluative symbols. Also, (5) selection and its effects on differentiation involve a series of reverse causal chains: Social differentiation reduces selection pressures by decreasing competition among social units in a particular resource niche (Durkheim [1893] 1933, p. 270); symbolic generalization, which itself is the result of selection pressures for some degree of symbolic unification under pressures for social differentiation, facilitates further differentiation by providing a repertoire of common abstract symbols among differentiating units; and networks of differentiated subgroups regulated by sets of domain-specific as well as by highly generalized evaluative symbols reduce selection pressures and competition for resources.

Functional and Ecological Views on Selection Processes

In looking back at Spencer's and Durkheim's models, many of the key elements of a macrolevel ecological theory can be found. What makes their theories ecological is the notion of "selection," but this concept denotes somewhat different processes in Spencer's and Durkheim's theories. One type of selection is Darwinian: Differentiation is related to the number of resource niches, the scarcity of resources in niches, and the level of competition and selection *among* social units or idea systems in these niches. Another type of selection is functional or organicist: Differentiation is related to disintegrative pressures in social wholes and selection *for* certain types of integrative social units and symbol systems. In the Darwinian view, selection operates under conditions of high density in a niche; in the more organismic approach, selection operates when there is low density, or even an absence of structures and symbols that can promote integration in the face of increased logistical loads and pressures for disintegration. For Spencer, there are non-Darwinian selection processes operating in the differentiation of a societal population; these involve selection for structural units that can resolve escalating logistical loads for regulation, production, and distribution. For Durkheim, there are also non-Darwinian processes revolving around selection for networks of subgroups and for layers of regulatory and evaluative symbol systems.

This distinction makes a great deal of difference in how macrolevel analysis is conducted. If one emphasizes Darwinian selection, then the key processes

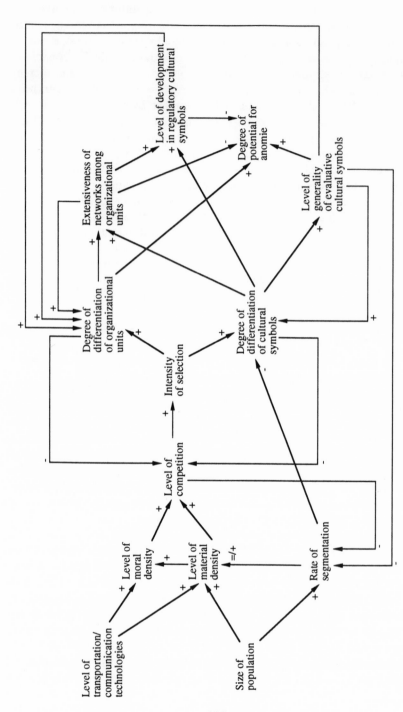

Figure 2. Durkheim's Ecological Model of Differentiation

are resource levels, resource niches, niche density, competition for resources, and selection *among* units; as a consequence, other macrolevel elements, such as population, production, distribution, power, war, territory, symbol systems, inequalities, and technology are viewed in terms of how they affect resource levels, niches, density, and competition. In contrast, if one stresses functional-organicist selection, the key processes are those disintegrative forces that generate selection *for* structures and symbols that can overcome these disintegrative forces; as a result, ecological processes revolving around niches, density, and competition are given less emphasis. Although present-day human ecology was initiated by the macrolevel functional theories of Spencer and Durkheim, it has developed on its own independently of the functional concerns of early theorists; over time, ecological theory has emphasized its affinities to bioecology (e.g., Hawley 1944, 1950, 1971/1981; Hannan and Freeman 1977). This divergence of ecological and macrofunctional theories has been useful in that the metaphorical and vague Darwinian arguments articulated by Durkheim and implied by Spencer have been made considerably more precise; therefore, it is useful to explore in detail prominent approaches in organizational ecology before initiating the task of reuniting them with selection arguments from macrofunctional theories.

THE DIVERGENCE OF ECOLOGICAL AND FUNCTIONAL THEORIZING

Hannan's and Freeman's Ecological Model

In Figure 3, Michael Hannan and John Freeman's theory on the differentiation of populations of organizations is reformulated at a more macrolevel.[3] In this model, the level of material and nonmaterial resources of a particular kind ultimately determines the number of organizational units in a resource niche. As organizational forms proliferate in a niche, a series of cycles revolving around rates of founding, legitimation, and structural inertia are initiated and sustained, providing selection something to work on once levels of organizational density and competition increase.

As niche density increases, competition within populations of organizational units is initiated, though if resource levels increase this competition will be mitigated. Increased production and political regulation can increase resources in a niche, but Hannan and Freeman do not elaborate upon these macrolevel forces in the same way as Spencer, Durkheim, or other contemporary macrolevel theorists. Markets can also increase resource levels, but their effects are somewhat contradictory. On the one hand, they increase resources and thereby lower competition but, on the other hand, they provide a mechanism for increased competition among organizational units in various niches.

The level of competition is also influenced by the rate and degree of variability (i.e., fluctuations and oscillations) in resources, both of which directly increase competition while having indirect effects on selection pressures. The rate of variation in level of resources has a direct negative effect on the size and generality of organizational units (conversely, slower rates will encourage these structural forms), but as this rate of variation is coupled with a high degree (or range) of variation, competition is heightened; as a result, larger and more generalized organizational units emerge (these processes were initially conceptualized by Hannan and Freeman [1977] as "niche width," a notion that now appears less central in their work than the older Durkheimian/ Darwinian notion of "density"). Also, under heightened competition, organizations in a population often work to form networks and confederations of various kinds in order to reduce competition, at least initially. Yet, such networks of organizational units ratchet up the size of organizational units to a higher level, potentially increasing competition and selection among organizational networks which invade, or overlap, each other's resource niches. At the macrolevel, however, organizational size, generality, and confederation into networks directly decrease the rate and level of differentiation by filling niches and, perhaps, invading and outcompeting additional organizational forms in other niches; at the same time, there is an indirect effect of these processes on reducing the competitive processes that encourage selection and differentiation of organizational forms.

When competition can increase, however, it escalates selection, especially when legitimating processes have created a high proportion of inertial to adaptive capacities in organizational units. Selection will increase rates of organizational failure which, in turn, will initially decrease the rate and degree of differentiation until failings reach a level where the niche becomes underutilized and, thereby, encourages new organizational forms to seek its resources. The degree of specialization of organizational units increases differentiation among such units, and degree of specialization is a positive function of the rate of variation in resources and a negative function of the extent of variation and fluctuation in resource levels. In sum, then, Hannan and Freeman provide many conceptual leads for a macrolevel ecological theory because their model fills in details on density, competition, and selection that neither Durkheim or Spencer were able to provide.

McPherson's Ecological Model

J. Miller McPherson and a number of his colleagues (see, e.g., McPherson 1981, 1983a, 1983b, 1988, 1990; McPherson and Ranger-Moore in press; McPherson and Smith-Lovin 1988; McPherson, Popielarz, and Drobnic 1992) have extended ecological analysis in an interesting direction, one implied by Spencer's discussion of social categories and, as I will examine shortly,

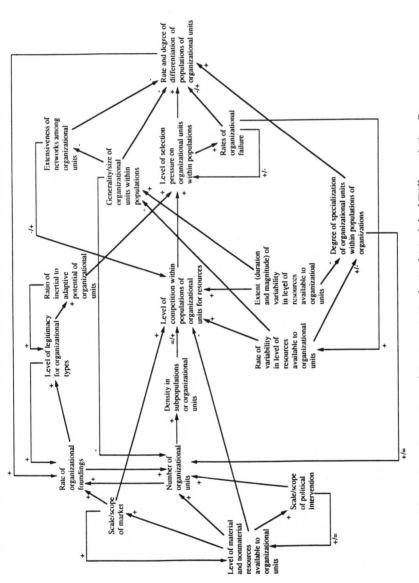

Figure 3. Hannan's and Freeman's Ecological Model of Differentiating Processes

121

Hawley's (1986) analysis of categoric units. His underlying model is delineated in Figure 4. McPherson introduces the notion of "Blau-space," named after Peter Blau's (1977) analysis of macrostructure. In McPherson's vision, system complexity creates individuals who can be distinguished in terms of many different attributes—age, sex, education, income, class, occupation, race/ ethnicity, residence, religion, and so on. What makes the conceptualization of Blau-space ecological is that the distribution of individuals with respect to some distinguishing characteristic can become a resource niche for organizational units, or what Hannan and Freeman term nonmaterial resources. The level of resources in Blau-space is a joint function of the total number of individuals in a population, the diversity of their characteristics, and the number of individuals in each diverse niche, whereas the number of niches is an inverse function of overall network density among members of a population and a positive function of the degree of diversity in the characteristics of individuals. When a niche is underexploited, there are many more individuals with particular characteristics than there are units organizing them. Under this condition of underexploitation, organizations will increasingly move into this niche, selectively recruiting members and clients in the niche. As more organizations move into a niche, however, the niche becomes overexploited— that is, the number of individuals in the niche is now less than that which can support all organizational units. The result is competition and selection in favor of those units that can successfully recruit and retain members and clients over those which cannot. Under competition and selection, the more "fit" organizations stay in a niche, while the less fit die; or, as is the more likely scenario for the voluntary organizations that McPherson studies, they can move to a new niche in Blau-space. Such movement is facilitated when there are adjacent niches in Blau-space that are underexploited and that do not require massive restructuring of the organizational unit. Thus, McPherson's model fills in details on the ecological dynamics generated by social categories, a task which Spencer left implicit and Durkheim ignored.

Strengths and Weaknesses of Organizational Ecology

These two theories of organizational ecology provide a number of important leads for developing an ecological theory of macrostructure: (1) Differentiation of structural units is related to resource levels and the diversity of niches composed of (a) material resources (e.g., members, clients, money) and (b) symbolic resources (e.g., cultural distinctions, social categories). (2) Density is a central dynamic because it sets into motion competition for resources and selection processes that force organizational units to adjust and adapt to available resources in a niche, move to a new niche, or die. And (3) out of competition and selection, social "speciation" or differentiation occurs.

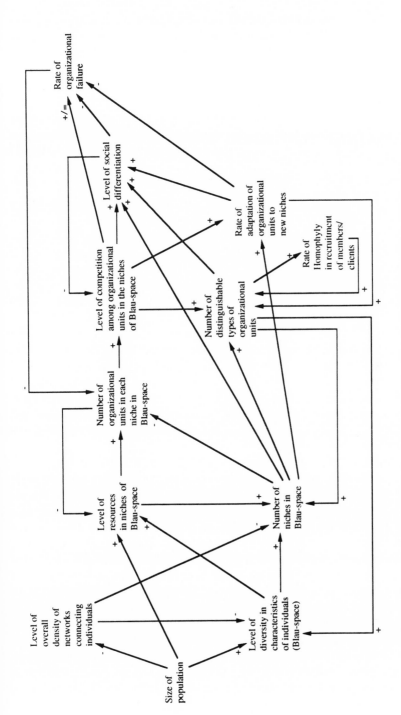

Figure 4. McPherson's Ecological Model of Differentiating Process

123

Yet, for all of the necessary detail that they add to a theory of ecology, these theories do not seek to explain all of those forces creating resource niches in the first place. In order to develop a more macrolevel theory, therefore, it is necessary to reconnect organizational ecology with more macrofunctional theories. Amos Hawley (1986) has initiated this theoretical project; I propose to take it a step further.

RECONCILING ECOLOGICAL AND ORGANISMIC ANALYSES

Hawley's Macrolevel Theory

In Figure 5, Amos Hawley's core ideas on the dynamics of macrostructural differentiation are modeled.[4] Hawley (1986) introduces what is an essential distinction in macrostructural analysis between "corporate units" and "categoric units"—one pursued by McPherson in his discussion of Blau-space and anticipated by Spencer in his brief portrayal of social categories. Differentiation of corporate units involves creating distinctive types of organizational structures, whereas differentiation of categoric units revolves around the emergence of social distinctions that classify individuals.

Technology, as it influences transportation, communication, and production, is one of the driving forces behind differentiation. Building on Durkheim's initial insight, Hawley sees mobility costs as a critical consideration because they set limits on how much differentiation and specialization of organizational units can occur; for without the capacity to move information, material, and actors, differentiation is not possible (a line of argument anticipated by Spencer's emphasis on distribution). The process of production directly increases differentiation of corporate or organizational units because of the increased efficiency of specialization; and this process is accelerated by the existence of markets, competition, and selection among specialized units which seek to find a stable and predictable resource niche. Population size, as it encourages expanded production and as it provides a larger social mass which can be divided up in more ways, also works to increase in the number and size of diverse units. Indeed, like Spencer, Hawley recognizes that larger populations must be divided into a greater number of organizational units if they are to be sustained. Yet, if population growth raises mobility costs in the absence of new technologies and increased production, then it works against differentiation of corporate units. Differentiation of corporate units and growing size of a population, along with the competition and threat generated by production and markets, increases the number and size of categoric units. In a manner reminiscent of Spencer's and Durkheim's functional arguments, the existence of many diverse types of corporate and categoric units creates selection pressures for their control through the differentiation of regulatory

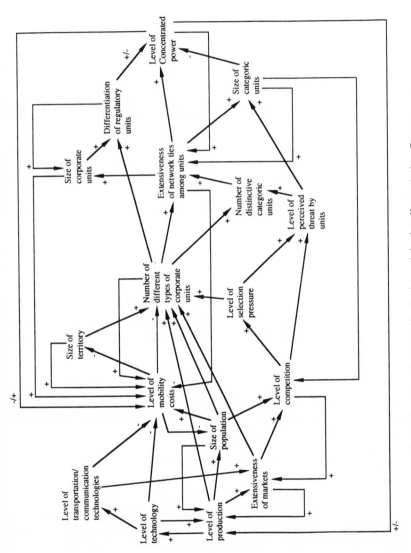

Figure 5. Hawley's Ecological Model of Differentiating Processes

125

units (i.e., concentrations of power) and through the consolidation of units in increasingly extensive networks. The concentration of power at moderate levels encourages further differentiation through its effects on capital formation in the productive sector. In turn, increased production causes further differentiation of corporate and categoric units, expanded numbers of network ties, and increased efforts at regulation and increased concentration of power (which eventually will work against increased production).

These theoretical leads in Hawley's (1986) scheme consolidate, to some degree, the ideas in Spencer's and Durkheim's functional approaches, while adding refinements. Yet, surprisingly, this more recent work moves more toward functional than ecological theory, analyzing differentiated units in terms of functions and key functions (Hawley 1986) for each other and for the maintenance of a system in its environment; as such, the scheme downplays somewhat Hawley's earlier emphasis on resource niches, competition, and selection (e.g., Hawley 1944, 1950, 1973). Indeed, it moves toward technology as the driving force behind differentiation, along the lines of Lenski (1966) and other evolutionary theories, but it does so by stressing transportation and communication technologies and their effects on mobility costs. Thus, once the unit of the analysis shifts from the meso level (i.e., communities and organizations) to the macro level (i.e., societal populations), ecological and organismic analyses begin to converge.

The Ecology of Macrostructure: A Synthetic Model

How, then, are we to take advantage of the conceptual leads provided by the theories modeled in Figures 1 through 5? In Figure 6, I have tried to pull these leads together in a model which reconciles the organicist selection arguments of functionalism with the Darwinian selection portrayals of human ecology. In the figure, three sets of selection processes are highlighted: those on the left pertain to first-order functional selection, those in the middle revolve around Darwinian selection, and those on the right pertain to second-order functional selection. These three blocks of selection processes will organize my discussion of the model in Figure 6.

First-order Functional Selection Processes

At the left of the model are a series of forces that set into motion what I term *first-order selection processes*. These processes involve selection for certain structures in the face of potential dissolution. Perhaps this emphasis is only a rewording of old functional arguments with all of their problems, but they are nonetheless fundamental to understanding the social organization of societal populations. Moreover, functional theories always implied a more ecological argument: Those societal populations that could meet requisites or

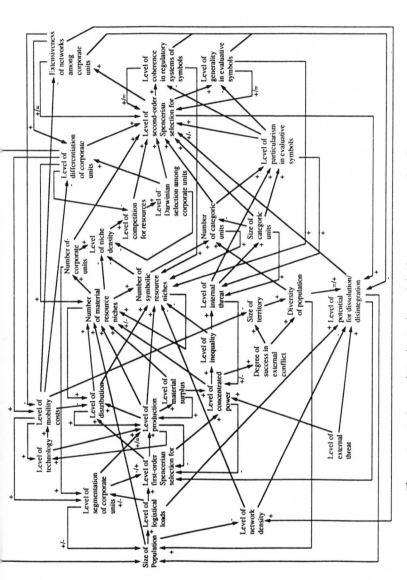

Figure 6. A General Ecological Model of Macrostructural Differentiation

needs were more likely to survive in an environment than those which could not do so. The model in Figure 6 simply makes this ecological portion of functionalism explicit by indicating that there are fundamental or first-order activities that, by intent or chance, must become structured if a population is to persist in an environment.

Most of these first-order selection processes were delineated by Spencer in *The Principles of Sociology* ([1874-1896] 1898), but I have added refinements suggested by others. With Spencer, I argue that first-order selection is ultimately caused by population growth. When a population grows, several forces are set into motion as a consequence of the increasing logistical loads for sustaining the population: (1) As Durkheim stressed, segmentation of like structural units is one response to growth; and as Hawley would argue, I think, such is particularly likely to be the case under conditions of low technology and high mobility costs (as denoted by the reverse causal arrow from mobility costs to segmentation). (2) As McPherson and various coauthors assert, population growth decreases network density among members of a population, thereby decreasing capacities for social control and, as Spencer (1862, [1874-1896] 1898) believed, setting into motion forces for movement and localization of subunits and subpopulations in new resource environments which cause either their differentiation from each other or their dissolution as a coherent system (such is possible, Durkheim averred, when there are few ecological constraints maintaining material density). As Mann (1986) and others (e.g., Maryanski and Turner 1992) have more recently argued, the "caging" of populations creates pressures for internal conflict and competition leading to differentiation, but the capacity of subpopulations to escape ecological and political cages also leads to differentiation by virtue of their localization in diverse environments. (3) Segmentation under conditions of population growth eventually becomes an inadequate response to mounting logistical loads, as both Spencer and Durkheim emphasized; as a consequence logistical loads escalate and the potential for dissolution increases.

Together, as is denoted by all of the direct, indirect, and reverse causal arrows into the level of first-order selection, these forces generate selection *for* expanded activity along the three principle axes suggested by Spencer: production, distribution, and regulation. The level of production must increase to support a larger population; distribution processes must expand to sustain the movement of goods and services among members of a population; and regulation through the concentration of power must increase in order to coordinate and control the increased volume of activities among a larger population. If these outcomes are not forthcoming, then mounting logistical loads cause the dissolution of the population.

Once increased production, distribution, and regulation (via concentrations of power) are set into motion, a series of interrelated processes delineated in the left-middle portion of the model in Figure 6 are initiated: (1) As Hawley recognized and Durkheim implied, increased production is both the result and cause of technological development which, in turn, causes mobility costs to decrease as new transportation and communication technologies are developed. (2) Lowered mobility costs facilitate expanded distribution, which then stimulates more production and technological development. (3) Expanded production increases material surplus which can be used as capital to expand production further, but as Spencer and more recent scholars like Lenski (1966) have emphasized, it is also usurped by centers of power and used to increase the concentration of power. (4) As power becomes concentrated, inequality escalates as Spencer and modern-day evolutionary-conflict theorists document (e.g., Lenski 1966; Turner 1984); as a consequence, internal threats ·increase and, ironically, lead to greater concentration of power in order to control such threats (up to the point where internal threats are so high as to create viable centers of counter-power). (5) As Spencer and more contemporary theorists like Lenski (1966) and Collins (1986) have recognized, the concentration of power is often related to geopolitical processes, because external threat increases concentration of power in order to mobilize, control, and channel resources to deal with the threat. In the long run, these processes aggravate the cycles that increase internal threat. Moreover, if external conflict ensues and society is successful in war, then the growing amount of territory, size of population, and diversity of this population all escalate logistical loads and first-order selection for increased power, production, and distribution.

Darwinian Selection Processes

The forces set into motion by first-order functional selection processes generate the resource niches within which Darwinian selection *among* corporate and categoric units takes place. That is, functional selection *for* increased production, distribution, power, and their effects on technology, mobility costs, inequality, and geopolitics determine the level and varieties of resources available for Darwinian selection among structural units organizing members of a population.

This outcome is the result of the obvious fact that to increase the levels of these functional processes involves growth and differentiation of structures and categories which, in turn, become resource niches for the Darwinian selection processes emphasized by ecological theories. These Darwinian dynamics are delineated in the middle-right portion of Figure 6. Increases in production, distribution and concentrations of power directly cause the number of resource niches to expand, although highly concentrated power will begin to decrease the political resources available to organizational units and, via the feedback loop to material resources, the material resources as well. These same forces will also expand the number of symbolic resource niches via the paths delineated in the model.

There is, however, a clear tautology in these generalizations: Increased levels of productive, distributive, and political activity involve the very differentiation that is to be explained by these levels. For most organizational ecologists, this tautology is not apparent because resource levels as generated by production, distribution, and power are, for the most part, exogenous variables or unexplained constants. But, when we seek to account for why resources exist at a given level and variety, creating resource niches that allow for differentiation of corporate and categoric units, we come face to face with the argument that differentiation of resource-generating processes produces differentiation.

In a real sense, this tautology is part of reality: Initial differentiation creates niches for further differentiation; in turn, this further differentiation increases the levels of those forces—production, distribution, and power—that generate more resources in existing niches while increasing the number of niches. Thus, differentiation is a self-escalating process, up to the levels that technology allows and up to the point where overly concentrated power works directly and indirectly (via causal processes delineated in the model) to decrease both the diversity and levels of resources. This is why Hawley (1986) argues that system complexity escalates to the maximum possible in terms of the levels of technology and environmental constraints. In the model in Figure 6, this self-escalating nature of differentiation is delineated by numerous reverse causal processes that directly and indirectly lead back to affect the number of material and symbolic resource niches, which then set into motion the Darwinian selection processes outlined by organizational ecology.

Turning first to the key causal processes revolving around material resources that are used by corporate units, several processes can be highlighted: (1) As the arrows flowing into this variable emphasize, material resources include human bodies (as members, clients, participants), money, products, goods, and other units of value that can be used to sustain a structure, physical objects and space, and coercive capacities, although these are almost always mingled together in some combination to produce a variety of resource niches. (2) As McPherson emphasizes, symbolic resources defining attributes of individuals in Blau-space also interact with material resources in creating niches for corporate units; also, as Spencer and Hawley recognized, inequalities and internal threats create categoric units that can become highly volatile and dynamic resources for corporate group formation (e.g., as a social movement or organized revolt). (3) As all ecological theory stresses, the number of corporate units expands to fill underexploited material resource niches, a process which is a form of segmentation that fuels, via the long feedback loop to segmentation and logistical loads, selection for those processes that increase the level and diversity of resources. Thus, segmentation is essential to differentiation by virtue of its effects on increasing niche density. (4) As the level of density increases, the degree of competition for resources escalates, leading to Darwinian selection among corporate units whose inertial tendencies give selection something to work on and whose adaptive abilities may allow them to readjust to an existing resource niche, or to find a new niche. (5) As competition and selection escalate, the level of differentiation among corporate units increases, feeding back to increase the number of resource niches. For as the differentiation of units occurs, the units often find or create new sources of resources, up to the limits of technology, concentrated power and, as Hawley stressed, rising mobility costs (and the effects of this force on distribution, production, material surplus, and power).

Let me offer a note on a particularly important process that accelerates the diversity of material resources and, I also argue, symbolic resources: distribution by markets. Markets are the critical mediating structure between technology, production, and material surplus, on the one hand, and the creation of resource niches on the other. Because markets connect individual preferences and demand to production, they can differentiate to meet the virtually unlimited preferences of individuals; in so doing, they can create "markets for" virtually any good, service, or symbol which, in turn, become resource niches for corporate units. As a result, markets can dramatically expand the number of niches, often without increases in aggregate production or material surplus (White 1981). For if markets are relatively open, their existence encourages sellers to seek "new markets," including the marketing of the terms of exchange (e.g., money, futures, options, etc.) in lower-level markets; in so doing, new resource niches are generated (Collins 1990). As a consequence, once markets reach a threshold of differentiation and evidence fiscal mechanisms (money, credit, insurance, etc.) that lower the mobility costs of transactions, they tend to expand and differentiate rapidly, up to the point where (a) the resource niches created by such differentiation become overexploited, (b) the level of speculation in such niches has produced goods and services beyond the level of demand, thereby setting into motion a market collapse, or (c) the level of demand for goods and services levels off, or declines. Capitalist markets take these dynamic qualities to the extreme, but they are inherent tendencies in all market systems that reach a certain level of differentiation. As the limits of (a), (b), and (c) above are reached, markets often collapse, thereby dramatically reducing the level of resources and the diversity of resource niches available to structural units.

Turning now to the key causal processes revolving around symbolic resources, several can be highlighted: (1) The number of symbolic resource niches is potentially greater than material resource niches, up to the limits of the number of individuals in a population and their imaginative capacities to create niches in Blau-space. (2) Production, distribution, and power all directly increase symbolic niches by virtue of the division of labor's partitioning effects on incumbents' experiences, a process that is expanded indirectly by the creation of material resource niches. (3) Lowered network density directly increases the number of symbolic niches by virtue of its effects on lowering interconnections among actors (both their "moral" and "material" density in Durkheim's terms), thereby reducing the effects of social control to enforce conformity to common symbols. (4) Concentrated power as it affects inequality and ethnic diversity (through geopolitics) is also a driving force behind the formation of symbolic niches. (5) The number of categoric units is related not only to the number of symbolic niches but also to the level of material resources (at a minimum, human bodies who are categorized but typically other material resources such as money, power, place in division of labor, etc.) necessary to sustain a category in Blau-space. (6) The size of categoric units expands as a result of internal threats which are fueled by inequality and ethnic diversity. (7) Categoric units, in turn, increase the symbolic resources available for corporate units. And (8) the ecological dynamics of competition and selection among categoric units are, I argue, related to the density of corporate units in symbolic resource niches; therefore, selection among categoric units occurs primarily when they have become wholly, or partially, imbedded in corporate units within densely populated symbolic resource niches.

In sum, then, Darwinian selection among corporate units and, indirectly, categoric units connected to corporate units, is circumscribed by first-order functional selection processes but, via a number of reverse causal effects delineated in the model in Figure 6, such Darwinian selection alters the course of these functional selection processes. One major reverse causal effect emerging from Darwinian selection is, as Spencer was most apt to emphasize, the capacity of a more differentiated set of corporate units to support a larger population and to organize this population in ways that respond to first-order functional selection pressures, thereby avoiding disintegration of the population. Another related causal effect occurs via what I term in the model in Figure 6, *second-order functional selection processes*.

Second-order Functional Selection

The processes delineated on the right of Figure 6 are second-order functional selection in this sense: The consequences of Darwinian selection within a population create a new level of escalated logistical loads revolving around how the differentiated corporate units are, themselves, to be integrated so as to avoid dissolution. This problem was initially given its most forceful expression by Adam Smith ([1776] 1805), but it was soon incorporated into the French lineage culminating in Durkheim ([1893] 1933).

We could argue, of course, that the process of differentiation creates resource niches for integrative structural units and symbol systems, but as with first-order functional selection, we can go only so far because we are addressing selection for sociocultural processes under conditions of low (or lack of) density among such integrative structural units. In broad contours, I think that

Durkheim ([1893] 1933, pp. 329-389, [1902] 1933) understood these processes best as a series of simultaneous processes for (1) the formation of larger networks of interdependence among corporate units which, as Hawley (1986) also recognized, is related to mobility costs; (2) the generalization of evaluational systems, or what Parsons (1966) later termed "value generalization;" and (3) the development of coherent regulatory symbols for (a) specifying generalized values and (b) articulating rights, duties, and obligations among corporate units. All of these processes are self-reinforcing because each generates selection for the other: Generalized systems select for regulatory symbols to fill in the relevant details (in order, in Durkheim's eye, to avoid "anomie"); regulatory symbols select for value premises to give them meaning and moral force; similarly, networks of organizational interdependency select for both specific and generalized symbols to regulate exchanges among units.

Yet, the level of inequality, the number of categoric units, and the size of such units (as fueled by internal threats) create particularistic evaluational symbols which work against generalized symbols and coherent sets of regulatory symbols. For inequality always creates structural divisions and symbols reflecting these divisions, and these more particularistic symbols (for classes, ethnic groups, religious groups, regional subpopulations, and the like) work as a counterforce to consensus over either regulatory or generalized symbols. At the same time, however, these particularistic symbols escalate second-order selection pressures for regulatory and generalized symbols—often without result, however. For particularistic symbols can overwhelm a population, subverting second-order selection and setting into motion dissolution and disintegration of a population.

All symbol systems become, as the reverse causal arrows emanating from them emphasize, symbolic resources for the formation of corporate units, such as administrative agencies in government, courts, law professions, political parties, religious sects, social movements, and other structures which make appeals to, or are organized around, particularistic, generalized, and regulatory symbols. Robert Wuthnow's (1987) ecological analysis of religious denominations is a good example of how these second-order functional selection processes become implicated in Darwinian selection processes among corporate units using symbolic resources to secure material resources.

CONCLUSION

In this paper, I have sought to reconnect functional and ecological theory in a way that produces a model suggesting the lines along which a more precise and robust theory could be developed. Analytical models like the one presented in Figure 6 are incredibly complex, but they offer a sense for the causal processes involved in the organization of societal populations. Such models can be decomposed into simpler submodels, reducing the sense of being overwhelmed by direct, indirect, and reverse causal arrows among so many forces (in a sense, I have done this by talking in terms of three blocks of processes—first-order, second-order, and Darwinian selection). These models can also be used to generate propositions that highlight important causal paths and that can serve as orienting ideas for constructing more specific hypotheses For, any set of causal paths in the model can be viewed as a potential set of propositions that can guide research, but since these propositions are extracted from a more robust set of causal configurations, they remain tied to more inclusive social processes. Thus, the model in Figure 6 represents a strategy for examining macrostructural processes in their most robust form, while at the same time suggesting ways to extract more delimited generalizations.

Figure 6 also emphasizes that the ecological analysis of macrostructure requires a reunification of the selection arguments in both analogies— organismic and Darwinian—from biology. As long as human ecology operates at the meso level of analysis, such reunification is not necessary, but as Hawley's (1986) more macroscopic turn suggests, functional ideas need to be reintroduced when larger-scale societal processes are examined from an ecological perspective. In broad strokes, the specifics of ecological analysis— the level of material and nonmaterial resources, the number of niches, the density of niches, the competition for resources, and the intensity of Darwinian selection—are variables whose values are determined not only by the indigenous dynamics of Darwinian selection itself but also by the outcomes of organismic selection for certain structures and symbols; conversely, the outcomes of first- and second-order organismic selection are circumscribed by the Darwinian selection processes that they set into motion. At the first-order level, organismic selection sets into motion forces—population growth, expanded production, concentration of power, market distribution, improved technologies—that, via their effects on each other and on stratification and geopolitics, influence the levels and kinds of resources in niches where Darwinian selection among corporate units operates. At the second-order level, differentiation of corporate units generates an additional set of forces— subnetworks, regulatory symbols, and generalized evaluative symbols—that, through complex reverse causal chains, feed back to exert further influence on both first-order functional selection and Darwinian selection among corporate units. It is time, therefore, that modern ecological theory as it emerged from the old functionalism of Spencer and Durkheim be reintegrated with neofunctionalism; the result will be, I argue in Figure 6, a more complete conceptualization of macrostructural dynamics.

NOTES

1. In recent years, there have been numerous extensions of the synthetic theory of evolution to sociological work, including sociobiology (e.g., van den Berghe 1978; Lopreato 1984), dual inheritance (e.g., Boyd and Richerson 1985), and coevolution (e.g., Durham 1991).

2. The model in Figure 1, as well as subsequent models to be presented, visualize time and processes as moving from left to right. The proximity of forces to each other and the configurations of the causal arrows indicate the intensity of the effects of these forces on each other. Of particular importance are reverse causal effects (Stinchcombe 1968), because most social processes are recursive. The signs on the arrows denote the form of the causal relationship: $+$ (positive), $-$ (negative), $+/-$ (positively curvilinear), $-/+$ (negatively curvilinear), $=/+$ or $=/-$ (lagged positive or lagged negative effect), $+/=$ or $-/=$ (positive or negative effect that levels off).

3. This model is a composite constructed from a number of works by Hannan and Freeman (1977, 1984, 1986, 1987, 1988, 1989).

4. This model is constructed from Hawley (1944, 1950, 1973, 1978, 1981, 1986).

REFERENCES

Alexander, J.C. 1985. *Neofunctionalism.* Newbury Park, CA: Sage.

Alexander, J.C., and P. Colomy, eds. 1990. *Differentiation Theory and Social Change.* New York: Columbia University Press.

Berry, B.J.L., and J.D. Kasarda. 1977. *Contemporary Urban Ecology.* New York: Macmillan.

Bidwell, C.E., and J.D. Kasarda. 1985. *The Organization and its Ecosystem: A Theory of Structuring in Organizations.* Greenwich, CT: JAI Press.

Bidwell, C.R., and J.D. Kasarda. 1987. *Structuring in Organizations: Ecosystem Theory Evaluated.* Greenwich, CT: JAI Press.

Blau, P.M. 1977. *Inequality and Heterogeneity, A Primitive Theory of Social Structure.* New York: Free Press.

Boyd, R., and P.J. Richerson. 1985. *Culture and the Evolutionary Process.* Chicago: University of Chicago Press.

Burgess, E.W. 1925. "The Growth of the City: An Introduction to a Research Project." Pp. 47-62 in *The City*, edited by R. Park, E. Burgess, and R.J. McKenzie. Chicago: University of Chicago Press.

Castells, M. 1985. "High Technology, Economic Restructuring and the Urban-Regional Process in the United States." Pp. 11-4 in *High Technology, Space, and Society*, edited by M. Castells. Newbury Park, CA: Sage.

———. 1988. "High Technology and Urban Dynamics in the United States." Pp. 85-110 in *The Metropolis Era: A World of Giant Cities*, edited by M. Dogan and J.D. Kasarda. Newbury Park, CA: Sage.

Collins, R. 1986. *Weberian Sociological Theory.* New York: Cambridge University Press.

———. 1990. "Market Dynamics as the Engine of Historical Change." *Sociological Theory* 8: 111-135.

Colomy, P. 1990. *Neofunctionalist Sociology: Contemporary Statements.* London: Edward Elgar.

Durham, W. 1991. *Coevolution.* Stanford, CA: Stanford University Press.

Durkheim, É. [1893] 1933. *The Division of Labor in Society.* New York: Free Press.

———. [1902] 1933. "Preface to the Second Edition." In *The Division of Labor in Society.* New York: Free Press.

Frisbie, P.W. 1980. "Theory and Research in Urban Ecology." Pp. 203-19 in *Sociological Theory and Research: A Critical Approach*, edited by H.M. Blalock, Jr. New York: Free Press.

Frisbie, P.W., and J.D. Kasarda. 1988. "Spatial Processes." Pp. 629-66 in *Handbook of Sociology,*
    edited by N.J. Smelser. Newbury Park, CA: Sage.
Hannan, M.T., and J. Freeman. 1977. "The Population Ecology of Organizations." *American
    Journal of Sociology* 82(March): 929-964.
_____. 1984. "Structural Inertia and Organizational Change." *American Sociological Review*
    49: 149-164.
_____. 1986. "Where Do Organizational Forms Come From?" *Sociological Forum* 1: 50-72.
_____. 1987. "The Ecology of Organizational Founding: American Labor Unions, 1836-1985."
    American Journal of Sociology 92: 910-943.
_____. 1988. "The Ecology of Organizational Mortality: American Labor Unions, 1836-1985."
    American Journal of Sociology 94: 25-52.
_____. 1989. Organizational Ecology. Cambridge, MA: Harvard University Press.
Hawley, A.H. 1944. "Ecology and Human Ecology." *Social Forces* 27: 398-405.
_____. 1950. *Human Ecology.* New York: Ronald Press.
_____. 1971/1981. *Urban Society: An Ecological Approach.* New York: Ronald Press.
_____. 1973. "Ecology and Population." *Science* (March): 1196-1201.
_____. 1978. "Cumulative Change in Theory and History." *American Sociological Review 43:*
    787-797.
_____. 1981. "Human Ecology: Persistence and Change." *The American Behavioral Scientist*
    24: 423-444.
_____. 1986. *Human Ecology: A Theoretical Essay.* Chicago: University of Chicago Press.
Kasarda, J.D. 1972. "The Theory of Ecological Expansion: An Empirical Test." *Social Forces*
    51: 165-175.
Lenski, G. 1966. *Power and Privilege.* New York: McGraw-Hill.
Lopreato, J. 1984. *Human Nature and Biocultural Evolution.* Boston: Allen and Unwin.
Mann, M. 1986. *The Social Sources of Power.* New York: Cambridge University Press.
Maryanski, A., and J.H. Turner. 1992. *The Social Cage: Human Nature and the Evolution of
    Society.* Stanford, CA: Stanford University Press.
McKenzie, R. 1933. *The Metropolitan Community.* New York: McGraw-Hill.
McPherson, J.M. 1981. "A Dynamic Model of Voluntary Affiliation." *Social Forces* 59: 705-728.
_____. 1983a. "An Ecology of Affiliation." *American Sociological Review* 48: 519-532.
_____. 1983b. "The Size of Voluntary Organizations." *Social Forces* 61: 1044-1064.
_____. 1988. "A Theory of Voluntary Organization." Pp. 42-76 in *Community Organizations,*
    edited by C. Milofsky. New York: Oxford.
_____. 1990. "Evolution in Communities of Voluntary Organizations." Pp. 224-245 in
    Organizational Evolution, edited by Jihendra Singh. Newbury Park, CA: Sage.
McPherson, J.M., P.A. Popielarz, and S. Drobnic. 1992. "Social Networks and Organizational
    Dynamics." *American Sociological Review* 57: 153-170.
McPherson, J.M., and J. Ranger-Moore. 1991. "Evolution on a Dancing Landscape:
    Organizations and Networks in Dynamic Blau Space." *Social Forces* 70: 19-42.
McPherson, J.M., and L. Smith-Lovin. 1988. "A Comparative Ecology of Five Nations: Testing
    a Model of Competition Among Voluntary Organizations." Chapter 6 in *Ecological Models
    of Organizations,* edited by G.R. Carroll. Cambridge, MA: Ballinger.
Park, R.E. 1936. "Human Ecology." *American Journal of Sociology* 42: 1-15.
Park, R.E., and E.W. Burgess. 1925. *The City.* Chicago: University of Chicago Press.
Parsons, T. 1966. *Societies: Evolutionary and Comparative Perspectives.* Englewood Cliffs, NJ:
    Prentice-Hall.
Smith, A. [1776] 1805. *An Inquiry into the Nature and Causes of the Wealth of Nations.* London:
    Davis.
Spencer, H. [1851] 1888. *Social Statics.* New York: D. Appleton.
_____. 1862. *First Principles.* New York: D. Appleton.

_____. [1874-1896] 1898. *The Principles of Sociology.* New York: D. Appleton.
Stinchcombe, A. 1968. *Constructing Social Theories.* New York: Harcourt, Brace.
Turner, J.H. 1984. *Societal Stratification.* New York: Columbia University Press.
van den Berghe, P. 1978. "Bridging the Paradigms." *Society* 15: 42-49.
White, H. 1981. "Where Do Markets Come From?" *American Journal of Sociology* 87: 517-547.
Wuthnow, R. 1987. *Meaning and Moral Order: Explorations in Cultural Analysis.* Berkeley: University of California Press.

EVOLUTIONARY TANGLES FOR SOCIOCULTURAL SYSTEMS:

SOME CLUES FROM BIOLOGY

Lee Freese

ABSTRACT

Drawing upon biology, I consider the problems that traditional social science and neo-Darwinian approaches must address in order successfully to theorize about sociocultural evolution. I imply that the problems are insurmountable within traditional approaches: first, because any choice of evolutionary models and units of analysis is unrealistic or undecidable; and second, because biological restrictions for interpreting a central evolutionary concept, adaptation to environments, as well as the organized systems in which evolution occurs, render the concept inadequate to serve as a paradigm for theorizing about evolutionary change.

INTRODUCTION

The theory of organic evolution by natural selection has been with us for well over a century. With the Modern Synthesis[1] of the theory in the last sixty years,

Advances in Human Ecology, Volume 3, pages 139-171.

the theory became very fine grained. Today, it is the reigning orthodoxy and provides the unifying paradigm in biological science. Theories of sociocultural evolution have been with us for about as long. But they are very course grained, and as undecidable as ever.

One reason, I shall argue, is that theories of sociocultural evolution do not permit us effectively to distinguish between evolution and development. Biologists employ a canon to distinguish these processes: Evolution is descent with modification from common ancestors across reproductive generations; development is modification over time within reproductive generations. The canon implies that individual organisms develop but do not evolve. Populations evolve.

Now, there is no a priori reason to take the biologists' distinction as canonical when analyzing sociocultural systems—indeed, no a priori reason to suppose that the sociocultural analysis of evolution ought to follow biologists' models at all. But that embarrassing difference in the progress the two bodies of theory have shown in the past century at least ought to lead social scientists to consider the biologists' distinction as a provisional guide,[2] even if the applicable criteria of distinction might need to be adjusted to sociocultural units of analysis. The canon at least enables us to formulate the significant question, "What, exactly, is the difference between sociocultural development and sociocultural evolution, and how could we tell if we were observing one process, the other, or both?"

It is a step forward, I think, and a necessary precursor to answering the question, to first scope the question (or at least some of it). By that, I mean it is necessary first to bracket salient issues that cannot be swept away if ever we are going to be able to tell the difference between sociocultural evolution and development. Analyzing why we cannot now tell and what we are going to need to know in order to tell—not the telling itself—is the purpose of this paper. All we seek here are some clues.

We shall look to biology to find them. We shall *overlook* tempting analogies. Our method is to follow some biological lines of thought about evolutionary change not with the thought of copying the lines, but with the thought of finding telling clues that could help us to avoid copying errors. My biases are two: Biological models cannot serve as proxies (let alone as mandates) for sociocultural theory, because the domains of interpretation are not the same; *but,* sociocultural theorizing about evolution cannot play to success until biological parameters are incorporated to enable theorizing about biosociocultural systems. I am assuming, but shall not here try to prove, that changes in sociocultural evolutionary regimes are nonlinear system responses to threshold changes in ecological regimes set in train by developmental changes. This paper tries to tell why I think we should cut straight to this scene.

First, a word about words. Problems of communication are inherent with social scientists' use of the terms evolution, ecology, and development.

Unintended meanings for these terms are often inadvertently read into their use, as social scientists supply their own implicit notions of the boundaries of the systems at issue. I shall not argue about intended meanings, but I do want to argue some about system boundaries. Different theoretical issues are brought into view as we extend our concepts to include more than sociologists, in particular, typically include. Typically, sociologists draw their system boundaries with respect to societies, institutions, organizations, and so forth, and their use of the word ecological is almost always strictly within their self-defined sociological framework. Here I shall draw boundaries wider so that ecology, evolution, and development are not understood to be limited just to what happens within societies, institutions, or organizations, or because of them, but apply also to what happens when these systems connect to others, specifically, to biophysical systems and their processes. That is required by any agenda that aims to advance biosociocultural theory.

EVOLUTIONARY TANGLES, I: MODELS AND UNITS

In attempting to explain sociocultural evolution we may point to two distinct strategies. One, the oldest and not much connected to the study of biological evolution, is to search for internal sociocultural system processes that generate evolutionary change. Another, the newest and deliberately connected to biology, is to describe the interactions of genes and culture that generate coevolutionary change. We shall consider both and try to highlight the tangles of each.

Endogenetic Evolution in Sociocultural Systems

For over 100 years, social scientists have organized, and have had organized on their behalf, a parade of sundry types of human societies or cultures that have in fact appeared in human history and which are supposed to have evolved. Sometimes, the types are listed according to the differentiation of leadership that is apparent, for example, in bands, tribes, chiefdoms, and states (Service 1962). Other times the types, such as Gehard Lenski's (Lenski, Lenski, and Nolan 1991), describe principal modes of human subsistence. Typologies based on modes of subsistence often mention societies that make their living by hunting and gathering, pastoralism and horticulture, agriculture, industry, and sometimes a modern variation on that last one, the so called postindustrial society; and sometimes these multifarious types are collapsed into fewer categories. But all are understood to be ideal types, since any particular case might show a mixture of different modes of leadership or subsistence. Notwithstanding how empirically messy that might be for analyzing a given case, a fundamental interest has been whether, when, and why particular cultures or societies change from one type to another. It is known to have happened, but it does not always. It is accepted now, though it was not when the parade began, that there is no empirically invariant progression from one type of society or culture to another. Also, there has not been established a satisfactory theoretical ground to suppose there should be an invariant progression. Yet, the idea that these (or other comparable) types represent an evolutionary sequence of stages of cultural or social evolution has long appealed to some social scientists.

There are, unfortunately, some serious difficulties that confront any stage theory of sociocultural evolution when formulated in traditional terms. Principal among the difficulties is to defend the claim that the theories describe evolutionary instead of developmental change.

Just because certain types of culture or society appeared in a certain order in the course of human cultural or social history does not in itself imply these are stages in the evolution of human culture or society. For a cautious sociologist, the theory of human society and the story of human cultural history are two different matters. Likewise, to a cautious anthropologist the theory of human culture is not the same thing as human social history. Culture and society—in the conventional wisdom of anthropologists and sociologists—are not two different names for the same thing even though they always go together. They go together because one cannot have a society without culture, and one cannot have culture without some social organization to support it. It follows that, in theorizing about evolution, an adequate evolutionary theory of culture might be entirely different from an adequate evolutionary theory of social organization. I shall here gloss over this serious issue by combining and simplifying so as to talk about sociocultural evolution.

There are other grounds for caution. Theories of sociocultural evolution that are grounded to types of human societies interpreted as sequential stages, are traceable to nineteenth-century social evolutionists such as Herbert Spencer and Lewis Henry Morgan. Stage theories are the classic theories of sociocultural evolution. The stage theories include the idea of descent with modification, fundamental to any evolutionary theory, but they carry with them some heavy extra baggage. Borne along with the tide of these classic theories, right to the present, is an ideological residue of the originals: the conflating of an evolutionary progression, such as an increase in sociocultural complexity (which can sometimes be observed), with social, cultural, and historical *progress*. The stages the nineteenth-century theorists thought they observed in the development of human culture were due, they thought, to a natural law of progress. Stage models are more sophisticated now, but the idea of progress is still very much a part of social science theories of cultural and social evolution (Dunnell 1988). For a long time, as we shall note later, biologists read progress into their interpretation of organic evolution, but now that notion has been expunged from the theory of organic evolution by natural selection. If we try to theorize about sociocultural evolution by using the idea of progress, we are really theorizing about what we think is good, not what we think is or has been. Fortunately, this ideological load is logically easy (if psychologically hard) to jettison. Unfortunately, that is the least of the problems.

It is questionable whether the historical emergence of the different types of primary subsistence in human society can be interpreted as evolutionary even though there may be descent with modification. We know the first human societies were hunting-gathering societies, then came horticultural, and then industrial, societies. But was that evolution? Perhaps, depending upon how we theoretically define an abstract evolutionary process and interpret the process for our choice of units. For cultures and societies, that is pretty hard to do, which is one reason there have been so many theories of the subject for so long. Tell, if you are persuaded by any of the modern stage theories, just what units are evolving in sociocultural systems. And tell what it is about those units and the process in which they behave, that enables us to call this evolutionary rather than developmental. With a different choice of units and a different theoretical model, what we describe in the course of sociocultural change might have to be construed as developmental not evolutionary. How shall we defend our choices?

I see some purpose to arguing about different units, but I see no way to do that without defining a model of the evolutionary process in which the units are supposed to behave. The evolutionary process at issue with the classic theories makes the choice of units very difficult, if not impossible. Let us first look at the process and then consider the obvious units of first choice.

The classic stage theories and almost all their modern versions define a process of internally generated evolutionary change. One term to describe that is endogenetic evolution, referring to gradual replacement from an internal core, in which something like an unfolding process similar to development can be observed. Endogenetic evolution is quite different from that found in organic evolutionary theory. There, the fundamental concept of evolution, descent with modification from common ancestors, is defined by the differential replacement of alleles as populations adapt to their external environmental conditions. Here, the fundamental idea is adaptation to *internal* system conditions, with external environments not influential. Such an idea has no uses to explain organic evolution, and it was long ago discredited when it went by the name orthogenesis.

It should be possible, as we shall see later, to rescue the idea of internally generated evolutionary change without resurrecting orthogenesis. It may be desirable to try, since indeed there may *be* internal evolutionary dynamics that drive sociocultural change, in addition to and distinct from internal developmental dynamics. If an endogenetic evolutionary process were to be described within the framework of the theory of complex (self-organizing) systems, which enables the formulation of stage theories, then perhaps we could tell what sociocultural units are evolving and how; but, so far sociocultural evolution theories have not been developed much in that framework.[3] As things stand now, we have no canonical means by which to decide whether we are describing an evolutionary or a developmental process if we are focusing on internally generated change.

Now to units of analysis. Whoever thinks they can tell the difference is obligated to say what the relevant units are, for between the units is where the difference should be observed. It is possible, of course, that exactly the same units could both develop and evolve. What sorts of units are cultures and societies that they might do both? We can tell, we think, that a horticultural society can replace a hunting and gathering society in response to population pressure on food supplies (Harris 1977). This pattern, to the extent it is empirically true, is suggestive but not definitive of evolution. Even if it were always true, using the same pattern of replacement and the details of it, we could infer development instead. It is often said by evolutionary theorists that evolution is a historical process, but which details of history are the details of evolution and which are the details of development? We cannot logically infer evolution or development or the difference, if any, from sociocultural history alone. Descent and replacement with modification may be necessary, but they are insufficient indicators of evolutionary change.

Assume we could sort the historical details of evolution and development according to their lawful connections to changes in ecological regimes. In other words, let sociocultural evolution be calibrated to ecological change. Now, if we could say something general and empirical about the ecological process by which some sociocultural systems change their modes of subsistence, we should be locating an evolutionary process in sociocultural change. Modes of subsistence, after all, are modes of ecological adaptation. But still we have the problem of units. It is not at all clear just how to define the boundaries for some sociocultural system in which an ecological-evolutionary process may be playing out. Culture itself will not do. Specific cultures will not do. Specific societies, defined by some political territory, will not do. All these boundaries are too vague. Vagueness we might tolerate for a time, for that is the lesser evil. The greater evil is that these boundaries are too delimited. At a minimum the concept of a bioregion (or something like it), which does not respect political, cultural, and social boundaries, is imperative. That implies we have to reckon how bioecological processes figure into interactions with sociocultural processes. Much stands in the way of that.

Cultures and societies are normally identified by social scientists strictly in human terms, according to what humans think, do, have, create, care about, relate to, and arrange with respect to each other. The social sciences are, in the first instance, single species sciences. Occasional deviants such as ecological anthropologists, like Jesuits in the Catholic Church, are permitted their say, but like the Church, the social sciences insist on a monolithic doctrine: human-centered system boundaries. The concept of a bioregion, within which a culture or society may be integrated (or disintegrated), is rarely employed. Thus, in social science theory, cultures and societies are usually interpreted as adaptations *to* biophysical systems, when bioecological matters are brought into theory and research at all. This treats cultures and societies as separate systems analyzable independently of biophysical systems. We could get away with this if we really thought their dynamics were independent of the dynamics of biophysical systems. But we know they are not. Since they are not, we ought to expect evolutionary continuities from biophysical systems to run a course through and to be modified by human sociocultural systems, should we not? If we should, then no historically defined social or cultural entity will serve well as a unit of sociocultural evolution. And if we cannot adequately define system boundaries for an evolutionary process we theorize to operate, nor say exactly what entities are behaving in the process, it is hard to talk with any precision about modified descent, is it not? If we are not sure what is descending from what, we cannot be sure what concatenation of variables might be critical to the process of evolutionary change, on one hand, and developmental change on the other.

Gene-Culture Coevolution

There are some modern theories that try to tell what is descending from what, and they seek to find greater partnership with natural selection. Until recently, cultural evolution theories never have borne much fidelity to the biological sense of evolution.[4] The modern theories are sometimes called theories of gene-culture coevolution (Durham 1990). The term coevolution, introduced for bioecological domains by Ehrlich and Raven (1964), is extended now to include the feedback that organic and cultural modes of inheritance are presumed to have on each other.

The concept of the coevolution of gene pools and cultures rests on several premises. One is that natural selection for genetic variants in a population is an ecological process. Another is that culture, at least in some of its facets, is an ecological adaptation. Both of these premises are rather old. A third has been given considerable attention of late: that culture arises in part from the biology of humans. That claim can be interpreted in different senses, but just one sense is needed to open the window to gene-culture coevolution. It is the sense that different populations of humans having alternative cultural characteristics may differentially survive, prosper, and reproduce, and thus perpetuate their culture, according as how environmental conditions may favor one set of cultural phenotypes over another. These interpretations, together with the foregoing two premises, enable us to speak of the natural selection of culture.

To speak thus is to speak of the coevolution of genes and cultures. There is no such thing as natural selection in the biological sense of the term without the differential survival of genes. When we allow—which the third premise above just did—that cultural characteristics are phenotypes of biological populations, we also allow culture to exert selection pressures on gene pools. But, to turn the looking glass around, gene pools also dispose humans toward some kinds of culture and prohibit other kinds. Not that genes determine or predetermine cultural phenotypes; rather, their encoding for biological development will produce organisms with an array of specialized cultural phenotypes that are in some sense or other adapted to biological phenotypes, and so are available for selection. In a sentence, genes adapt to culture all the while that culture adapts to gene pools or, in a word, genes and cultures coevolve.

How they do this is not so simple to discover, but a number of investigators have been trying (Alexander 1979; Durham 1979, 1991; Boyd and Richerson 1985; Lumsden and Wilson 1981, 1983; Pulliam and Dunford 1980; Cavalli-Sforza and Feldman 1981). The approaches differ, but all attempt in one way or another to connect biological and cultural evolution. The difficulties are formidable, perhaps more so than some of the theorists wish to admit.

All recognize a couple of prime facts. One is that biological and cultural evolution proceed on vastly different time scales, the former being much slower than the latter. How can we effectively theorize about the interaction of evolutionary selection processes that behave at such different rates? Nobody is sure. Another confounding fact is this: For culture to be treated as a system of inheritance, it is necessary to account for how symbolic information, learned by individuals and socially transmitted, is inherited. The problem this presents is that the acquired characteristics of a culture can be socially transmitted or, in other words, cultural inheritance is Lamarckian. Fully aware that genetic selection is nothing of the kind and bearing in mind the different time frames for cultural and biological evolution considered separately, the more cautious of the modern theorists hesitate to affirm that natural selection among populations of organisms and natural selection among (or within) cultures is exactly the same process. Some explicitly affirm that the selection process is different for enculturated compared to unenculturated organisms. Most do not take cultural selection to be perfectly analogous to, or strictly derivative from, organic selection.

Yet, in another respect the modern cultural evolutionary theorists all throw caution to the wind. They want to describe the evolutionary *interaction* of biological and cultural systems of inheritance, and for cultural inheritance they are not satisfied with analogy and the purloining of biological terms. This means they have to concern themselves with inheritance derived from common cultural ancestors. The problem of the choice of evolutionary units now becomes much more difficult. Now, the choice is constrained by the unit used to describe genetic inheritance, the Mendelian gene, which somehow must be integrated with the chosen unit of cultural inheritance. Here, we should extend our sympathy, for there may be no more difficult problem for a theory of sociocultural evolution to solve.

The presumption that human cultural systems are related by descent to common ancestor cultures in principle should enable cladistic analyses of the branchings of human culture, given enough data and *provided* one could be sure which units of cultural transmission to use to organize the data. How difficult would that be? Forget the particulars, whose difficulty alone would rush many cultural anthropologists and archaeologists into premature retirement. There are a priori problems of theory and method that are well nigh unsolvable.

For a full appreciation, we must remember that the organic theory of natural selection *is* a theory of descent with modification from common ancestors, where the lineage is traceable by shared gene proportions. The proportions diminish with distance from some arbitrarily chosen point of origin, and the genes are Mendelian—a hypothetical abstraction that enables genes to be interpreted as distinct, countable entities. The measurement interval is the reproductive generation, and the measurement unit across the interval is the changing frequencies of genes in the gene pool of a population.

If we think we can copy that or invent something like it, or correlate what we invent for use in sociocultural evolution theories, then we need to formulate in theory the appropriate "generations" and countable measures of changes between them. Should we attempt a strict extrapolation of the biological approach, we may find ourselves compelled into a logic that leads to the Durham hypothesis: All human cultures are descended from a single common culture. Now, the Durham hypothesis could well be true, and Durham (1991) has shown how to work with it empirically. But, try to trace the strict patterns of descent with a cladogram—a procedure whose application is implied by the hypothesis! For the inheritance of organic phenotypes, clades can be used to reconstruct phylogeny on the assumption of declining gene frequencies with greater distance from common ancestors. The archaeological evidence that would be needed to construct historical clades adequate to establish the Durham hypothesis is forever unrecoverable. Worse for the plan, *Homo sapiens* was not the first species to have had some culture that would have to be traced. But, putting aside the who, when, and where of it all, try even to say exactly what ought to be traced.

For coevolution theories to specify what, exactly, is descending from what, they have first to explicate the "material" that is supposed to be descending. Descent with modification implies something that is inherited in some mode or other. The inheritance of what and by what means, of course, are problems that have not been overlooked. But the first-generation efforts to solve them clearly pose a difficulty as formidable as Durham's wished-for cladogram. Here is why.

The genetical theory of natural selection is said to deal with inheritance that is particulate. This is derived from the notion that Mendelian genes are particles or units, and are inherited just so as they replicate. Alleles do not blend when chromosomes match.[5] They recombine or get mixed in different distributions. There they maintain their identity and definition as units. By way of analogy, imagine we took 100,000 seeds of many different varieties and randomly mixed them. Afterwards, with great difficulty, should we desire to do so, we could unmix them—sort them out again by type into their original groupings. We did not change their constitution, only their arrangement. But suppose next we mixed together eggs, flour and water. Now we cannot get the eggs back. In this kind of mixing, a blend, we changed their constitution. The analogy may be completed as so: The transmission of cultural symbols is mostly a blending mode of inheritance, not a particulate mode of inheritance. As it is culturally diffused, symbolic information tends to combine so that we get a phenotypic blend that could be selectable in some sense, but could not be reducible to original constituents. Cultural traits are "emergent" phenotypes.

As a general matter, to extend the theory of genetical selection straightway to human culture is to apply a theory of mixing to a process of blending. In the present instance, theoreticians want to show how genetic and cultural inheritance interact. They have therefore to settle on some unit of cultural inheritance—a blending process—that can accommodate and correlate with the accepted unit of genetic inheritance, which is particulate.

The most obvious approach to this problem, adopted by some sociobiologists, is also the clearest candidate for failure—although, curiously, its manifest shortcomings have not halted the effort. The obvious approach to try is to formulate a unit for sociocultural transmission that is perfectly homologous in its properties to the theory of natural selection. Homology would be present if sociocultural evolution operated on particles—that is, if cultural units of inheritance could be conceived so that symbols were particulate, well individuated, replicating entities. Dawkins (1989) had just this in mind when he talked about memes, as did Lumsden and Wilson (1981, 1983) when they talked about culturgens—cultural replicators that are supposed to behave just like the replicators of organic evolution, the genes. The memes or culturgens are interpreted as well-defined units of culture that can be symbolized and transmitted to others, imitated and elaborated by others—and thus replicated, inherited, and selected.

This plan for theorizing, and any like it, cannot possibly succeed. The symbolic information that marks cultural inheritance, which blends with other information of its kind and spreads by social transmission processes (such as diffusion), may indeed be selected in some manner or other—but not in the form of countable units. It is one thing to count Mendelian genes. Those are well individuated, definite entities that are amenable to the calculus of arithmetic. To count memes or culturgens or any of the other proposed units of cultural transmission is to count *indefinite* entities whose replication, if that is what it is, produces a *blending* inheritance of *acquired* characters. This requires an arithmetic we do not have. Matters go downhill from there. Unlike genetic inheritance whose countable units are measured across reproductive generations, cultural inheritance cannot be measured in discrete reproductive intervals except on some fully arbitrary choice.

Without countable units and discrete time frames, there is no cultural calculus to apply to cultural inheritance. Minus that calculus, there is no method by which to cladistically array units of cultural inheritance so that patterns of descent can be displayed. We cannot get Durham's cultural cladogram without the requisite theoretical measurement with which to construct it. And without it, how can we tell if we are describing evolution or development? There is no way.

EVOLUTIONARY TANGLES, II: ADAPTATIONS

We ought, therefore, to explore other angles. It is logical to wonder if some trail can be blazed by means of the concept of adaptation. This, after all, provides a paradigm for theorizing about evolution across the sciences. Again, however, we shall stand down from straightway extrapolations of biological concepts, because our domain is not the same as theirs, even while we search for clues that can highlight some issues salient to ours. We have now to move through a thicket of adaptations or, more accurately, of adaptation concepts—and further tangles.

The concept of adaptation to environments provides a root for all ecological and some social science. It derives from organic evolutionary theory and was snapped up by social scientists for use early and late in theories of sociocultural evolution, ecology, and development. By now, the concept has many intended meanings—too many. It means less to evolutionary biologists and philosophers, who in the past 25 years have given the concept a hard look. It should be helpful to look where they have, and then to look where they have not.

Evolutionary Adaptations

To make sense of the idea of adaptation, it helps to remember that evolution and selection are two different matters, since one can happen without the other. Evolution has the connotation of descent with gradual changes. Selection is not always for changes. The theory of evolution and the theory of natural selection, accordingly, are not one and the same. They intersect at evolutionary selection, which is selection for heritable, gradual changes.[6]

Everybody since Darwin has thought that adaptations are central to evolutionary selection. Unfortunately, it is not so easy to establish whether some phenotypic trait is an adaptation or which traits have been naturally selected. There are, however, some accepted parameters for interpreting all this. What can current theory tell us about some perennial questions? In what follows, I draw heavily (but not exclusively) from G.C. Williams (1966).[7]

One perennial question is whether adaptations are beneficial for the organisms that have them. The answer is: sometimes, but not always. Some genes, called pleiotropic for their multiple effects, may confer adaptive advantages on one character but disadvantages on another, especially when different parts of the life cycle are implicated by the different characters. Therefore, the evolutionary benefit conferred upon one trait may be a selective disadvantage for another, and the given adaptation may not necessarily be optimal for the organism as a whole. If the mean effect of a pleiotropic gene is favorable and the gene is selected, its unfavorable effects will be selected too. A question of evolutionary benefit has to turn into the question, beneficial for what?

Perhaps for the survival and reproduction of the population or species. Yes, often, but not always. The presence of an adaptation in a population normally can be assumed to produce an increase in numbers, not necessarily in the same habitat, for that may be governed by other considerations (such as density); but, on the whole, compared to the absence of the adaptation, the species may become more widespread. Any Darwinian theory would be in deep trouble if this were not normally so because, if it were not, there could be no adaptive radiation—no gradual evolution of different species from a common ancestor as descendants adapted to different habitat niches. The adaptive benefit conferred, when there is any, concerns quantitative increase per unit area, per unit time, for a population. Utilitarian interpretations to individual organisms— for example, to infer there accrues something desirable, preferable, or profitable to individuals—are unwarranted. Also unwarranted in the neo-Darwinian theory is to infer an adaptation just because some character evidently confers some benefit. Some evolutionary reproductive benefits occur by accident.

Are beneficial adaptations functional? This depends entirely on what is meant by functional. At table always with invitations to functions are three places to be carefully set: function that does what, functional for what, and functional because of what? A function that does x in y is not necessarily functional for y. It may destroy y. Here we must understand the phrase "functional for y" as "promoting the survival and reproduction of y," because that is where all the issues are grounded in neo-Darwinian theory. Understanding that, we tacitly commit ourselves to some notion of functional design: some organization of related functions the design of which promotes survival and reproduction. A functional design we are to understand to be an organization of functions that *functions for* differential survival and reproduction, at least for a time. According to Williams, the presence of some functional design is implied by the theory of natural selection and is necessary for evolutionary adaptations to be inferred. It is an empirical question whether some hypothesized function functions in an organized design so as to benefit (read: increase) reproductive advantage.

Can we impute purpose—it seems we are—to a design of evolutionary adaptations? This gets to the question, functional because of what?

We can impute purpose to anything we wish, but that does not mean a design of evolutionary adaptations evolved to serve any purpose. We can always say that birds fly south in the winter in order to avoid freezing and starvation. It is not clear, however, from the point of view of evolutionary selection, what this could intelligently mean. The evolutionary chances are that many birds that did not fly south froze, starved, and failed to reproduce themselves; many that flew south did survive and reproduce; and we are left now with those that are genetically predisposed to come in out of the cold. *They* may have a purpose in flying south. The natural selection of that behavioral character had none. Flying south is functional for keeping the birds alive and it serves that "purpose." But no notion of purpose is required or implied by the theory we invoke to explain why these birds are now widespread or this adaptation maintained. The presence of a functional design of evolutionary adaptations does not require a designer with a purpose.

Are functional adaptations progressive over the course of evolutionary time? Again, it depends on what one means. There is much evidence for an increase in complexity in all sorts of phenotypes and their organization. However, all this means is that their number, kind, organizational forms, and relations have increased. This increasing complexity, to be adequately described, would require a very large array of quantitative distributions. It is not at all clear outside a mathematical context what it means to describe as "progressive" some distribution of increasing quantities. It should be clear, I would think, that some increase or progression in complexity does not enable one to infer some increasing state of *perfection*—some order of progression from lower, and less valuable, to higher and better forms. That would be reading into the natural order of things something that nature can neither confirm or deny. But, as we remarked earlier, that reading has been given.

At times in the past, and sometimes still, progressive has meant "better" from a human point of view. But natural selection is not undertaken from a human point of view. Artificial selection is. The idea of desirable progress toward perfection in the evolution of forms is a conceptual residue left from the worldviews of earlier times, in which evolution and progress were often equated. This derived from, and was at the time of Darwin intertwined with, the Enlightenment vision of the perfectibility of humankind. Some early evolutionary theorists looked at the world and saw, they thought, evidence of increasing progress and perfection purposely designed no longer by God but "naturally." Thus spoke Darwin in one of the most quoted of all sentences in *The Origin*:

And as natural selection works solely by and for the good of each being, all corporeal and mental endowments will tend to progress towards perfection (1985, p. 459).

Darwin and his contemporaries were seeing in nature the reflections of their own minds, which put *Homo sapiens* at the pinnacle of evolution. We ought not to fault them for this, since *Homo sapiens* in Western societies had in its own mind been at the pinnacle of existence at least since the Book of Genesis was written, and Darwin himself had already done a great deal to challenge age-old prevailing conceptions of God's design. But the attitude reflected in this statement is a simple anthropocentric affirmation of self-designated worth. It certainly is not substantiated by modern ecological science in which, taking survival and its functional consequences as criteria, the phytoplankton are probably the most valuable of organisms. We can believe in evolutionary, goal-directed progress toward perfection if we wish, but we cannot accurately believe that it derives from the synthetic theory of evolution by natural selection. It does not.

The synthetic theory provides assorted parameters for interpreting the idea of evolutionary adaptation. They include the following: The reproductively beneficial adaptations among a set of local habitat alternatives are naturally selected, *if* there are selection pressures at all; there may not be. Not every phenotypic trait is an adaptation, not every adaptation is selected, not every trait was selected, not every trait selected is an adaptation, but a trait counts as an adaptation *only* if it was selected. It is generally agreed that adaptations will not necessarily appear or, should they appear, be preserved just because some population faces an extinction crisis; or, if preserved, prevent the extinction. No adaptation is assumed to appear without some functional design—some organization of functions that promotes survival and reproduction. Should an adaptation appear, this can only be inferred by its subsequent effects in the organized design, but from the effects one cannot necessarily infer *why* the adaptation evolved. A trait might not be an adaptation when it first appears, for whatever reason it appears, but it might become an adaptation over time as it gradually fits into an evolving organized design. Since it may be entirely fortuitous whether a trait becomes an adaptation, organisms may or may not be active adapters.

The crucible in the neo-Darwinian theory is that all evolutionary adaptations must relate to reproduction and genetic inheritance. Otherwise, there could be no natural selection for adaptations. When there is, selection is said to operate on individuals not populations (while populations not individuals evolve). Adaptations are incorporated into the genotypes of the individual members of a population; however, a population itself does not have a genotype and so, strictly speaking, it cannot adapt. The synthetic theory applies to populations of adapted individuals, not to adapted populations of individuals. Since individuals are the carriers of genes, whose changing allelic frequencies measure evolution, it can also be said that alleles are selected. The natural selection of Darwinian adaptations is the natural selection of genetic variants. These caveats for interpreting adaptation are the product of numerous analysts, but as I indicated, they owe much to George C. Williams. His classic 1966 treatise, *Adaptation and Natural Selection,* in retrospect was a watershed for evolutionary analyses in the framework of the modern synthesis. This work, and that which followed it, was so cogent that the theory of natural selection is now coming to be interpreted by many for just the purpose Williams said it should be: not as an explanation of evolutionary change, but as an explanation for the maintenance of adaptations and the spread of new variants. This, it seems, is at odds with Darwin, who thought his theory could explain the origin of species by showing how heritable variation between individuals would gradually convert to fixed variation between populations.

Something here seems to be not quite right.

Evolutionary and Ecological Adaptations

On some of the recent interpretations for the synthetic theory, which is now the reigning orthodoxy, there comes a break in the flow from Darwin. The break occurs at the idea of adaptation, for this is two ideas masquerading as one.

Darwin derived the assumption of adaptation of organism to environment apparently from reading William Paley's *Natural Theology* ([1802], 1970). In the process of adaptation, Darwin reflected, could be found the origins of evolutionary design.[8] It is worth remembering that Darwin had God, that Great Designer in the Sky, on his mind and was seeking an alternative source of evolutionary design. Putting Paley and T.R. Malthus together, he hit upon the natural selection of adaptations. Why did he call it natural? To distinguish it from human-controlled (artificial) selection, and to suggest that selection was not divine. Since then, except for the notice afforded this by creationists (and they, as usual, notice the wrong things), all the attention has focused on selection with its naturalness taken for granted. Ignoring the issue of divine origins, something else here cannot be taken for granted.

In publishing and explaining his theory, it is now well known, Darwin had troubled himself over his choice of terms. The word ecology made its appearance only toward the end of Darwin's days, and was not until later widely diffused into English-speaking cultures. But suppose it had been. Suppose, instead of "natural selection," Darwin had had available and had settled on "ecological selection." This would have been in keeping with his theory—a struggle to survive, won through phenotype adaptations to biophysical habitats, which enables the relatively fit to differentially reproduce. Such populations therefore would be "naturally" selected, but he might have said ecologically selected. "Ecological" applies because the selection is a natural product of ecological dynamics—a complex of organism-habitat interactions and changes, the directions of which are candidates for selection if they relate to heritable traits. It is, of course, not uncommon to find the thought that natural selection is an ecological process, or that natural selection is the ecological moment of evolution—the moment when adaptations are selected.

Now, in the lexicon of the synthetic theory, try substituting "genetical selection" for "natural selection." This works, too. Selection for alternative alleles is the effect of marginally superior adaptedness in habitats. In the synthetic theory, allelic replacement is the measure of evolution and reproductive generations the interval for the measure. What happens between the intervals? The struggle to survive and obtain reproductive opportunities— all those ecological dynamics whose effects are selected for or against, to be measured on alleles. The genetic interpretation at the core of the Modern Synthesis would not be the reigning orthodoxy if it did not work better than what it replaced.

Okay, now try substituting "genetical selection" for "ecological selection." This does not work. The genetic measure does not sample the ecological property space. It is not defined on the same spatial or temporal scales at which ecological processes operate, and it does not admit of linear scale transformations. The interval does not measure ecological dynamics, being designed instead to measure a variable property of species rather than the ecological complex whose dynamics affects species' variable values of the property. It is worth remembering that reproduction is not the same thing as the struggle to survive, and ecological dynamics involve more than species populations. Populations, in response to a combination of biotic and abiotic conditions, have to function and survive before and after they reproduce. That is where the action is—in the dynamic motion between the intervals.

In virtue of the measurement model it incorporates, the genetical theory of natural selection is not an ecological theory of natural selection. At its best, the genetical theory presumes ecological dynamics but can cover only the reproductive ecology of species. It tells what happens at reproduction. It does not tell about the time in between reproduction episodes. At its worst, the genetical theory conceives ecological dynamics as just so many details to be sorted out at reproductive intervals and confines ecological principles to a black box whose contents can be glimpsed only as an outcome at those intervals. If the genetical theory cannot explain how organisms adapt to habitats and habitats to organisms, and for the most part it cannot, then Eldredge (1985) was right to complain that ecological entities are not addressed in the Modern Synthesis.

The idea of adaptation seems to be cracking a bit. It should be easy now to break it into two.

If organic evolution is a process of adaptation by natural selection, it cannot be *evolutionary* adaptations that are naturally selected—not in the framework of the synthetic theory and its modern caveats about adaptations. Among the currently accepted caveats about evolutionary adaptation is the one that has us unable to tell, perhaps not until long after origins, whether a trait actually is an adaptation; there could be hundreds of reproductive generations before we could say, depending on the trait's post-factum role in the scheme of things. In the meantime, while we wait, assorted functional activities of the population and its interactions with its habitat—adaptation in process—will change the values of variables that become candidates for selection. What are we to call these ongoing functional activities? A reasonable answer is ecological adaptations. We cannot be sure if they are or will become evolutionary adaptations. We can be sure they are adaptations of a sort—physiological, morphological, or behavioral changes made by organisms in response to habitat conditions that ebb and flow over life courses and cycles, and which affect the courses and cycles with implications for the organisms' descendants. These ecological adaptations, when they succeed in the short term, are the causes of the long-term evolutionary adaptations. That is not to say they *become* the evolutionary adaptations. They are distinct ecological adaptations that may be selected as feeders for a cumulative evolutionary trajectory measured by quite different adaptations. Evolutionary adaptations cross the generations. Ecological adaptations might or might not.

The theory of natural selection is usually presented as a theory for long-term evolutionary adaptations selected from heritable variants during short-term reproductive moments at ecological sites. In itself, that idea is not problematic, but the *presentation* of it often confuses evolutionary and ecological adaptation. The confusion issues from two mistakes of interpretation that are commonplace with the theory of natural selection. One mistake is to think of natural selection as a dynamic causal force, and the other is to suppose there is some unit on which the force acts.

Biologists frequently speak of natural selection (directional selection usually is the referent) as a causal force in the changing of gene frequencies. It takes a philosopher to show just how this idea can be made coherent (see Sober 1984a), and some biologists (Sober and Lewontin 1984; Endler 1986) also agree it is confusing and misleading to think of directional selection as "causing" evolutionary change in the sense of "producing" it. Natural selection is one (but just one) statistical outcome of the process of evolution. It is not a causal force. It is more accurate to think of evolution as *described* by natural selection than evolution as *explained* by natural selection. The "forces," such as they are, materialize from an interaction of genetic and ecological processes, with evolutionary selection a sometime result, whose interactive causal "force laws" are not as well understood as the analogy to mechanical forces would suggest. A mechanical force produces motion, but natural selection is a constraint on motion already produced (Swenson 1991).

For the sake of argument, however, let us compound the error and suppose there are selection forces. Then, there have to be units of selection; for, without units it is impossible to get forces to materialize. The telling point about units of selection, amid all the hullabaloo about the subject, was made by Michael Ghiselin (1981). Ghiselin wanted to know, with apparent sarcasm in his heart, why his shirt should be thought of as a unit of undressing. Undressing did not take his shirt off, he observed, he did. His point, sarcasm aside, was that selection is a process that defines relations.[9] Well, what relations? Units of *analysis,* which any theory and measurement model presume, are not necessarily isomorphic with epistemic units on which real forces act. Genetical selection theory defines its relations by quantitatively comparing reproductive generations for allelic substitutions, its unit of analysis. It describes a statistical outcome of epistemic relations that themselves may issue from forces, but the choice of unit of analysis prevents the theory from describing the forces per se. The theory does not explain how or why some adaptation was marginally superior so that alleles to maintain it were substituted.

If there is any coherence to saying that allelic replacement happens *because* of selection, it comes only if we understand the "natural" in natural selection to mean that ecological adaptations are selected. If our formulation says that evolution is a process of adaptation by *ecological* selection, then indeed we have a theory of forces. We also have a formulation in which adaptation takes on ecological as distinct from evolutionary meaning. Darwin, indeed, meant ecological. In his theory of evolution, natural selection was a causal force. But the genetical interpretation of selection theory took it out. By the theoretical logic of the Modern Synthesis natural selection is an effect, not a cause, of two sets of evolutionary forces that interact: molecular gene mutations and ecological variation. Unfortunately, as John Endler admitted, "We are most remarkably ignorant about the ecological aspects of natural selection" (1986, p. 248).[10]

So, the synthetic theory is not a theory *of* adaptation in the sense that it can tell us about adaptive ecological dynamics. It is a theory that presumes ecological adaptations before it can tell us anything at all. Then, it can tell us about the maintenance, spread, and loss of *evolutionary* adaptations. Organic evolution conceived as a process of the natural selection of Darwinian adaptations is a deep cover for ecology. Lift the cover and we find that the respective theories of population genetics and ecology do not enable a one-to-one mapping. The relations are many-to-many. Matters would be simplified if we could conceive ecology as just so many short-term evolutionary details, especially the activities pursuant to reproduction. Unfortunately, we cannot. Many ecological details are not incorporated into the evolutionary process and its results, and anyhow, there is more to ecology than its details. Evolutionary and ecological phenomena behave at different spatial and temporal scales of resolution. The theory, measurement, and data that would enable scale transformations is very tentative and incomplete. So, between evolutionary and ecological theory there is something of a break.

No biologist doubts the connection of ecology to evolution, because habitats are the sites of evolutionary selection. However, biologists employ numerous concepts of adaptation. What I have called ecological adaptation some call ontogenetic adaptation, and biologists are familiar with the idea of acquired adaptations from work by C.H. Waddington. Physiologists speak of adaptation differently. They mean to refer to the tendency of tissues, organs, or organ subsystems to functionally adjust to changes in the internal or external environments of somas—adaptation as compensation.

Social scientists have used the term adaptation for whatever has suited their purposes. Social science concepts of adaptation are highly metaphorical and sometimes analogical, and often nothing more is meant than some adjustment made by some entity to an environmental stimulus. At other times, what social scientists mean by adaptation is something entirely vernacular, such as the coping responses of individual humans.

We arrive at an easy conclusion: The concept of adaptation—if unexplicated, unexpurgated, and unexpunged—can provide no theoretical basis for sorting between sociocultural evolution and sociocultural development. Try it yourself. Assume that some sort of adaptation process is operating for both evolution and development. What sort of adaptation process do you have in mind? Is it the same process for evolutionary, ecological, and developmental change? These, too, behave at different rates and on different scales. How do they connect by way of your adaptation process(es)? Is your concept nothing more than the intuitive idea of a response to changed or changing conditions?

The concept of adaptation is not a ticket to ride very far, but perhaps we should follow one train of thought. Perhaps we should temporarily retain an ecological concept of adaptation, since it seems we would be helpless to make sense of sociocultural evolution, ecology, and development without one. Very well. Now let us delude ourselves into thinking that our concept is general, clear, consistent, and coherent. There follows immediately another idea that we have to make sense of and settle upon, without which our concept of adaptation could not possibly be coherent: the idea of some environment for our unit of adaptation, whatever it may be, to be adapted to.

EVOLUTIONARY TANGLES, III:
ADAPTATIONS TO ENVIRONMENTS

Sociocultural theory proceeds as if sociocultural systems are developing *in* various environments, by adapting *to* various environments, some of which are sometimes but not always acknowledged to be biophysical; and that cultures and societies may evolve as they develop and adapt. Now, I shall argue that this paradigm for theory construction is too simplistic to be effective for describing evolutionary, ecological, and developmental change in sociocultural systems. The paradigm was inspired by, if it does not have clear roots in, Darwinian theory; and so I shall argue the point by again turning to the strongest possible case that illustrates the complexities that make the paradigm too simple: the case of biological organization inasmuch as its design is evolutionarily and ecologically adaptive.

Now, however, we shall lose some analytical precision. The restrictions that apply to interpreting the concept of evolutionary adaptation cannot be applied straightway to ecological adaptations. We shall have now to employ the term adaptation in a more intuitive sense, consistent with the practice in social science. For the present purpose this should do no harm; in fact, it should help establish that the concept is too weak.

Multiple Environments For Adapting Entities

A continuing process of adaptation, involving some sort of entity-environment interaction, is a necessary condition for evolutionary selection and ecological functioning. To make sense of evolutionary-ecological organization, it is necessary to know with respect to just what environments are what sorts of entities adapting? It is just as reasonable to think that genes adapt, are adapted, and are adaptable as it is to think that those predicates apply to organisms, and it may be reasonable to apply them to ecosystems. Yet, it is plain, these different entities could not possibly adapt, be adapted, or be adaptable to the same environments, since they do not have the same environments. We know there are several kinds of environment in which both genes and their carriers are situated, and the environments of each extend so far as the environments themselves are nested. And nested they are. Matters now become uncomfortable.

The proximal environment of a gene is the chromosome on which it is arrayed. Except for RNA viruses, the hereditary material for all organisms is found in its nuclear DNA. So, chromosome, genome, nucleus, and cell represent four physical environments for a nuclear gene (and I cannot say that list—or any that follows—is exhaustive). For multi-celled organisms, other, distal physical environments for a gene include the tissue, organ, and soma of the organism that carries it.

There are theoretical environments. Every gene functions in the environment of its genotype. It does not function alone. Its contribution to the organism's cell growth, regulation, differentiation, or development, as the case may be, is affected by the functioning of specific forms of other genes that belong to the same genotype. The genotype of diploid organisms, deviant cases notwithstanding, is a unique combination resulting from the equivalent of a Great Genetic Crap Shoot at the time of reproduction. Then and there, another theoretical environment for a gene materializes: the gene pool. Since the somas that carry genes have environments of their own, we have also to observe that genes are remotely nested in those.

The most obvious environment for an organism or population of them is its biophysical habitat, but just to talk like that gives the wrong impression, as if organisms' habitats were monolithic and fixed. Normally, they are not—again depending on the time frame, the species, and the parameters one chooses to look at. Some habitats change daily, even hourly, for certain populations. Within the same habitat as viewed from the human eye, assorted microhabitats can sometimes be observed—for instance, microclimate differences issuing from variable amounts of sunlight. In any case, the local biophysical habitats in which organisms make their immediate living are embedded in larger ones from which come flows of energy and materials that provide suitable living conditions. The larger environments range from biomes to ecosystems to the biosphere. All these are environments to which an organism or population must directly or indirectly respond. For some organisms, there are even more to consider. For the enculturated social species, two of the environments to which they must respond are the forms of social organization and culture, the presence of which defines them as enculturated and social.

Genes and their carriers have different environments to which they perforce respond, just to continue functioning if nothing else. That much we could manage to understand well enough, but we have a further, very serious, complication: Genes, organisms, and local habitats all respond to each other. They interact. With the important exception that acquired traits do not change the germ line, the effects of all are mediated by the effects of the others. These effects are extraordinarily complex and, in many instances, the details of the interactions are unknown.

It is known that genes are not always phenotypically expressed. The habitats of organisms or the metabolism of somas, or the interactions between those, or the presence of other interacting genes, may foreclose the phenotypic expression of a given gene. The characters for which genes encode are realized depending upon the environments available for their realization, and the relevant environmental parameters vary with the gene and character at issue. Some genes have effects on more than one character. Some characters, to be phenotypically realized, depend upon the interactions of multiple genes. Some single genes encode for single characters, but most do not. There are multiple gene-gene, gene-soma, and soma-habitat interactions, some sequential and some simultaneous, that intervene between molecular genes and their expression as Mendelian phenotypes. This is what is meant by saying that the relations are many-to-many, without known isomorphic transformations.

If a genotype is analogized to a computer program, which it sometimes is, then like a program, a genotype may produce variable output according to the nested, multiple, and interacting environments in which the program is running. If a genotype is like a computer program, however, it is at least a program whose commands do not change. In this, a genotype differs from a biophysical habitat, whose commands often are not the same from one run to the next. The command lines in the programs of biophysical habitats may be substituted in sporadic fashion to varying degree, with some command lines always the same except in large geologic time frames, but with additional lines being periodically substituted as habitat stabilities, operative for portions of the run, are perturbed by virtue of changes in biome, ecosystem, or biosphere. Organisms are provided with a fixed (if flexible) genotype. Put them in a changing environment, in which somehow they must survive, and they are made to work with a program that changes as they use it.

The biophysical habitats in which genes are remotely nested eventually can alter population gene distributions. Imagine, to make the point, a habitat in which stabilities are normally distributed with low variance—a habitat occupied by populations with stable life cycles, to which members are well adapted through dispositions provided by their fixed genotypes. Then subject the habitat to rapid, severe, and permanent climatic change. Now, apply the theory of natural selection. If there are properties of the habitat *with respect to* some character of physiology, morphology, or behavior *such that* a reproductive advantage ensues for some moment, the relative frequency of the gene for that character will increase in the gene pool. Extend the moments and the magnitude of increase is extended. Population gene pools stand to be reconstituted now, because some populations may prosper while others should perish in the changed climatic conditions. In an intuitive manner of speaking, genes "adapt" to habitats inasmuch as gene pools are affected by habitat variability and the match, or lack of it, that a population has with its habitat at a given time. It would be more strict to say that genes are adapted rather than say they adapt, since they are not active adapters. All it means is that, as habitats change, a population's gene pool distribution "responds" to the changes.

We are not finished. An important class of interactions I have yet to mention—the most important from an ecological point of view—is habitat changes that happen *because* of the activity of organisms. We know, for instance (and there are many instances), that oxygen became prevalent in the atmosphere, where originally there was almost none, as a result of organic activity back long before you and I came along. That fundamentally altered the course of organic evolution because it effected so many fundamental habitat changes, creating new evolutionary opportunities and closing others off, and making it possible for you and me to come along. The activity of living organisms changes the conditions for their own natural selection, and for the selection of others. Habitats respond to their organic populations every bit as much as populations respond to habitats. This is another class of interactions about which many of the fine details are unknown.

In theory, if organisms create their own habitats, so to speak, and organisms carry genes that set parameters for their own functioning, we can turn this observation around: The evolution of habitats is a somewhat-removed adaptation to genes. The organizational properties of habitats are partly shaped by the complex of interactions involving genotype and organism.

These are just some of the serious complications that arise when we consider—and I admit the consideration is abbreviated—the structure of bioecological organization. Genotype, phenotype, organism, and habitat behave in multiple, simultaneous, interdependent interaction processes because of the multiple, nested environments that come into play for these entities. But matters get more complicated still: The processes do not behave at the same rates nor within the same time frames. Genotypes incorporate adaptations to past environments, evolved over the long term. The evolved adaptations represented in genotypes enable phenotypes to be more or less adapted to current habitats in the short term. Better-adapted phenotypes make for more successful organisms. But successful organisms change biophysical habitats. The reciprocal adaptations of habitats to organisms provides a continuing mandate for organisms to further adapt to habitats, thus changing gene frequency distributions, on penalty of surrendering fitness and going extinct. This is the origin of ecological dynamics.

Where does natural selection fit into all this? About where Swenson (1991) said it does—as one means, restricted in its sphere of influence and operation, by which order is produced within larger evolving systems, whose tendency toward maximum entropy production permits order to be selected from disorder. Organic selection is a specific case of a more general physical selection process (Swenson and Turvey 1991).

Dimensions and Limits of the Adaptation Paradigm

However necessary it may be, the concept of adaptation to environments is by itself too ambiguous to do justice to biological organization that results from evolutionary-ecological processes. Insisted-upon qualifications for interpreting evolutionary adaptations do not apply straightaway for interpreting ecological adaptations—certainly if there is any thought to including humans in ecology. This is as it ought to be: To look at *any* unitary adaptation of some organic entity to any *one* of its environments is to look at just one among many simultaneous, interdependent adaptation processes behaving at different rates in a complex field of interacting environments. To look at single entities in all their adaptation glories would likewise distort by simplification what is inordinately complex. The point holds for aggregations of single entities. Especially it holds for sociocultural entities. To use "adaptation to environment" as some general paradigm for theorizing about evolutionary change, where sociocultural systems are included in the scope of the change, and to expect that it should be a paradigm sufficient to do the work, is to be placed in the uncomfortable position of having to explain how the work has worked to resolve the issues. The issues remain because the work has not worked.

Adaptation is a multidimensional concept if ever there was one. Which dimensions are relevant to us?

At least four different adaptation processes can be argued to be relevant in one way or another to sociocultural evolution. Each behaves at different rates, with different results. Each has a different origin, with a different mandate to adapt, directed to different adapting entities.

1. *Evolutionary adaptation* originates in the collision of two phenomena: genetic variation and habitat variation. Evolutionary adaptation serves a mandate to adapt for fitness. The mandate applies to genes and is executed by organisms, and the results are changed allele distributions. Evolutionary adaptations cross the generations. Evolution is about ancestors and descendants and the reproduction of them, and gradual changes in their forms through the reconstitution of gene pools.

2. *Ecological adaptation* originates in the variable resource conditions that ebb and flow within organisms' life spans, in localized habitats. No long-term gene frequency changes are at issue. Short-term physiological and behavioral compensations, within reproductive generations, are. Ecological adaptation serves a mandate to adapt for survival. The mandate applies to individual organisms or to populations of them. It is executed by utilizing whatever resources are available in the web of connections that evolutionary adaptations have provided to phenotypes in local habitats. The results are changed population dynamics, changed biota, and changed habitats. Ecology is about eating and being eaten.

3. *Socioecological adaptation* originates in the outcomes of the evolutionary and ecological adaptations of populations of social animals, humans in particular. It serves a mandate to subsist within the parameters of the biophysical resources the population's habitat provides or the population itself is able to improvise with its forms of sociocultural behavior. Solutions to the problem of subsistence encountered by the human species in its biophysical environments are provided by its cultural forms of societal development and, within those, its forms of social organization—especially its political, economic, and urban forms, which we shall call *sociotypes.* In principle, sociotypes connect to phenotypes and genotypes because they behave in an evolutionary-ecological process. Sociotypes are first-order derivatives of ecological adaptation within the parameters set by evolutionary adaptations. Socioecological adaptation applies to collectivities, although its execution devolves on individuals whose behavior shapes the form of the collectivities. The results are changed resource distributions, changed population dynamics,

changed biophysical environments, and changed sociotypes. Socioecology is about the provision, by means of collective social and cultural organization, for collective biophysical subsistence.

4. *Sociocultural adaptation* originates in the outcomes of socioecological adaptation.[11] Provided with sociotypes to ensure continuing human subsistence, humans incline out of self-interest to enhance their material conditions. So, they contrive enduring sociocultural forms that function purely in terms of each other. They contrive the voluntary associations, formal organizations, mores, traditions, information networks, and institutions familiar to sociologists and anthropologists. These sociocultural forms beget more of their own kind. Social science itself is about these self-generating social groups and their symbolic relations, in which sociocultural environments are constructed and to which affected individuals and aggregates must adapt in the short term to ensure the maintenance or enhancement of their positions in sociocultural groups. The groups, systems, and symbolic relations among them that come into being from the mandate to adapt socioculturally, kinship relations excepted, are far removed from direct ecological influences. They are n-order derivatives of an ecological process, to be sure, and may be changed because of that; but, as they come and go, they are spin-offs mostly of each other. Sociocultural adaptation is to social, cultural, economic, and political, not to physical or biological, niches. The mandate for sociocultural adaptation derives strictly from sociocultural forms themselves. It applies to individuals as well as aggregates, but is reflected in aggregates. The results are changed cultures, changed societies, and changed subsystems within those.

Evolutionary, ecological, socioecological, and sociocultural adaptation processes are nested, but not like so many Chinese boxes. They are hierarchically ordered, but not so that any process is under the control of the others. Their effects are not unidirectional or linear. They behave simultaneously, but at different rates, on different time scales, ranging in the order listed from the very slow to the very quick. Depending upon the closure conditions defined for them, some evolutionary adaptations can take millions of years while some sociocultural adaptations can occur within a matter of minutes. The different adaptation processes issue from different mandates to adapt, which is just to say they have different origins and their operation sets different initial conditions to which organisms or populations of them must respond. All these adaptation processes connect and interact so as to change each other. We do not know exactly how, but let us think for a moment how complicated and sophisticated must be the theory to establish their connections and describe their interactions and effects.

We could think of evolutionary and ecological adaptations as if they were different-sized gears that turn each other. Organic evolution occurs in habitats, from ecological action on phenotypes with genetic variants. Without ecological adaptation in the short term, there can be no evolutionary adaptation in the long term. Socioecological adaptation functionally depends upon how those two gears turn. Its own gears are turned by, and its sociotypes evolve from, the product of the interaction of evolutionary and ecological adaptations. However, evolved though they are from that interaction, nevertheless they produce feedback for it because sociotypes change biophysical habitats and the ecological interactions therein.

Sociocultural adaptive forms, though they are utterly dependent upon the functioning of the other three adaptation processes, in the short term can be self-generating. It is in this sense, for instance, that formal organizations may meaningfully be said to be adaptive, but this is a purely sociocultural adaptation since these forms have no origins in any evolutionary mandate for reproduction, or ecological mandate for survival, or socioecological mandate for subsistence. Sociocultural forms of adaptation nevertheless can produce direct and immediate consequences for biophysical habitats, so this adaptation process is not self-contained either. None of them are.

To say that these different processes of adaptation interact is one thing. To mathematically model their interactions is something else again. Assorted bodies of theory and evidence can be and have been brought to bear to address each of the different dimensions. There is considerable consensus that genic selection theory explains the maintenance of organic adaptations, but that it omits to explain the adaptation *process,* since the natural selection of evolutionary adaptations is an effect not a cause of the process. This omission is a prime impetus for the dissatisfaction some have with the Modern Synthesis. There is a growing body of theory for ecological adaptations themselves, which eventually may help to alleviate the omission. Unfortunately, much theory that would be needed to connect evolutionary to ecological adaptations is not yet developed. It is not all that easy to produce connective theory for the interaction of multiple processes that behave at substantially different rates.

Why, then, should we suppose that a focus on adaptation, seemingly central to any evolutionary theory, will suffice to produce effective theories of human social and cultural evolution? Distinguishing socioecological and purely sociocultural adaptations might help. We could provide the assumptions that socioecological adaptations are factors in evolution not development, and sociocultural adaptations are factors in development not evolution. But even so, to provide satisfactory social and cultural entities that could evolve or develop, as well as measures of the processes and intervals for them, and measures for the interaction of the processes, may be an insurmountable charge. We must, following the present line of thinking, accept the charge to connect sociocultural systems to biophysical processes and regimes. Existing theories of sociocultural adaptation, by which I mean to include almost all the purely sociological, anthropological, economic, political, or historical theories of social change, do not connect at all. We could attempt a preemptive bid. We could model theories of social and cultural evolution on natural selection theory. Unfortunately this fails because organic inheritance is particulate and sociocultural inheritance is not. There, more or less, is where matters rest.

Is there reason to suppose that *any* concept of adaptation, or all of them together, will suffice for theorizing about sociocultural evolution and development? I suggest that adaptation-based explanations are coarse-grained beginning bids, not fine grained finished contracts. As we are dealing with different kinds of systems, the sociocultural and the biophysical, and we wish to understand their connections, it is elemental that we must bid to describe their *mutual* adaptations, or interactions. But when we admit the idea of interaction, we tacitly commit to a concept of mutual *internal* not external adaptations, because we arrive at an explicit contract to investigate *systems* of *biosociocultural* connections. How can we make that contract? Only by playing to the analysis of mutual interactions, or system integration (and disintegration). If it is coherent to maintain that sociocultural systems evolve, then the concepts we employ to understand their evolution have to be ratcheted up something like that, from adaptation to interaction to integration. Then, sociocultural evolution can be comprehended as one means of order production within more comprehensive natural systems. Sociocultural evolution cannot be understood on its own terms, because it does not happen on its own terms.

Smart Wagering On Sociocultural Evolution and Development

There remains to suggest a workable alternative to following the traditions of social scientists and the models of orthodox neo-Darwinism. The alternative is to formulate sociocultural evolution theories within the framework of complex, self-organizing, evolving systems. The clues biology has to offer I take as pointing unmistakably in this direction.

Without committing to anything canonical, some differences between evolutionary and developmental processes nevertheless can be assumed for sociocultural systems if experience with biological systems is any guide—or, at least, can be assumed for the purpose of smart and not-so-smart wagering.[12] Smart money follows an evolutionary process that is contingent, in that the process incorporates chance factors into its trajectory, with the trajectory sometimes irreversibly altered because of them. Not-so-smart money follows evolution as if it has a normal trajectory. Though it may seem normal for evolution to result in greater complexity, one has to ask: normal compared to what? The answer is: Compared just to the historical record of all those incorporated contingencies. There are no other means to calibrate.

Smart money has normality and contingency behaving differently in developmental processes, with other means to calibrate. First, developmental processes *can* be evaluated against a norm. This is routine, even with the development of certain pathologies; one may, for instance, speak (if morbidly) of the normal development of Tay Sachs Syndrome. Smart money would avoid any wager that developmental trajectories are "necessary" in some deterministic sense or that they have any "purpose" to them. (Wagering on necessity or purpose in evolution is a pure sucker's play.) Second, the effect of contingencies on developmental processes is largely to disturb them—largely to change the normal trajectory. We can wager smartly that developmental outcomes are confined to tighter ranges than evolutionary outcomes just because they are evaluable against a norm that is internal to the developing system. It is possible to evaluate the "success" or "failure" of a developmental process by taking into account the accumulated contingencies and measuring their departures from the norm. An evolutionary process that is taken to be "normal," with a tight range of outcomes having specifiable trajectories, is an orthogenetic evolution. Definitely not smart.

Developmental outcomes, therefore, ought to be much more predictable, and attract more wagerers (if wagerers are rational), than evolutionary outcomes. To wager on specific evolutionary outcomes or whole evolutionary regimes is not so smart. The regulation of evolution is largely an externally driven process for systems that may show transitory similarities as they or their subsystems diverge over longer time frames. The regulation of development by means of a system's internal norms of organization and functioning enables distinct developing systems that are fundamentally alike to appear to be superficially dissimilar (commercialized cultures, for instance [see Bodley, 1994, this volume]).

Now, it would be not-so-smart to bet that the external regulation of evolution and the internal regulation of development provide a canon to distinguish the processes *unless* we are willing to assume that exactly the same kinds of units are capable of evolving and developing. I am not willing. I suggest that specific cultures and nameable societies are perfectly capable of developing in ways that social scientists now take them "normally" to do, while I reaffirm our earlier conclusion that evolution cannot occur for such units. Why should we suppose that the kind of unit that is amenable to evolution is anything at all like the kind that is amenable to development?

Suppose sociotypes can develop. I suppose—to complete the earlier bidding— that it takes *biosociocultural types* to evolve. These are entities for which we do not now even have names, let alone measures for identification. But, to review, we do know that sociocultural systems are connected to ecological systems, which are connected to organic evolutionary processes. If we believe there is a process (or more than one) of sociocultural evolution, we have to bet that evolving units incorporate all those dimensions (best, probably, in some hierarchical organization). This extends the domain of appropriate analysis to encompass a greater range of interacting environments in which a unit may evolve, compared to a unit that may develop. Now, we may define a system in which evolution is internally regulated, not by the evolving unit per se as with development but by the system within which the evolving unit is a functional assembly. Insofar as we conceive evolutionary change as internally driven, it seems not so smart to look for internal *norms* for regulation but, rather, to look for system sensitivity to initial conditions that gives rise to spontaneous self-organization far from equilibrium. It would be smart, then, to allow a wide latitude for nonlinearity in the description of evolutionary change. In a nonlinear system far from equilibrium, the "external" norms for regulating the evolution of subsystems are internal to the system itself.

If a canon to distinguish sociocultural evolution and development and the means to describe their interactions are desirable, then this has to issue from theory adequate to disentangle the complexities of the simultaneous processes, which almost certainly behave at different rates and on different scales. Where should the smart wagerers go to find out how smart their wagering really was— where should they go even to place their bets, let alone to be paid off? The sciences of complexity,[13] implicated in the preceding paragraph, provide the only game where the true odds can be set and the payoffs determined—the only theoretical paradigm that can possibly accommodate the unknown complexities and interactions of evolution and development, generally speaking, and the known complexities of sociocultural evolution and sociocultural development in particular. However, as Dyke (1994, this volume) makes clear, even our concepts of explanation, not just our choice of models and units, have to change to work within this paradigm. Paradoxically, the paradigm permits sociocultural evolution theory to return to its origins—to theories of endogenetic evolution, even to stage theories if we wish, and even to Spencer, where all this began— for here the concept of adaptation has internal applications without inevitable orthogenetic implications. The results of theorizing in this paradigm, however, could not be anything like the patterns of explanation we are now familiar with, for here we commit ourselves to describing nonlinear dynamics. Such are probably the true dynamics of the evolved and developing sociocultural systems that have captured our attention to date.

ACKNOWLEDGMENTS

The author is grateful to C. Dyke and A.R. Maryanski for advising him about the contents and presentation of this paper.

NOTES

1. The term Modern Synthesis refers to an array of theoretical and empirical developments in biology, which occurred roughly in the period 1930 to 1950 and have continued periodically thereafter, by means of which population genetics and systematics became fully intergrated with

the original Darwinian theory. Ever since, the modern theory of evolution by natural selection has been called the neo-Darwinian, the genetical, or the synthetic theory.

2.   They did not come by the distinction easily. To pre-Darwinian biologists, evolution often meant a process of development unfolding, consistent with the Latin root for the word evolution. The concepts of evolution and development began to be sorted out when the works of Darwin and Herbert Spencer became influential, but the sorting continued for a long time and continues still, as in Hall (1992), who reviews the tangled and difficult history in terms of which biologists settled upon the distinction.

3.   There have been some suggestions how to start, but no finished results. See Adams (1988), Freese (1988), and Olsen (1993a, 1993b), but none of these give any indication of the complexity of the theoretical project.

4.   This may be understating matters. One student of the subject goes so far as to say that "cultural evolution and biological evolution do not share the same metaphysical view of the nature of realtiy" (Dunnel 1988, p. 171).

5.   This claim and the point made in connection with it apply to Mendelian genes, which are the relevant units of analysis. Molecular genes, the biochemistry of whose combinations may under certain conditions render this bald claim arguable, are not at issue. The Mendelian gene is not the same concept as the molecular gene. Though certainly not disjoint, there does not now exist a body of integrated formal theory that permits isomorphic transformations from the language of molecular theory to the language of Mendelian theory. How molecular genes translate into Mendelian phenotypes depends upon an array of contingent developmental and environmental processes that intervene to effectively prohibit a one-to-one mapping.

6.   Biologists recognize four types of organic evolutionary change, only one of which is natural selection. The other three are mutation, migration (also known as gene flow), and genetic drift (also known as the Sewall Wright effect). Biologists also recognize four types of natural selection: directional, stabilizing, balancing, and disruptive (also known as diversifying) selection. There can be evolution without selection and selection without evolution. Evolutionary selection is evolutionary change in the directional or disruptive modes (see Grant 1991).

7.   I also draw from Bowler (1984), Brandon (1990), Dawkins (1982, 1984), Denton (1985), Eldredge (1985), Endler (1986), Ho and Fox (1988), Levins and Lewontin (1985), Levinto (1983), Mayr (1982, 1988), Oyama (1988), Plotkin (1988), Sober (1984a), and the Sobre anthology (1984b), in this and following sections.

8.   Two central ideas of Darwin's theory, adaptation and struggle for existence, had prior to Darwin been grounded in theological explanations of nature's design (see Bowler 1985, pp. 95-99).

9.   Patrick Bateson (1992) made the same point with a different analogy. Why, he wanted to know, if food consumers began to prefer crusty bread to the flabby variety, should they be said to be selecting the recipes? It made no semantic sense, he averred, to think of selfish recipes manipulating consumers—a reference, of course, to Dawkins' concept of selfish genes.

10.   I am quoting Endler slightly out of context here, but I do not think I am abusing the sense of his remark. See his discussion (1986, ch. 2) on why natural selection cannot be interpreted as a force.

11.   Olsen (1993a, 1993b) uses similar terminology to sort socioecological from sociocultural processes and organization, and his views about their interaction are similar to some I expressed elsewhere (Freese 1988). However, Olsen's theory rests on a fundamental difference in interpreting the relative significance of the two kinds of organization. He views the two as parallel and, in a sense, as coequal in a system of mutual causation. I view them as serial because of an asymmetric dependence: Sociocultural organization cannot function without effective socioecological organization to support it, whereas socioecological organization does not require much sociocultural organization in order to function. To my way of thinking, sociocultural adaptations are (nonlinear) spin-offs of socioecological adaptations because sociocultural systems are spin-offs of biophysical systems. Olsen rejects the idea of hierarchical order, while I accept it.

12. The following conclusions owe much to discussions with C. Dyke, who helped to clarify, articulate, explicate, stimulate, and suggest them, along with caveats I ignored.

13. No sampling of references can represent this burgeoning literature,which originated with the physical theory of nonequilibrium thermodynamics and includes the subject of chaotic motion. Prigogine and Stengers (1984), Nicolis and Prigogine (1989), and the anthology of Dalenoort (1989) give some indication of the physical scope of the sciences of complex systems. Weber, Depew, and Smith (1988), Wicken (1987), and Brooks and Wiley (1986) use the paradigm to explore the limits of neo-Darwinism and desired extensions of evolutionary theory. Ulanowicz (1986) develops evolutionary applications for ecological systems, Adams (1988) for sociocultural systems, and Dyke (1988) for biosocial systems. The comprehension treatment by Jantsch (1980), which came early in the genre, is still very informative. A recent major effort is Kauffman's (1993).

REFERENCES

Adams, R.N. 1988. *The Eighth Day: Social Evolution as the Self-Organization of Energy.* Austin: University of Texas Press.

Alexander, R.D. 1979. "Evolution and Culture." Pp. 59-78 in *Evolutionary Biology and Human Social Behavior,* edited by N.A. Chagnon and W.G. Irons. North Scituate, MA: Duxbury Press.

Bateson, P. 1982. "Behavioural Development and Evolutionary Processes." Pp. 133-151 in *Current Problems In Sociobiology,* edited by King's College Sociobiology Group. Cambridge: Cambridge University Press.

Bodley, J.H. 1994. "A Culture Scale Perspective on Human Ecology and Development." Pp. 92-112 in *Advances In Human Ecology,* Vol. 3, edited by L. Freese. Greenwich, CT: JAI Press.

Bowler, P.J. 1984. *Evolution: The History of an Idea.* Berkeley: University of California Press.

Boyd, R., and P.J. Richerson. 1985. *Culture and the Evolutionary Process.* Chicago: University of Chicago Press.

Brandon, R.N. 1990. *Adaptation and Environment.* Princeton, NJ: Princeton University Press.

Brooks, D.R., and E.O. Wiley. 1986. *Evolution As Entropy: Toward A Unified Theory of Biology.* Chicago: University of Chicago Press.

Cavalli-Sforza, L.L., and M.W. Feldman. 1981. *Cultural Transmission and Evolution: A Quantitative Approach.* Princeton, NJ: Princeton University Press.

Dalenoort, G.J., ed. 1989. *The Paradigm of Self-Organization: Current Trends in Self-Organization.* New York: Gordon and Breach.

Darwin, C. 1985. *The Origin of Species by Means of Natural Selection.* London: Penguin (Originally published 1859, London: John Murray).

Dawkins, R. 1982. *The Extended Phenotype: The Gene As The Unit of Selection.* Oxford: Oxford University Press.

_____. 1984. "Replicators and Vehicles." Pp. 161-180 in *Genes, Organisms, Populations: Controversies Over the Units of Selection,* edited by R.N. Brandon and R.M. Burian. Cambridge, MA: MIT Press.

_____. 1989. *The Selfish Gene.* New ed. Oxford: Oxford University Press.

Denton, M. 1985. *Evolution: A Theory in Crisis.* Bethesda, MD: Adler and Adler.

Dunnell, R.C. 1988. "The Concept of Progress In Cultural Evolution." Pp. 169-194 in *Evolutionary Progress,* edited by Matthew H. Nitecki. Chicago: University of Chicago Press.

Durham, W.H. 1979. "Toward A Coevolutionary Theory of Human Biology and Culture." Pp. 39-59 in *Evolutionary Biology and Human Social Behavior,* edited by N.A. Chagnon and W.G. Irons. North Scituate, MA: Duxbury Press.

————. 1990. "Advances in Evolutionary Culture Theory." *Annual Review of Anthropology* 19: 187-210.

————. 1991. *Coevolution: Genes, Culture, and Human Diversity.* Stanford, CA: Stanford University Press.

Dyke, C. 1988. *The Evolutionary Dynamics of Complex Systems: A Study In Biosocial Complexity.* Oxford: Oxford University Press.

Dyke, C. 1994. "The World Around Us and How We Make It: Human Ecology As Human Artifact." Pp. 1-22 in *Advances In Human Ecology,* Vol. 3, edited by L. Freese. Greenwich, CT: JAI Press.

Ehrlich, P.R., and P.H. Raven. 1964. "Butterflies and Plants: A Study in Coevolution." *Evolution* 18: 586-608.

Eldredge, N. 1985. *Unfinished Synthesis: Biological Heirarchies and Modern Evolutionary Thought.* New York: Oxford University Press.

Endler, J.A. 1986. *Natural Selection in the Wild.* Princeton, NJ: Princeton University Press.

Freese, L. 1988. "Evolution and Sociogenesis: Parts 1 and 2." Pp. 59-108 in *Advances in Group Processes: Theory and Research,* Vol. 5, edited by E. Lawler and B. Markovsky. Greenwich, CT: JAI Press.

Ghiselin, M.T. 1981. "Categories, Life, and Thinking." *Behavioral and Brain Sciences* 4: 269-313.

Grant, V. 1991. *The Evolutionary Process: A Critical Study of Evolutionary Theory.* 2nd ed. New York: Columbia University Press.

Hall, B.K. 1992. *Evolutionary Developmental Biology.* London: Chapman and Hall.

Harris, M. 1977. *Cannibals and Kings: The Origins of Cultures.* New York: Random House.

Ho, M., and S. Fox, eds. 1988. *Evolutionary Processes and Metaphors.* Chichester: Wiley.

Jantsch, E. 1980. *The Self-Organizing Universe: Scientific and Human Implications of the Emerging Paradigm of Evolution.* Oxford: Pergamon.

Kauffman, S.A. 1993. *The Origins of Order: Self-Organization and Selection in Evolution.* New York: Oxford University Press.

Lenski, G., J. Lenski, and P. Nolan. 1991. *Human Societies: An Introduction to Macrosociology.* 6th ed. New York: McGraw Hill.

Levins, R., and R.C. Lewontin. 1985. *The Dialectical Biologist.* Cambridge, MA: Harvard University Press.

Levinton, J.S. 1983. "Stasis in Progress: The Empirical Basis of Macroevolution." *Annual Review of Ecology and Systematics* 14: 103-137.

Lumsden, C., and E.O. Wilson. 1981. *Genes, Mind, and Culture.* Cambridge, MA: Harvard University Press.

Lumsden, C.J., and E.O. Wilson. 1983. *Promethean Fire: Reflections on the Origin of Mind.* Cambridge, MA: Harvard University Press.

Mayr, E. 1982. *The Growth of Biological Thought: Diversity, Evolution, and Inheritance.* Cambridge, MA: Harvard University Press.

————. 1988. *Toward A New Philosophy of Biology: Observations of an Evolutionist.* Cambridge, MA: Harvard University Press.

Nicolois, G., and I. Prigogine. 1989. *Exploring Complexity: An Introduction.* New York: Freeman.

Olsen, M.E. 1993a. "Components of Socioecological Organization: Tools, Resources, Energy, and Power." Pp. 35-67 in *Advances In Human Ecology,* Vol. 2, edited by L. Freese. Greenwich, CT: JAI Press.

————. 1993b. "A Socioecological Perspective On Social Evolution." Pp. 69-92 in *Advances In Human Ecology,* Vol. 2, edited by L. Freese. Greenwich, CT: JAI Press.

Oyama, S. 1988. "Statis, Development, and Heredity." Pp. 255-274 in *Evolutionary Processes and Metaphors,* edited by M. Ho and Sidney Fox. Chichester: Wiley.

Paley, W. [1802] 1970. *Natural Theology: Of Evidences of the Existence and Attributes of the Deity collected from the Appearances of Nature.* London: Farnborough, Gregg.

Plotkin, H.C. 1988. "Behavior and Evolution." Pp. 1-17 in *The Role of Behavior in Evolution,* edited by H.C. Plotkin. Cambridge, MA: MIT Press.

Prigogine, I., and I. Stengers. 1984. *Order Out of Chaos: Man's New Dialogue With Nature.* Toronto: Bantam Books.

Pulliam, H.R., and C. Dunford. 1987. *Programmed to Learn: An Essay on the Evolution of Culture.* New York: Columbia University Press.

Service, E. 1962. *Primitive Social Organization: An Evolutionary Perspective.* New York: Random House.

Sober, E. 1984a. *The Nature of Selection: Evolutionary Theory in Philosophical Focus.* Cambridge, MA: MIT Press.

————, ed. 1984b. *Conceptual Issues in Evolutionary Biology: An Anthology.* Cambridge, MA: MIT Press.

Sober, E., and R.C. Lewontin. 1984. "Artifact, Cause, and Genic Selection." Pp. 210-231 in *Conceptual Issues in Evolutionary Biology: An Anthology,* edited by E. Sober. Cambridge, MA: MIT Press.

Swenson, R. 1991. "End-Directed Physics and Evolutionary Ordering: Obviating the Problem of the Population of One." Pp. 41-59 in *The Cybernetics of Complex Systems: Self-Organization, Evolution, and Social Change,* edited by F. Geyer. Salinas, CA: Intersystems Publications.

Swenson, R., and M.T. Turvey. 1991. "Thermodynamic Reasons for Perception-Action Cycles." *Ecological Psychology* 3: 317-348.

Ulanowicz, R. 1986. *Growth and Development: Ecosystems Phenomenology.* New York: Springer-Verlag.

Weber, B.H., D.J. Depew, and J.D. Smith, eds. 1988. *Entropy, Information, and Evolution: New Perspectives On Physical and Biological Evolution.* Cambridge, MA: MIT Press.

Wicken, J.S. 1987. *Evolution, Thermodynamics, and Information.* New York: Oxford University Press.

Williams, G.C. 1966. *Adaptation and Natural Selection: A Critique of Some Current Evolutionary Thought.* Princeton, NJ: Princeton University Press.

HUMAN ECOLOGY: LOST GRAIL FOUND?

A CRITICAL REVIEW OF PROGRAMS TO ADDRESS HUMAN-ENVIRONMENT RELATIONSHIPS

Jeremy Pratt

ABSTRACT

A plethora of regional, national, and global programs have been announced within a short time, signaling a quantum leap in the treatment of complex environmental problems. For the most part, these are commons problems and, since they concern relationships between humans and their environments, they are by definition problems of human ecology. These new programs express a growing awareness that failure to address them as such will probably mean failure to solve them. The objectives of the new programs are to develop integrated, interdisciplinary, and *sustainable* solutions. This paper reviews several leading programs that share these objectives, including the Sustainable Biosphere Initiative published by the Ecological Society of America in 1991 and extended internationally by ecologists from 14 countries in a recent workshop in Mexico; the United Nations Conference on Environment and Development; the proposed

Advances in Human Ecology, Volume 3, pages 173-247.

new United States National Institutes for the Environment; the U.S. Man and
the Biosphere Program's Human-Dominated Systems Program; the report of the
National Research Council Committee on Human Dimensions of Global Change
and the associated National Science Foundation's Human Dimensions of Global
Change Program; and Green Plans published by the governments of Canada,
Norway, the Netherlands, the United Kingdom, and Austria. Common themes
are found throughout all of these programs. Largely unacknowledged roots in
human ecology are identified in all of the programs as well. A disturbing tendency
is found: while attempting to reinvent human ecology, little awareness is shown
of the groundwork that has been laid. Few display comprehension of human
ecology's scope and legacy and all fail to cite the field's principal literature. I
probe these findings by critically examining the ongoing development of these
programs and initiatives, their potential contribution to human ecology, and the
field's struggle to apply its ideas.

INTRODUCTION

The 1990s have seen sustainability attain exceptional status as a value in
American culture and throughout the West. The idea of using resources at levels
that can be maintained indefinitely without long-term degradation has become
something of a grail of late; it is fast becoming a hallowed tenet whose
realization is expected to "restore the wasteland."

Veiled in the train of sustainability, however, are two other notions whose
controversies and consequences have been far less eagerly embraced. One of
these is the concept of capacitance. Sustainable use implies knowledge of the
capacity of the environmental system to absorb a continuing level of use
without loss of essential qualities. This, in turn, implies an acceptance of limits.
The other idea is that of the commons, described in Hardin's seminal article
(1968). The environmental capacities of greatest concern are almost always
capacities of commons—of resources shared in common among all members
of society. Both ideas imply a critical interdependence between humans and
environment.

Clearly, these notions are inextricably bound together. As planners,
scientists, and decision makers prepare to implement a "sustainable future"—
and all this implies—they find themselves increasingly in need of a framework
that can articulate the links between these concepts. More than that, they need
a framework to direct both research into the human-environment relationships
underlying these concepts and management of the critical problems they
present.

Human ecology supplies such a framework (cf. Young 1989). Developed in
a number of applied and theoretical disciplines over the past 70 years (Young
1974, 1983), human ecology concerns itself with the relationships between

humans and their environments. Attempts to build the needed framework are epidemic. Everywhere, problem statements are formulated and applications designed which parallel the central principles and approaches of human ecology. This occurs so broadly one might believe human ecology is the lost grail found—except that the field itself is almost never cited and never acknowledged.

Thus, I have two fundamental messages in this paper, the first directed toward those who are building new frameworks, the second intended primarily for human ecologists. The first is that we are witnessing the wholesale reinvention of a field of study which has been developing for more than half-a-century. It has endured serious pitfalls along the way; those now engaged in the recreation of human ecology could be spared these trials by examining its history and integrating the hard lessons and seminal work that have gone before.

Second, if human ecologists do not respond to this challenge, they will simply be left behind, their problems, methods, and principles taken over by more dynamic enterprises. These efforts are well underway. Many of them are practical, well conceived, and hardnosed. They have picked human ecology up by the ears and are running toward an applied state of the art at a breakneck pace most human ecologists will find hard to sustain—and which may invite very real dangers as well. Human ecology has been wrested from bickering academicians and thrust into a very real world of application, policy, and decision. Nothing could be healthier for the field, but human ecologists must realize that claims of academic primacy have no bearing in this world. There is no particular reason why they should consult and advise on these new endeavors, if others can and will.

THE BREAKING-IN OF A PARADIGMATIC REVOLUTION

A sure sign that something new is in the air—that a crucial need has reached a critical mass—is that expressions of that thing (or the need for it) begin to flower everywhere at once. Such delicate metaphors are admittedly misplaced, since the thing itself explodes onto the scene like a runaway train into a crowded station, an event better phrased in more careful and technical terms, such as "paradigmatic revolution" (cf. Kuhn 1962; Pratt 1988, in press).

The wafting of new ideas into mass cultural consciousness is, of course, small news to those who have sniffed them in the air for some time—sometimes for decades. These are the ones whose work underlies and has prepared the ground for the events the work heralds. As the cognoscenti are aware, a revolution has broken in upon the late twentieth century, as evidenced by sundry diverse but related events. This revolution can be found in the language of the Sustainable Biosphere Initiative (SBI) published by the Ecological Society of

America (ESA) in 1991 (Lubchenco et al. 1991) and extended internationally by ecologists from 14 countries in a recent workshop in Cuernavaca, Mexico (Huntley et al. 1991). It underlies the United Nations Conference on Environment and Development (UNCED) (see, e.g., Valentine 1991), the proposal for a new U.S. National Institutes for the Environment (NIES) (Howe 1990, 1991, 1992; Howe and Hubbell 1990; CNIE 1992), and the Santa Fe workshop that anticipated them (Brown and Roughgarden 1990). The U.S. Man and the Biosphere Program's Human-Dominated Systems Directorate Core Project (USMAB) (Harwell et al. 1991; USMAB 1991a) is an impressively detailed study program addressing it. Proposals for research into it are sought under the auspices of the new National Science Foundation (NSF) Human Dimensions of Global Change Program (NSF 1992a). The National Research Council Committee on the Human Dimensions of Global Change probes this revolution in a new book (Stern, Young and Druckman 1992) which develops a set of recommendations for a national research program addressing it. And, it is reiterated in "green plans" published by a half-dozen nations (see, e.g., de Jongh 1992; Hofseth 1992; Schreiber 1992; Slater 1992; Stoker 1992; Canada 1990; The Netherlands n.d.; Norway 1989; United Kingdom 1990) and throughout the burgeoning literature on sustainable development and common property resources. Others working on this revolution include the Human Interactions Panel of the Committee on Global Change (organizing U.S. participation in the International Geosphere-Biosphere Programme); the Committee for Research on Global Environmental Change established by the Social Science Research Council; and the Standing Committee on the Human Dimensions of Global Change of the International Social Science Council.

All of these programs and plans, conferences and agendas, share one epistemological theme: They all call for an integrated, interdisciplinary approach to complex problems of human-environmental relationships. This theme will be immediately recognized by the practitioner of a certain interdisciplinary and, unfortunately, marginalized field—human ecology. Indeed, rarely has a field so poorly positioned itself or been more unprepared for an explosive demand for its services than this one. On the other hand, the shared need for, lack of recognition of, and attempt to reinvent human ecology testifies to its marginalization within both academia and the practical world of environmental policy and decision making, which may account for the widespread unawareness on the part of those programs and plans that now seek to reinvent it in time of need. Such an oversight, if that is what it is, on the part of some of the world's preeminent scientists in their proposals to lead national and international research initiatives into what amounts to human ecology, exhibits disturbingly poor scholarship to say the least.

KEY THEMES OF THE NEW PROGRAMS AND INITIATIVES

Appendices A-F summarize statements extracted from the programs[1] reviewed in this paper and illustrate selected key themes shared by them all.[2] The first theme I discuss is the need they have expressed for the kinds of services, framework, and approach that should be provided by a mature human ecology. The second theme, a call for interdisciplinarity, is a logical corollary of the first. A third theme is the recognition of anthropogenic environmental change in the commons, generally associated with a recognition of strained support (or carrying) capacity, the fourth theme. The fifth theme responds to these conditions with a call for sustainability. Finally, the sixth theme recognizes the need to affect environmental policy and decision making.

Theme 1.   Problem Statements and Expressions of Need for Human Ecology

Much of what I am terming a revolution in thought regarding human-environment relationships has stemmed from the recognition of global change. It is the *scale* of human impacts on the environment, coupled with the desire to manage these effects through an appropriate mix of policies and other institutional responses, that has occasioned most of the calls for the framework human ecology supplies.

Intensified attention to global problems of environmental change may have its most important effect on the scale at which people live and think. People are asked to think in terms of generations and to relate to planetary environmental concerns. In effect, we have been asked to raise the level of our participation in our environment from short-term, local scales to long-term and worldwide ones. This elevated perspective focuses attention on a complex network comprised of multiple interacting factors or driving forces, a system which has been the domain of human ecology for some time. Thus, it is no accident that, in exploring the human dimensions of global change, investigators have articulated problem statements and conceptual frameworks so reminiscent of human ecology.

Because the focus of serious attention on these planetary-scale problems is new in many quarters, there is a propensity to view integrated approaches to them as also new, but today's needs and the responses to them are little different from those that surrounded Earth Day more than two decades ago. Indeed, human ecology—understood by its content, not its title—may be said to have entered the international environmental policy arena in large part via the debate on global change. Accordingly, this review repeatedly returns to the global change agenda as it has been unfolding in both policy and research.

Brown and Roughgarden (1990), reporting on a December 1988 Santa Fe workshop,[3] anticipated the recent spate of global change research agendas which recognize the role of humans in ecological systems. Their identification of global change phenomena, call for interdisciplinary collaboration, delineation of human dimensions, and discussions of problems of scale and of the need for a national environmental data repository, all anticipated the Sustainable Biosphere Initiative (Lubchenco 1991), the National Research Council report on global environmental change (Stern et al. 1992), and the proposal for the National Institutes for the Environment (CNIE 1992)—often in very specific terms. Remarkably, none of these programs or reports cite either Brown and Roughgarden or the Santa Fe workshop.

Paraphrases of human ecology and expressions of need for human ecology emerging in the years since the Santa Fe workshop typically identify the need for a framework that will enlarge the perspective or expand the scope of ecology to include interactions between humans and the biosphere or relationships between human activities and their environments. The desired framework is envisioned as comprehensive or integrated. The human-environment relationships of interest are characterized as complex, simultaneous, and occurring at many spatial and temporal scales. The need to address them is formulated as a response to intricate, anthropogenic, and global environmental problems.

The first point to recognize about these generalized conceptualizations is their congruence with the ways in which human ecology has defined itself. Such formulations are not new. Young's (1974, p. 3) seminal review, *Human Ecology as an Interdisciplinary Concept,* traced "wide-scope statements on the general application of ecological concepts to man" as far back as Lindemann (1940).[4] A broad survey of research institutions, departments, and associations by Tengström (1985) revealed that the usual way in which practitioners of human ecology define their field is simply as a study of human-environment relationships. Similar conclusions emerged from a three-day workshop in 1988 attended by 130 human ecologists from over 20 nations (Pratt and Young 1990).

These generalized statements of scope—which the programs reviewed here hurry to reinvent—have been roundly criticized because they accommodate so broad a diversity of fields and methods that it has not been very apparent how to use the resulting integration. This difficulty led Wolanski (1989, p. 153) to remark, "If we consider all environmental aspects of the existing domains of knowledge to constitute human ecology, the latter would account for over 50 percent of all human knowledge. Such an approach would be nonsensical...[and] such a classification would be simply useless." Ehrlich (1985, p 379) has stated a similar misgiving:

> In its broadest definition, human ecology would deal with all interactions between human beings and between each person and his or her environment. It would subsume virtually the entire body of human knowledge, including history, languages, accounting, engineering, and so on. Such a broad definition, however, obviously cannot form the basis of a coherent discipline.

Wolanski's point is that a good deal of what makes up human ecology concerns what he terms linear interactions between environment on the one hand and the content which lies within the domain and competence of other fields on the other. This, he states, should not be now artificially retitled. He urges that the name human ecology be reserved for those occasions on which a systemic and synthetic perspective is applied to "man and his culture as a dynamic part of ecosystems" (Wolanski 1990, p. 214). None of the programs reviewed appear to be aware of this debate.

Generally, Wolanski's suggested boundaries make good sense. Most generalist treatments in human ecology have been flawed by shallow reading and simplistic systematizing, manifested in a propensity to reduce human ecology to superficial lists or acronyms (e.g., Duncan 1959). Some, such as Ehrlich's (e.g., Ehrlich and Ehrlich 1970; Ehrlich, Ehrlich, and Holdren 1977), concern an important subset of problems, but are more of an urgent agenda than a fully developed treatment of human ecology. Nevertheless a few have met Wolanski's criteria by presenting integrative approaches to human ecology (e.g., Boyden 1986; Jungen 1986), and at least one (Young 1989) provides a unifying structure by examining fundamental concepts shared in common among the diverse interpretations and approaches that make up contemporary human ecology. Yet, none of these efforts are cited by the various programs reviewed.

A possible reason for the omission of scholarly work in human ecology can be deduced from the contrast between the statements of need which introduce the programs reviewed here and that which introduces Young's framework. As noted, most of the programs under review are motivated by a global scale of change in critical environmental parameters. They are rooted in an urgent action agenda to address these changes, which are perceived to threaten quality of life in a very fundamental way, if not human survival altogether. As such, they reflect the success of the so-called environmental movement in achieving higher visibility for its agenda. But, as Young has commented elsewhere, there has never been a great deal of exchange between academic human ecology and the environmental movement:

> The so-called..."environmental" movement did stimulate some activity in human ecology, but it is ironic that there has been really so little connection between the two, that human ecology has played so small a role in the ecological awakening of recent decades (1983, p. 1).

Young's conceptual framework is not an ivory-tower piece, unaware of urgent real-world environmental dilemmas, but neither does it offer the standard statement of pressing crises as its raison d'etre. His sense of need is much broader and more basic. It is founded on the simple observations that humans interact with their environments, participate in functional relationships with them, and are organized at various levels in them. The avoidance of a statement of need based on contemporary crises and the agendas of the moment places Young's conceptualization on a timeless footing rather than in the passing position of current urgency. It may be that many of the programs under review cannot afford to occupy such high ground, but none of them would fail to benefit from orienting their action imperatives within the framework-building that has gone on in human ecology (cf. Fulton 1992).

Most of the programs reviewed echo ongoing developments in human ecology in their heuristic models of human-environmental interaction and feedback (e.g., Boyden 1986; Pratt in press, 1991, 1992; Young 1989). They are aware that interactions occur between human and environmental *systems*, and that a wide variety of subsystems are implicated on both sides of the equation. Often feedbacks between these systems are noted, sometimes in the context of a simplified control-systems model. There is broad awareness that these feedbacks entail both human impacts on environments and environmental impacts on humans, to which humans respond. It is sometimes realized that the latter may be an effect of the former (i.e., that some responses are to environmental impacts which we ourselves created) and that humans may act reflexively to intervene in these feedback loops and redirect them. However, there is little appreciation (with the exception of the NRC [Stern et al. 1992]) that these responses are themselves part and parcel of human ecological processes.

Although the role played by values, beliefs, and perception (sometimes identified as "cultural and behavioral factors") in human-environment relationships is widely recognized, most of the programs fall short in specifying their approaches to this aspect of human ecology. The roles of values, attitudes, and knowledge itself as processes in human ecology have received intense attention in the field (e.g., Arler 1991a, 1991b; Carpenter 1988, 1989; Meeker 1974; Pratt 1991, 1993; Rothenburg 1988, in press; Steiner 1990; Steiner, Furger, and Jaeger in press; Skolimowski 1991; Stewart 1986; TeHennepe 1991; Visvader 1986; Ward 1991, 1992), but this literature, outside of sociology, is not well integrated.

Theme 2.   Calls for Interdisciplinarity

Calls for interdisciplinarity are rife throughout the programs reviewed. Often phrased as calls for integrated research programs, they echo a theme that has been a fundamental organizing principle in human ecology for some time (see, e.g. Young 1974; Pratt and Young 1990). Such calls are made in recognition of the need to address complex and comprehensive environmental problems on a global scale involving both natural and social sciences. Sometimes, though not often, the role of the humanities is recognized. At times, there are allusions to economics, physical sciences, engineering, and cultural and policy studies.

The best thought-out programs recognize that interdisciplinary research presupposes a problem orientation (cf. CNIE 1992; Stern et al. 1992; Pratt and Young 1990). According to Dietz, the NSF has been successful in promoting interdisciplinary research under its human dimensions program:

> The program makes use of disciplinary experts in reviewing proposals. But it also insists on interdisciplinary review of proposals and has given such broader expertise weight in making decisions. Just such special efforts are required to insure that funds are supporting truly interdisciplinary efforts that will generate new and useful knowledge rather than simply re-enforcing conventional wisdom from traditional fields (1992, p. 5).

However, neither recognition of the need for interdisciplinarity nor the issuance of calls for it provide any guarantee that it will be achieved, whether in these national and international research programs which so studiously avoid the term human ecology, or in human ecology itself. Things may no longer be as bad as they were at the time of Crowe's (1969) critical review of Hardin's *Tragedy of the Commons,* when he pointed out that both the social and the natural sciences had isolated the same subset of problems as insoluble and relegated them to the other camp for solution. Two decades later copious calls for interdisciplinarity may have torn down the fence between the social and natural sciences, but little has been done to actually integrate them beyond erecting a new fence to enclose both together. Inside, a multidisciplinary melange remains.

Program builders appear unaware that true interdisciplinary work may not go on among the members of a multidisciplinary team—though it may be stimulated, encouraged, and facilitated in such a setting. Interdisciplinary work is synthetic in a way that requires more than several persons from different disciplines working together. It goes on *inside* the minds of individuals who have learned important parts of more than one discipline and who sweat to relate them.

None of the programs reviewed do much to include the humanities, and in all of them, the social and natural sciences usually touch upon one another only as, to use the National Research Council's term, "bordering multi-disciplinary complexes." Each recognizes the other as necessary to solve global environmental problems, but no one knows what to do with this unfamiliar newcomer that has married into the family. Programs put forward by biological ecologists (e.g., SBI) focus on biology; those offered by social scientists (e.g., the NRC Committee on Human Dimensions of Global Change) have a social science perspective. The former focus on the physical environment and biology, the latter on human dimensions; both fail at the full integration of the natural and social sciences *and* the humanities so necessary for genuine human ecology.

Human ecology, by contrast, provides the framework for an interdisciplinary approach to the study of human-environment relationships. It is important to stress that human ecology is as much *meta*disciplinary as interdisciplinary

(Young 1989; Pratt and Young 1990). Ignoring human ecology or relegating it to the status of a so-called small subfield of one of the two primary sciences that need to be integrated (cf. Stern et al. 1992) are equally fatal. Human ecology as a "transfield," rather than a subfield, can act as an integrating catalyst; it supplies the perspective requisite to carry out the crosscutting synthesis that can transform these neighboring "multidisciplinary complexes" into a genuinely interdisciplinary approach to global environmental problems (cf. Jüngen 1986; Daysh 1988; Young 1989).

Theme 3.   Recognition of Anthropogenic Environmental Change in the Commons

If the phrase "human dimensions of environmental change" is an euphemism for human ecology, then the phrase "global environmental change" contains a second euphemism. Global change refers to global commons. Fully translated, the term means: human ecology applied to changes in global commons.

Environmental changes of global extent, by definition, affect commons. The programs discussed in this paper reflect a growing sense of responsibility for these changes, coupled with alarm at their dimensions. The affected commons comprise the major environmental systems of the earth: oceans, the atmosphere, fresh waters, and terrestrial ecosystems. The changes of concern are generally recited in introductory statements which lay out the need and rationale for each program. The issues are the familiar ones that have captured worldwide attention recently—climate change, ozone depletion, deforestation, desertification, and the loss both of crucial habitats (e.g., wetlands) and of diversity in the earth's gene pool.

Again, insight into human modification of natural systems on a grand scale is not new; it can be traced as far back as George Perkins Marsh (1864). More than a few grasped the global implications of Marsh's insights, not needing to see the consequences they foretold come to pass first, but for most it has taken more than a century and the actual initiation of global environmental change for the significance to sink in. One way of identifying human ecologists might be to say that they were the ones who were studying these problems before they became politically popular. Nevertheless, realization of the magnitude of anthropogenic stress in global commons is now dawning, as illustrated by this sampling from the programs reviewed:

While we know that a nuclear war will make the earth uninhabitable, we are just beginning to appreciate that the cumulative effect of our day-to-day activities might be just as severe (Brown and Roughgarden 1990, pp. 173-174).

Virtually every ecosystem on Earth has been influenced, to some extent, by the activities of humans.... Human activities are currently leading to unprecedented changes in the Earth's...environments (Lubchenco et al. 1991, pp. 392, 386).

The scale of anthropogenic alteration of nature...promises to present policy decisions unprecedented in the human experience (Howe 1990, p. 31)

We are actually changing the global environmental conditions that originally permitted our emergence as a species (USMAB 1991c, p. 1).

Human beings, both individually and collectively...for the first time...have begun to play a central role in altering global biogeochemical systems and the earth as a whole (Stern et al. 1992, p. 17).

Statements such as these underscore that it is only the unprecedented scale and scope of these changes in global commons that have brought us to take environment and ecology as seriously as welfare and warfare. However, while the study of common property resources has become an established field in its own right in the past few decades, the term commons appears almost as rarely in these program narratives as does "human ecology." Affected environments and resources are not identified as commons, and problems of global environmental change are not well analyzed in terms of their common pool or common property dimensions. Such issues as access, definition, and monitoring of boundaries, and mutually agreed rules for the use and allocation of commons resources—central concerns of common property studies—are either tangentially implied or, if the program addresses them directly, they are not explicitly connected to the idea of the commons and the body of research into common property.

From a human ecology point of view, this is particularly distressing because if commons are not recognized as such, then the intricately interwoven human dimensions of global change governing them will almost certainly go unfathomed and perhaps be misinterpreted. For example, a recent statement by Akio Morita, chairman of the Sony Corporation suggests the degree to which the market itself is a commons. Discussing changes needed in Japanese business strategy to reduce trade frictions, he said, "Given the current corporate environment in Japan, every company would hesitate to make the change first. Any company that unilaterally scaled back its quest for market share would be eaten alive by competitors" (McCarthy 1992, p. 12). This not only portrays the classic commons dilemma, it also illustrates how difficult it will be to internalize externalities without applying principles of common property theory. An interdisciplinary synthesis of economics, business, sociology, and anthropology must be applied to the biological and physical resource problems to determine how functional common property regimes can be reconstructed in contemporary international markets.

Theme 4. Recognition of Strained Support or Carrying Capacity

Commons remain invisible, taken for granted, until some stress makes problematic their capacity to continue to provide some accustomed human use of them. The ideas of stress and capacitance are corollary concepts in human ecology (Young 1989). Most programs acknowledge this linked pair in their overview statements, citing such things as the earth's life support capacity or life support systems, the carrying capacity of natural systems, the carrying and absorptive capacities of the earth's natural systems, or the life-sustaining qualities of the earth. Some awkward (and anthropomorphic) formulations are found, such as "human-supporting capacity" (Huntley et al. 1991) or "capacity to support human endeavors" (Howe 1990). Others trivialize the ecological into the economic by referencing only the "productive capacity of natural and managed ecosystems" or "yields" (Howe 1990, 1991).

Human population density (or sometimes, the growing human population), together with increasing use and misuse of resources, were commonly identified as sources of stress. UNCED (UN 1992b) divided resource use into unsustainable patterns of production and consumption, in keeping with its theme. Rarely was "quality of life" recognized as a key element in the delineation of human carrying capacity; sometimes, this concept was fuzzed into "habitability."

While recognizing stresses as severe, the nature of stress-capacitance relationships between population, environment, resource use, and quality of life were usually described—if at all—in only the most general terms. Sometimes these were as simplistic as the recognition that the earth's resources are finite or that humans overexploit them. Statements such as "the earth cannot provide infinite natural resources or endlessly assimilate our wastes" (M. Strong, UN press release, May 1992) are illustrative. Stress/capacitance was often dealt with by passing reference to resilience, assimilative capacity, ecosystem processes, and regulatory functions of the environment.

Only Harwell et al. (1991) address systems integration of stress/capacitance functions, and they circumambulate the concept somewhat, including indicators of ecosystem stress/capacitance within the unwieldy term ecological endpoints. The fact that the idea surfaces in the USMAB working model (Harwell et al.), a team with strong biological ecology representation, but is left out where social scientists predominate, may be an indication of the continuing failure to integrate across disciplines. Although the NRC Human Dimensions of Global Change Committee (Stern et al. 1992) presents the best developed model of human-environment interactions, the model is marred by the lack of a distinct concept of capacitance. The NRC Committee notes the nonlinear responses of environmental systems but does not connect these responses with carrying capacity thresholds. Perhaps because the idea of carrying capacity has its roots in natural resource management, it may not come to mind as naturally to the NRC's social science-oriented committee.

On the other hand, the NRC Committee, together with UNCED, stood out for their recognition of the importance of "lifestyle"—a critical variable in any human carrying capacity model. Although absolute physical limits do exist, most of the important questions regarding human carrying capacity concern relative values operating within broad ranges. Interpreted in terms of quality of life or lifestyle, carrying capacity analysis quickly moves into values questions because human life can persist under an extremely wide range of physical conditions. UNCED's tenacious focus on environment and development persistently reminds us of the functional relationship between lifestyle values and environmental quality. However, it is not merely a matter of unsustainable patterns of production and consumption, which UNCED ties so well to environmental problems, but of the underlying values that drive them. The NRC Committee has a handle on this piece of the puzzle but does not clearly grasp its connection to carrying capacity. In many respects, the values dimension is a relative one, since decisions establishing carrying capacity thresholds are themselves relative. None of the programs differentiate between absolute limits and relative values in human carrying capacity.

Theme 5.   Calls for Sustainability

Sustainability is more eulogized than used in most of the programs reviewed. Although most are founded on the principle of sustainability and have at their center some concept such as sustainable development or sustainable use, none offers a definition of the term or even much hint as to what it means to the framers of the broad goals that invoke it. For example, if any distinction was drawn between the notions of development and growth, none made it explicit.

This observation indicates the degree to which sustainability is serving more as an icon than an operational tool. The USMAB (Harwell et al.) draws attention to the popularity of the term sustainability and the correspondingly loose way in which it is used:

> its meaning can vary from utilizing only renewable resources at rates compatible with long-term ecological health to exploiting resources extensively, limited only to not causing system collapse (1991, p. 14).

Thus, the USMAB prefers to call its objective "ecological sustainability," but it is not clear that this use of the term is meaningfully distinguished from other uses. Harwell et al. state that their goal is not to "derive the maximal resources from the ecosystem without exceeding some threshold of ecological damage" but "rather, the goal is set from the ecosystems' perspective, allowing only those human interactions that will not impinge on ecosystem health over the long term" (1991, p. 14). Again, it is far from clear that such a distinction means anything, particularly since ecosystem health remains a matter of human judgement and the difference between "exceed some threshold of damage" and "not impinge upon ecosystem health" is not specified.

Their point that "ecological sustainability must be defined in terms of specific ecological endpoints [i.e., characteristics]" (Harwell et al. 1991, p. 14) is a useful one, however. Harwell et al. again stand apart in their acknowledgement that the concept itself must be specified in much more detail in order to be used. In contrast, the Canadian *Green Plan* (Canada 1990) identifies sustainable development as a philosophy but not as an action plan.

The International Association for Ecology (INTECOL 1991a, p. 3) traces the concept of sustainability through "a sequence of comparable terms, which started with 'limits to growth' about 20 years ago,[5] followed by 'wise use' or 'organic development' in a 'balanced environment,' and eventually arrived at 'sustainable development' as recommended by the Brundtland Report, Our Common Future." INTECOL considers the term to mean something analogous to "self-organization and self-maintenance of natural systems" (1991a, p. 3). Most others, if they define the concept at all, simply cite the Brundtland definition (World Commission on Environment and Development [WCED] 1987).[6] Some (Strong 1992, INTECOL 1991a) recognize that, as with carrying capacity, dimensions of perceptions, values, beliefs, and cultural styles are indispensable to a full understanding and application of sustainability.

Redford and Sanderson's (1992, p. 36) criticism that "policy makers have turned what were academic working concepts into funded programs" and, in the process, "disconnected them from their scientific advisors" would seem particularly apt here, but I have not found the scientists themselves using the term any more precisely than the policymakers. With that caveat, the Redford and Sanderson critique applies:

> Over the past decade, a policy-making consensus has developed that conservation of biological diversity and promotion of sustainable development not only can, but must go together...a joint mission of combining biodiversity and sustainability has been declared and heavily funded....But because of the fuzzy definition and operationalization of the concepts...dangerous confusions pervade the discussion (1992, p. 38).

Interestingly, Redford and Sanderson's own statement on sustainability includes a strong dose of human ecology, as indicated by their recognition that it is "a direct function of a wide band of possible social goals in human-impacted ecosystems and cannot be separated from more global considerations of politics" (1992, p. 37). Wide interest in sustainability among human ecologists was catalyzed by the Brundtland Report, surfacing as a theme of interest for the first time at the U.S. Society for Human Ecology conference held the year after it was released (Pratt and Young 1990). The idea of sustainability implicit in such concepts as carrying capacity and commons can be followed much further back, of course.

Theme 6.   Objectives to Affect Environmental Policy and Decision Making

The penetration of the concepts identified in Appendices A-F into the action agendas of those who set policy and make decisions may be one reason why the early 1990s sometimes sounds like an echo of the early 1970s (which, in turn, contained echoes of Leopold, Thoreau, Muir, Pinchot, Marsh, and others). Janetos' (1992) recent note on the sustainable biosphere initiative (SBI) and federal agencies exemplifies the degree to which federal agencies are now "hearing" these themes. Interestingly, Janetos attributes the success of the SBI to its articulation of priorities and its provisions of *reasons*—an argument or rationale—for pursuing the SBI priority areas, for funding, and for cooperation among federal agencies.

Perhaps the most basic concern shared by all programs is that decisions be informed, that ecological knowledge be incorporated into policy, and that decision makers possess a fundamental understanding of the interactions between human and environmental systems. The SBI (Lubchenco et al. 1991) notes that thousands of decisions affecting human ecology are made every year by policymakers, regulatory agencies, planners, resource managers, business and industry, consulting firms, and conservation groups. Decision-support systems and better communication are proposed as the best ways to counsel and guide these decisions.

The list of things on which decision makers needed to be informed included the current state of the national and global environment and progress toward solutions to environmental problems (CNIE 1992) and the implications of technical fixes (Howe 1992). The NRC suggested that another important services which could be provided was soliciting appropriate outputs for decision making and policy analysis in global change research (Stern et al. 1992).

A focus on decision-making processes and institutions as well as on the decision maker was apparent. Some specific statements of objectives concerned improving the process of identifying and ranking problems to set a national environmental agenda (Howe 1990), providing a simulation model for examining alternative policies (Harwell et al. 1991), allowing a prescriptive rather than ad hoc response to environmental change (Howe 1992), or improving the mechanisms by which science makes available its advice (M. Strong, UN press release, May 1992).

Several programs identify scale as an important consideration. On the one hand, the necessity to relate scientific input and advice to the scale at which management decisions are made is noted, and on the other the need to link the actions of global decision makers with those of global peasants (Huntley et al. 1991).

While all programs sought to influence the development and implementation of policies, the UNCED literature and the so-called green plans were, not surprisingly, the most focused in terms of their policy and decision-making goals. This included such specifics as promoting the development of international law, arriving at specific agreements by governments and intergovernmental organizations, generating political will, using regulations and markets to direct behavior, and raising taxes to finance agreed actions.

Howe (1992, p. 4) notes that "the technical literature does not and cannot provide what is needed by society and lawmakers" and several programs discuss developing a decision-making "calculus" that integrates all of the domains from which interdisciplinary contributions are needed to improve environmental policy. Others seek to directly link science and policy research or to move environment and development issues into the center of economic policy and decision making (M. Strong, UN press release, May 1992). With this so-called decision-making calculus we return full circle, to the call for human ecology again.

A CRITIQUE OF THE NEW INITIATIVES

Sustainable Biosphere Initiative (SBI)

The SBI seeks to acquire fundamental ecological knowledge in three priority areas: global change, biological diversity, and sustainable ecological systems (this last includes elements elsewhere called human dimensions or human-dominated systems). In addition to research, the program recognizes the importance of education and environmental decision making and devotes brief statements to them.

The SBI's ground-breaking statement has already begun to raise consciousness on the importance of maintaining sustainable ecological systems, and nothing in this review is intended to diminish that. However, its seminal value notwithstanding, the SBI is seriously flawed by a severe disjunction between its problem statement and its research program. Though it articulates global ecological problems in stirring terms, clearly recognizing that they are fundamentally matters of human ecology, the SBI's research agenda is comprised of nothing but state-of-the-art biological ecology.

This logical discontinuity may arise from its authorship. Prepared by the Ecological Society of America's Committee for a Research Agenda for the 1990s, the SBI does exactly what that committee was commissioned to do: It serves the ESA membership by promoting an investigator-initiated, peer-reviewed biological research agenda. An effort has been made to be interdisciplinary, but this appears to have been limited to subfields of biology. With evident pride, the preface describes how the SBI was developed with wide participation by ecologists in an array of disciplines. However, no reviewer aware of developments outside of biology can fail to note the glaring omission of the ecological perspectives of researchers working in nonbiological disciplines.[7] Thus, the SBI loses an important degree of credibility among those engaged in or aware of the very active and fertile inquiry into ecological questions taking place outside of biology proper.

A narrow focus on biology is, of course, entirely appropriate for an association of biological ecologists and, to its credit, the SBI issues more than a dozen calls for or statements of interdisciplinary intent (see Appendix B). Nevertheless, it is fundamentally *not* an interdisciplinary program. This disjunction between stated interdisciplinary intent and actual achievement mirrors and underlies the larger one between problem statement and research program. Perhaps the authors of the SBI, lacking the scope, depth, or charge to deal with the full interdisciplinary implications of their problem, intended that the program would be broadened in the future—as implied by frequent allusions to the need to integrate the social sciences, economics, and so forth (see Appendix B).

One of the chief criteria used in the SBI to evaluate research is "the potential to respond to major human concerns about the sustainability of the biosphere" (Lubchenco et al. 1991, p. 374). This statement exemplifies the broad, overarching language of the SBI's introduction and implies cognizance of human dimensions. However, in moving on to identify research priorities, the SBI surveys a dozen "intellectual frontiers in ecology" (p. 381) without once touching on an issue or problem of human ecology. The criteria used in selecting these "frontiers" were not themselves restrictive; they were: (1) that the questions were synthetic, and (2) that they involve a search for general principles that can unite disparate studies and provide the basis for extrapolation and prediction. Under either of these criteria, the larger problems of human ecology better fit the bill with respect to the large questions that introduce the SBI than do the narrow biological topics fleshing out its "frontier" research agenda.

A table of key research topics follows the discussion of "intellectual frontiers;" again, nowhere in 10 main topics and 55 research questions can one find the kind of problem statement that would effectively carry forward the broad issues of human ecology to which SBI ostensibly responds. Citation analysis reveals that only four of the 110 pieces of literature referenced depart from narrow biological topics (one of these is on the politics of biodiversity, another on the ethics of sustainability, a third on the ecological origination of the Soccer Wars, and a fourth is titled "What does global change mean for society?"). None of the seminal literature in human ecology is cited, nor do any leaders in the field appear in the citations list.

Whether in the final analysis the SBI will be anything more than a "sustainable *research* initiative" to fund "business as usual" in biological research—as has been charged by Watson (1991, p. 204)—will depend upon whether it transcends its horizons to carry its broad goal statements into a research program that reaches beyond the various subdisciplines of biological ecology. The SBI presents itself as "a call-to-arms for all ecologists" (Lubchenco et al. 1991, p. 373)—but leaves out some of the ecologists who have been most active in researching the questions upon which the need for this initiative is premised. With this initiative, the ESA says it intends to "lead its members into a period of introspection, in which the whole realm of ecological activities would be examined" (p. 371)—but it proposes a research agenda that leaves out some of the ecological activities central to the problem statements upon which the need for that agenda is predicated. In light of these omissions, the opening words of the SBI preface, informing us that "this document is unprecedented in its scope and objectives" (p. 371) are overblown.

As it stands, the SBI is in essence a biological research agenda, albeit a strong agenda put forward by a committee comprised of some of America's preeminent biological ecologists under the auspices of the United States' foremost professional society of biological ecologists. In calling for "advances in understanding basic ecological principles...if environmental problems are to be resolved" (Lubchenco et al. 1991, p. 380), it is clearly biological processes that are intended. While the biology of processes involved in global change, biodiversity, and sustainability are undeniably important (and too often neglected or grossly misinterpreted by "ecologists" working outside of biology), it is in the understanding of processes in human ecology that knowledge is arguably most deficient. Furthermore, that deficiency will be determinative: If those problems to which the SBI refers in defining its own mission, purpose, and goals are not resolved *as problems of human ecology,* then the biological data may amount to little more than so much museum information.

Watson gropes toward this insight in her cogent critique of the Sustainable Biosphere Initiative:

> we have a good understanding of the most important global concepts—limits to growth, sustainable yield, waste assimilation capacity, diversity and flexibility. The main questions that need to be answered to manage ecosystems (and ultimately the biosphere) in a sustainable fashion are fairly local, site-specific questions.... Answering such site-specific, management-oriented questions often involves application of accepted concepts and methods to a specific local situation. Such work is not considered to be cutting-edge research and is less fundable, less publishable, than the development of new basic concepts.... Yet these are precisely the sorts of questions with which society needs much more expert help (1991, p. 204).

What Watson does not recognize is that the local, site-specific questions entail a host of human-environment relationships that are simply left out of the SBI agenda. Her theme is echoed by Brewer et al., who ask:

> Is basic ecological research really central to solving environmental problems? In many cases, a sufficient foundation of ecological information already exists that should be used in environmental restoration, remediation, and management...it is unfortunate that applied research seems tangential to basic research in SBI. Shouldn't applied research questions actually be a central theme (1992, p. 24)?

The SBI is vulnerable to this type of critique precisely because its research agenda does not address its problem statement. Both Watson and Brewer et al. are correct in noting that more basic biological research is neither needed nor particularly helpful in addressing what are essentially problems of much broader scope and—paradoxically—more local application. In the case of Brewer et al., the entire debate misses the point, as indicated by their statement, "Virtually all ecologists can find their research interests embedded in the 'Intellectual Frontiers of Ecology' [of the SBI]" (1992, p. 24). This ironic testament to a fundamental ignorance of the scope and content of human ecology—while raising definitive problems in the field—illustrates how even those engaged in cogent criticism of such programs can be unaware of the actual omission that validates their criticism. Had the SBI directly addressed human ecology in its research agenda, it would not have been vulnerable to such criticism, nor would Watson or Brewer et al. been moved to offer it.

International Sustainable Biosphere Initiative (ISBI) and Related Events

One of the eight action items proposed by the SBI was realized when 14 ecologists from around the world met at Cuernavaca, Mexico, in June 1991, to take up the SBI on an international basis. The workshop, funded by the MacArthur Foundation, recommended the establishment of a cooperative international sustainable biosphere program (ISBI). The central goal of the ISBI is to "facilitate the acquisition, dissemination, and utilization of ecological knowledge to ensure the sustainability of the biosphere" (Huntley et al. 1991, p. 7)

Although very similar to the SBI in structure and presentation, the ISBI differs in one essential respect: its third priority area for research has been renamed Human Dimensions of Sustainability and contains a much better developed research agenda in applied human ecology (see Appendix A). While the brief synopsis of the meeting is not sufficient to judge the participants' actual awareness of human ecology (and leaders in human ecology were absent from the workshop), the ISBI appears to have considerably remedied the disjunction between problem statement and research agenda that mars the SBI. This difference between the international and U.S. programs is not surprising, as it parallels the generally more advanced development and recognition of human ecology internationally.

The statement made by the Cuernavaca group was subsequently picked up by INTECOL and published as a special issue of *Ecology International* (Huntley et al. 1991) together with the original SBI. Subsequently, INTECOL and the International Union of Biological Sciences (IUBS) held a workshop on sustainable development in Paris (November 15-17, 1991). Workshop participants issued a statement defining sustainable development in terms of the responsive capacities of human and environmental systems, organized into hierarchies and interacting with one another in dynamic, ever changing and responsive ways (INTECOL 1991b). In this, the Paris workshop presages the National Research Council's more elaborated formulation of human dimensions of global environmental change (see below). Both describe human ecology in its metadisciplinary, interaction based, and systems oriented aspects. The Paris workshop stated:

> Fundamentally, the issue of sustainable development involves bringing together, and integration of, all the diverse sources of information, experiences and theories relevant to the human environment problem in its broadest aspect. It is necessary that we break out of the bounded structures that were created to solve other problems and create new, broader, more integrative points of action to understand and solve problems of sustainable development (INTECOL 1991b, pp. 2 and 5).

The human-environment problem in its broadest aspect *is* human ecology. This again represents a call for human ecology and implies that successful implementation of sustainable development will require a mature, operational human ecology.

Shortly after the Paris workshop, the International Council of Scientific Unions (ICSU) held its International Conference on an Agenda of Science for Environment and Development into the 21st Century (ASCEND-21) in Vienna. ASCEND-21 stressed the need for international and interdisciplinary cooperation in the analysis and evaluation of policies affecting environment and development. In preparation for UNCED (see below), members of the scientific community participating in ASCEND developed a list of major problems affecting the environment and hindering sustainable development. The topics are substantially the same as those motivating most of the programs reviewed here, and include primarily commons problems such as population and per capita resource consumption; depletion of agricultural and land resources; climate change; loss of biological diversity; water scarcity; industrialization and waste; energy consumption; and inequity and poverty. In addition, ASCEND participants recommended intensified research into the carrying capacity of the Earth and ways to slow population growth and reduce overconsumption (INTECOL 1992).

Participants in the Cuernavaca workshop recommended developing the ISBI program under the auspices of the ICSU and promoted workshop findings for inclusion in ASCEND-21. A final objective of the Cuernavaca workshop was realized with the presentation of the ISBI to the ICSU Scientific Committee on Problems of the Environment (SCOPE) at their January 1992 in Spain, where it was adopted as a new project.

U.S. Man and the Biosphere Directorate on Human-Dominated Systems

The mission of the U.S. Man and the Biosphere Program is "to foster harmonious relationships between humans and the biosphere through an international program of policy-relevant research which integrates social, physical, and biological sciences to address actual problems" (USMAB 1991a, p. 1). Within the USMAB, the Human-Dominated Systems Directorate is charged with focusing interdisciplinary research "on the problems arising from human activities that profoundly modify or dominate underlying ecosystems and related life support systems" (USMAB 1991a, p. 2). This Directorate focuses on human settlements or intensified activity across ecosystems and tends to be preoccupied with urban ecology and intensively managed resources such as agriculture or forestry. Emphasis is "on the role of natural systems in human activity and the threats to natural systems in human-dominated areas, and on research to identify methods of integrating harmonious ecosystem functions with intensified human activity" (USMAB 1991a, p. 2).

The Human-Dominated Systems Directorate's Core Project is a well conceived and detailed carrying capacity study program (Harwell et al. 1991). Its central theme is ecological sustainability, a concept that the core project attempts to define while examining a variety of human institutions and policies that impinge upon it. The project's focus is on three case-study Biosphere Reserves (the Everglades, New Jersey Pinelands, and Virginia Coastal Reserve) and it is divided into two phases. The first phase develops and refines conceptual models and builds a case-study database using GIS (geographic information systems), and the second would perform simulations and scenario testing, with specific hypothesis testing on causal links and feedbacks between ecological and human systems. A conference (reporting commissioned papers on ecological/societal linkages) and a workshop (elaborating and developing the model) are called the anchors for the Directorate project during Phase I.

The core project is notable for its recognition of the role of human institutions in creating environmental stress and in dysfunctional environmental feedback loops. One desired outcome is to "specify the institutional and policy regimes necessary to attain ecological sustainability" (Harwell et al. 1991, p. 4, see also pp. 19-21, 37-38). Other goals are to specify sustainability "in terms of particular levels of selected ecological endpoints;"[8] "evaluate patterns of human uses of environmental resources and other anthropogenic stresses imposed on...ecosystems; examine societal and institutional factors influencing ecological sustainability; and assess their compatibility with essential characteristics of ecological sustainability" (USMAB 1991b, p. 40652).

The conjunction between biological ecology and human uses, values, and institutions implicit in these goal statements promises a degree of integration that should characterize cutting edge, applied human ecology. The proposed approach combines biological ecology objectives (e.g., to characterize case-study ecosystems in terms of important so-called ecological endpoints, identify specific desirable qualities about the selected ecosystems) with human ecology objectives (e.g., understand how human institutions and policies interact with ecological systems, identify changes in them that can achieve ecological sustainability, describe their evolution as they interact with case-study environments).

While these are promising signals, the USMAB core project's so-called conceptual paradigm for human biosphere interactions disappoints, in its reduction of the human element in its systems model to what are termed societal controls. There is very much the flavor of the technological fix here, applied to social, political and economic problems. For example, the authors display a rather facile willingness to trust transferable development rights to solve "conflicts between individual wealth positions and the maintenance of a healthy ecological regime" (Harwell et al. 1991, p. 20). More importantly, they imply that scientists can and should set what they call ecological sustainability goals—explicitly defined as statements of desired *qualities,* that is, statements bearing on quality of life. In reserving these decisions to professional hands to establish for society, the authors display a certain arrogance.

The core project proposal notes that "little is known about feedbacks from natural systems to *modern* human systems beyond the fact that such feedbacks exist" (Harwell et al. 1991, p. 19). This marks the most problematic part of the USMAB model and deserves thorough attention. As might be expected from the criticism above, the approach is weighted heavily toward economic externalities,[9] regulatory regimes, property rights, zoning, and the like. This approach has the virtue of capturing a very practical and necessary facet of applied human ecology, but it neglects ecological roles of institutions in their deeper cultural or symbolic aspects. Further, the goal of the case-study exercise is unclear: Is it to manage the use of, or to characterize, a system? Measuring sustainability goals in terms of indicators of "ecological endpoints" does nothing to relate levels of use to changes in indicator values within the commons, and is not a sufficient basis for the management of dynamic human-environmental systems with regard to these desired "endpoints."

To its credit, the core project recognizes that it must address the key question of interactions between institutions and the commons. The project statement notes:

> For most aspects of the economic system and the legal (regulatory) systems, a study methodology already exists.... However there are more fundamental questions about the nature of the human system. Among these is the question of whether only coercive elements have operated to restrain over-exploitation of these commons. Alternatively, it is possible that some "larger hand" is working, something incorporated in community mutualism or societal altruism, that may come into play as resources are perceived to be extremely limiting (Harwell et al. 1991, p. 35).

Here, the USMAB verges on, but does not quite raise, problems of how limits are known, how that knowledge is expressed, and how such expressions serve to regulate human-environment relationships as processes in human ecology.

Like the SBI, both the USMAB Human-Dominated Systems Directorate mission statement and its core project proposal indicate no awareness of the program's multiple roots in human ecology or of work already done that may have partially satisfied its goals. The literature cited, though, is far broader and more truly interdisciplinary than that in the SBI; it even includes the work of a few important human ecologists in the areas of sustainability and commons (e.g., McCay and Acheson 1988). Moreover, in raising such questions as, How do human/societal endpoints interact with ecological endpoints?, and seeking to link human-related and natural-science components for study, the Human-Dominated Systems Directorate comes down foursquare upon central issues of human ecology. In its discussion of sustainability goals, the core project clearly recognizes that both biological and social questions are raised. The third sentence of the Directorate's Executive Summary virtually defines human ecology: "Central to the Directorate are interdisciplinary issues at the interface between ecological systems and society" (Harwell, et al. 1991, p. 1). The fifth paragraph of the Executive Summary is a cogent statement of central problems in human ecology:

Interdisciplinary research is never easy. Understanding diverse ecosystems, their important characteristics and natural variability, their response to stresses, and their recovery processes is extremely challenging. Adding to this diversity of simultaneous anthropogenic stresses, direct and subtle feedbacks from ecological responses to society, a continuously changing physical and societal environment, and the desire to manipulate and manage societal policies and institutions to achieve a particular ecological outcome is truly daunting. Yet the present scale and intensity of human-caused stresses on the biosphere and the rate at which valuable ecological resources are becoming impoverished nationally and globally, demand an understanding of those relationships and complexities if a high quality of life for humans and the other biota on Earth is to be achieved and sustained (Harwell, et al. 1991, p. 2).

Similar concerns underlie the core project objective to establish an Ecological/Societal Interface Workgroup. This group seeks to:

assure appropriate communications and understandings across disciplines—getting scientists and policy specialists to understand each other's terminology and percepts and facilitating exchange of information is essential to successful execution of interdisciplinary activities (Harwell et al. 1991, p. 33).

This and other objectives of the Interface Workgroup echo long-standing developments in human ecology (cf. Jungen 1986; Pratt and Young 1990). Such exchange and communication has been an explicit objective of several U.S.

Society for Human Ecology's international conferences over the past decade. The core project notes that "differences in utility of the methods of economists, sociologists, and historians, and the methods of natural scientists need to be understood and each used appropriately" (Harwell et al. 1991, p. 35), but, for example, Young's (1989) framework-building work integrating them is not recognized.

In summary, the USMAB program distinguishes itself by not only recognizing questions of human ecology, but by attempting to address them in its research program. However, the research program could be measurably strengthened by a fuller awareness of developments in the field of human ecology, especially in the USMAB's formulation and modeling of its conceptual paradigm for human/biosphere interactions. There is a single-minded focus on impacts as virtually the only way in which humans enter the system of interest. Thus, the USMAB Human-Dominated Systems core project largely leaves out the very organism which dominates the systems to which this directorate addresses itself.

United Nations Conference on Environment and Development (UNCED)

The United Nations (UN) General Assembly called for UNCED in 1989 to "elaborate strategies and measures to halt and reverse the effects of environmental degradation in the context of strengthened national and international efforts to promote sustainable and environmentally sound development in all countries" (Res. 44/228, United Nations 1989, p. 3).

Billed as the Earth Summit and "convened to consider the future of humanity as it struggles to balance development pressures against an increasingly imperiled global environment" (Valentine 1991, p. 1), UNCED was the largest and possibly most influential human ecology conference ever held—although of course it was not identified as such.

In what UN press releases termed "a defining moment in the history of the planet and its people," the heads of state from most of the nations on the planet met in their capacity as chief stewards of their environments to discuss plans of action that would balance equity and development with environmentally sound policies. They considered relationships between the needs of people and environments, and the pressures that are placed by each upon the other. These included stresses in global commons, the capacities of environments and resources to absorb continued use and abuse, and prospects for sustainability. In short, they took up important elements of an agenda that has preoccupied human ecologists for decades, though with considerably greater capacity to act upon it.

Among UNCED's accomplishments were an Earth Charter (also called the Rio Declaration), which is a "declaration of basic principles for the conduct of nations and peoples in respect of environment and development to ensure the future viability and integrity of the earth" (United Nations 1992a, p. 5); an action plan called Agenda 21, which presents a detailed work program for the international community to follow in addressing key environmental issues (United Nations 1992b); international conventions on climate change and biodiversity; and a statement on forest principles (United Nations 1992c).

UNCED addressed the core themes of the programs reviewed in this paper. The resources with which the UNCED conventions and agendas struggled are primarily commons resources (e.g., global climate change and transboundary air pollution; oceans; the gene pool upon which biodiversity is based; and forests and fresh waters, which are held in trust by governments for their peoples). Global commons have been of serious concern to the United Nations since its 1972 Stockholm Conference on the Environment, which was the first international forum to promote a global perspective on environmental problems. UNCED commemorated the twentieth anniversary of the Stockholm Conference, and the continued deterioration of global environmental since then is noted with concern throughout UNCED documents, including the enabling resolution, draft Rio Declaration, and statements by the Secretary General for UNCED (UN 1989 and 1992c; Strong 1992).

Global commons problems frequently enter the arena of international concern precisely because environmental thresholds—carrying capacities—have been exceeded. Again, this is recognized in the enabling resolution, Agenda 21, and in various statements by the Secretary General Strong (United Nations 1989, 1992b, 1992d; Strong 1992). A vision of sustainable development has underlain the United Nations approach to commons and carrying capacity problems since the UN-appointed World Commission on Environment and Development issued its report, *Our Common Future* (WCED 1987). This report (also known as the Brundtland Report) was instrumental in placing the questions of environment and development in a common frame and underlies, at least philosophically, many of the initiatives reviewed here. It, too, is explicitly noted in the enabling resolution and elsewhere as a forerunner of UNCED.

There are, however, few calls for interdisciplinarity in UNCED documents. The dimension of cooperation and integration which most concerns conference organizers is not among the disciplines of knowledge, but among the nations of the earth, in particular between developed and developing countries. The lines of tension that define these international polarities reflect the deeper issues of human ecology at stake and reveal just how much the UNCED debate was shaped by the very pressures and strains that form the questions of human ecology.

While the specific agenda of UNCED was comprised of such vital environmental issues as climate change, biological diversity, forest management, and so forth, the pivotal issue on which every agenda turned was the split in perspective between the North and the South, the developed and the developing nations. The UNCED enabling resolution identifies unsustainable patterns of production and consumption, particularly in the industrialized countries, as a major cause of continuing environmental degradation, and stresses the link between poverty and the deteriorating environment.

The developed countries, concerned about the deteriorating state of the environment, sought to keep the agenda focused on the technical aspects of that topic. The developing countries, not less concerned, saw the environmental issues as more complex and interdependent with other social, political, and above all economic issues. They were, in a sense, the spokespersons for human ecology at this conference, because they were radically aware of the degree to which environmental degradation is inextricably interwoven with all aspects of human systems and the human condition, particularly the dynamics of poverty.

Here, we may gain some insight into the unacceptance of human ecology in certain quarters. Human ecology implies profound responsibility on the part of the Western industrialized nations, the United States first among them. Their levels of consumption, flows of resources and wastes, and the underlying social, political, and economic organizations that support them, leave no doubt about their leadership in stressing the global commons and transgressing carrying capacity. Thus, human ecology could be construed as supporting the position of the developing countries; its application leads to the conclusion that the developed countries bear responsibilities that will be enormously costly. Were such a conclusion to be acknowledged, it would undermine the developed countries' strategy of focusing on technical aspects of environmental management, technical analyses of physical systems, and the engineering of technical fixes for environmental problems. It would greatly expose their vulnerability.

The emphasis placed upon the comprehensive treatment of environmental, economic, and social issues as an integrated whole indicates that UNCED's agenda was motivated by the same holistic concerns and recognition of interrelationships that also underlie human ecology. The questions of environment and development were explicitly linked in UNCED, as they are in human ecology. However UNCED, like the Green Plans reviewed below, pushed beyond sweeping calls for new frameworks or generalizing about global commons or carrying capacity, to lay out detailed blueprints for an applied human ecology based on a systems analysis of human-environmental relationships. Few overarching theoretical formulations are to be found, but simply very plain statements summarizing these relationships. The tone is very much one of getting on with urgent business. The short summaries of eight key problems contained in *Earth Summit Issues in Brief* (United Nations 1992e), for example, each are short human ecology problem statements. It would be possible to design a very workable world model of human-environmental relationships and contemporary lines of stress in them simply by sketching the linkages identified in the 31 proposals of Agenda 21 (United

Nations 1992b). The best illustration of the relationship between the UNCED vision and the key themes of this paper would be to quote the entire program.

U.S. National Institutes for the Environment (NIE)

The NIE, recently being studied by the National Academy of Sciences (NAS), was formally proposed by the Committee for the NIE (CNIE) at a meeting of distinguished scientists, conservationists, and policymakers in late 1989.[10] Structurally modeled after the National Institutes for Health (NIH), it would be an umbrella for extramural, peer-reviewed research on fundamental and applied environmental problems involving the human condition, as well as biology and the physical environment. Its mission would be to develop scientific information on the environment relevant to public policy. The NAS feasibility study was authorized and funded by Congress in 1990 under the sponsorship of the Environmental Protection Agency, with additional funds provided by the National Science Foundation and the Departments of Interior and Energy. The NAS report was supportive of NIE concepts in many ways, though it recommended much more drastic institutional changes to achieve them.

In many ways, the NIE proposal moves to fill the niche which the ESA's The Institute of Ecology (TIE) tried unsuccessfully to occupy during 1971-1984. With proposed operational funding via Congressional appropriation, it clearly would avoid one of the major factors leading to TIE's demise (Doherty and Cooper 1990). The other key factor identified by Doherty and Cooper— support from the community of scientists based on their active involvement in institutional design and program planning—also has been well addressed in the NIE's extensive involvement of the scientific community.

The NIE proposal was motivated by inadequate funding for ecological research and the need for a comprehensive understanding of global environmental problems. The CNIE point out that federal funding for ecological research is scattered over many agencies, is ill coordinated, and devotes only tiny amounts to the social sciences. By comparison, "the United States spends billions of dollars each year to clean up and litigate environmental disasters" and "poorly conceived regulations" cost "billions more" (CNIE 1992, p. 3). What research is funded rarely offers an integrated, interdisciplinary approach. These funding concerns may seem peripheral, but they are not. An exceptionally plain spoken statement by Howe and Hubbell (1990, pp. 71-72) makes clear why:

> Government funding priorities in the USA determine the quantity and quality of research undertaken; the hiring, promotion, and agendas of research universities; and, by example, the priorities of teaching universities and colleges. Government research funding also determines the relative success of competing research areas within and between

disciplines.... Funding disparities also distort university priorities. Research areas within disciplines that receive substantial governmental support [and pay the university's overhead] are viewed by university administrators as "hot," while those with less funding are viewed as "old-fashioned," "peripheral," or simply as financial liabilities.... In discipline after discipline, government priorities relegated environmental specialties to the realm of minor grants, simplistic theory, inadequate empirical tests of unrealistic hypotheses, preoccupation with disciplinary subjects bordering on scholasticism and a continuing struggle among practitioners to justify their existence rather than to master the environmental challenges that face society.

No factor is more important in explaining the marginalization of human ecology than this one. This theme is taken further by Howe (1992, p. 6), who addresses the powerfully distorting effect of funding priorities can have:

Funding priorities of DOD, DOE, and NSF skew university science faculties in favor of non-environmental engineering, physics and chemistry far out of proportion... because generous funding programs...define a clear...source of support to university administrators....[F]unding priorities limit or, as is often the case, eliminate courses and programs in environmental biology or other environmental disciplines.... If support exists only for basic disciplinary research of no direct relevance to pressing environmental problems, our educational system produces "the wrong stuff"...faculty and students concerned with narrowly defined applied problems may lack the breadth...to grasp and address problems.

The model for the NIE reviewed for this paper responds to these distortions with a proposal for six institutes. The Institute of Human Environments would sponsor research on the interactions of human societies with their environments. The Institute of Biotic Resources would concern itself with biological diversity, with an agenda similar to parts of the SBI. The Institute for Ecosystem Management and Restoration would seek to better understand ecological processes, ecosystem function, and interactions between species, environments, and humans. The Institute of Environmental Change would support study of global processes of environmental change in relation to natural and human systems. The Institute for Sustainable Resources and Development would take on the theme of sustainable use. Finally, the Institute for Pollution Prevention and Management would consider the impact of pollution on natural and human systems and resources. Additional intramural support centers would include a National Library for the Environment, an Office of Environmental Education, and an Office of Fellowships and Grants. Several of these institutes—the Institute of Human Environments, in particular— would have missions which encompass much or all of human ecology.

The NIE proposal and various articulations of its rationale teem with calls for interdisciplinary collaboration and contain many problem formulations that indicate a need for the framework which human ecology provides. The NIE's approach would be problem oriented rather than narrowly disciplinary, because environmental problems are complex and require contributions from multiple disciplines. Their purview would include social as well as biological science, and it would encourage cross-disciplinary research. Howe (1992, p. 5), in a draft of a rationale for the NIE, elaborates the following example of the interdisciplinary nature of the problem:

> To illustrate the point, real solutions to even a seemingly limited environmental problem, such as groundwater contamination, must involve chemists and biochemists, environmental engineers, and geologists to monitor and eventually mitigate contamination; environmental toxicologists and ecologists to determine how toxicants move through ecosystems and affect plants, microbes, and animals; epidemiologists to determine how particular toxicants affect people; geographers, agronomists, economists, and political scientists to determine how pollution changes social and economic conditions; economists, historians, philosophers, and political scientists to interpret human responses to change; legal experts and specialists in conflict resolution to determine how disputes can be resolved; and communicators capable of translating technical issues to the public and policy-makers. Simple technical fixes are insufficient and sometimes dangerous panaceas.

While Howe recognizes that "problems grow out of control for lack of understanding of all aspects of complex environmental issues, including social, political, and economic aspects as well as technical issues" (1992, p. 5), he does not specifically call for the conceptual framework that would integrate all of these contributing disciplines. However, he does propose an institutional framework in which to coordinate their research. It would seem a small step from the NIE materials to recognition of the role and need for the integrating approach that human ecology supplies, albeit a step that has not been taken. Nevertheless, the framers of the NIE show deep appreciation of the human dimensions of environmental problems; their problem orientation is the sine qua non for genuine interdisciplinary research. The NIE's robust awareness of these elements of human ecology may be due in part to the balanced composition of the CNIE, which has strong multi-disciplinary representation and includes several prominent human ecologists.[11]

The needs statement for the Institute of Human Environments, which is the one closest to the scope of human ecology, presents environmental management as its central problem—an orientation that would make for a rather truncated vision of human ecology. However, the impacts of human activities on many environmental dimensions, and the feedback effects of changing environments on social and other human dimensions, comprise a common thread running through the needs and mission statements of the proposed institutes. These interactions form the substance of human ecology and their emphasis throughout the NIE proposal is encouraging. The NIE framework could be substantially strengthened, however, were it to incorporate the foundations that the field of human ecology has laid on these very themes. Ignorance of this work is troubling in a proposal for an institution whose very role would be to nurture and advance American research and scholarship in neglected fields.

However, Howe and Hubbell (1990) make the point that a NIE could build an infrastructure of support for human ecology and the environmental sciences in universities and other research centers, much as the NIH has done for the biological sciences. In that respect, a NIE may do more than any of the other programs or plans reviewed here toward the long-term understanding of global commons problems, management of carrying capacity, and fostering of sustainable development.

National Science Foundation Human Dimensions of Global Change Program

The Human Dimensions of Global Change (HDGC) program is lodged within the NSF Directorate for Biological, Behavioral and Social Sciences, Division of Social and Economic Science. The goal of the Division is to "develop basic scientific knowledge of human social behavior, interaction, and decision-making and of social and economic systems, organizations and institutions" (NSF 1992b, p. 1). The two programs within the NSF under which HDGC is most likely to be funded are Geography and Regional Science and Sociology. The former supports research on geographical differences in economic, social, cultural, and physical phenomena, including interrelations between human activities and the natural environment. The latter program is concerned with problems of human social organization, demography, and processes of individual and institutional change.

An initiative of the executive branch, the HDGC competition was established in 1989 "to encourage the participation of social scientists and scientists in related disciplines in research on the myriad ways that human systems affect and respond to changing natural and physical systems." It is oriented toward an understanding of "how individuals and institutions affect and respond to environmental processes at a multinational or global scale" (NSF 1992a, p. 1).

The FY 1990 list of awards made under the HDGC program are a diverse group, including work on:

- Perceptions and attitudes;
- Geography and land use;
- International agreements and global change programs;
- Institutional analysis;
- Natural resource management and planning;
- Processes of change and human responses to it;
- Environmental conflict and national security;
- Economics of global and resource productivity;
- Urbanization/development; and
- Common property resources.

Some of the HDGC first-year funding was given to the National Academy of Sciences (NAS) for the National Research Council (NRC) Committee on the Human Dimensions of Global Change to produce a report and recommendations advising on approaches and topics of critical importance.[12] The committee's fourfold charge was to undertake:

> an assessment of previous social science research on topics related to global change; an evaluation of extant data resources for social and behavioral research on global change; a consideration of how collaborative research on global change might influence the generation of knowledge in the social sciences as well as attract social and behavioral scientists to apply their knowledge to global issues; and the development of a research agenda that can be implemented over a period of years (Stern et al. 1992, p. vi).

The committee has produced a book on the human dimensions of global environmental change (Stern et al. 1992) which articulates a six-point recommendation for a national research program. The NRC research proposal has many similarities with the NIE, and it is to be hoped that a unified national research program can be forged. Although the NSF has no necessary mandate to accept the NRC recommendations, they are expected to be taken very seriously.

The NRC committee sees its efforts as distinguished from those of others at work on the human dimensions of global environmental change, in their attempt to lay the intellectual groundwork for the development of the subject as a well-defined and professionally recognized field of study. They state:

> Our product reflects a sustained commitment on the part of all participants to the creation of a new field of study drawing on the intellectual capital of numerous disciplines but dominated by none (Stern et al. 1992, p. vii).

However, the field of study that the committee labors to create is not new at all; again, the call is for something very similar to the field of human ecology itself. While on the one hand, the scant materials provided by the NSF concerning its HDGC program betray no very deep appreciation of human ecology, on the other hand, the NRC committee, of all the programs reviewed in this paper, has the clearest conception of the links and feedback loops between human and natural systems which are definitive of human ecology:

> To explain or predict the course of the present global environmental changes, one must...understand the human sources, consequences, and responses, some of which can alter the course of global change....To understand global environmental change, it is necessary to focus on the interactions of environmental systems, including the atmosphere, the biosphere, the geosphere, and the hydrosphere, and human systems, including economic, political, cultural, and sociotechnical systems. Human systems and environmental systems meet in two places: where human actions proximately cause environmental change, that is, where they directly alter aspects of the environment, and

where environmental changes directly affect what humans value. The main questions about human causes concern the underlying sources or social driving forces that give rise to the proximate causes of global change (Stern et al. 1992, p. 1).

The committee is cognizant that almost all human activity has some potential relevance to global change and its simple model, implied above, links both human causes and human responses to environmental change. The NRC committee's strategy for scientific analysis of global change develops this model by specifying environmental and human systems (including what are called human response systems).[13] Each human system is seen as having "its own dynamics, and each also interacts with other human systems and the environment" (Stern et al. 1992, p. 33). This is human ecology, by whatever label. The committee states that understanding the feedback mechanisms between subsystems is key to their research strategy. Feedback occurs at two critical interfaces: (1) where human actions cause environmental change, and (2) where environmental conditions affect what humans value. Feedback modulation of stress/capacitance is not explicitly acknowledged or incorporated, however.

The committee's model contains the crucial recognition that "human forces that cause environmental change may also be affected by it" (Stern et al. 1992, p. 3) Their near-term research agenda would "emphasize processes of human response to the stresses [of] global environmental change" in recognition of the fact that "many of these responses may indirectly affect the driving forces of global change" because "human responses to global change are likely to feed back into the processes at work to amplify, dampen, or redirect [them]" (pp. 4, 24). The committee recognizes, with Liverman (1991, p. 71), that

the impact of global change is likely to depend more on the vulnerability of the social systems that are affected than on the physical magnitude of the environmental changes in themselves.

This recognition of the interaction of natural and human systems and the detailed specification of linkages and feedbacks between them sets the NRC effort apart from the others (although the USMAB Core Project has a similar objective and may yield equally impressive results), as does the extensive attention paid to the role of values, cultural beliefs, and attitudes. The committee acknowledges that "it is human behavior itself that must be controlled if we are to succeed in ameliorating or redirecting global change" (Stern et al. 1992, p. 27) and recognizes the role of knowledge itself as an actor in human ecology. Thus, human ecology as a field is itself understood to be a part of human ecology as a process:

the reflexivity of human activity makes knowledge itself a driving force of the system that is the object of that knowledge.... The problem of reflexivity in human activity adds a unique theoretical challenge: because people respond to their own understanding, research on global change is itself an influence on the human response (pp. 167, 174).

However, in its treatment of human ecology itself, the committee report falls far short. While the NRC committee report does refer to human ecology several times, each time it is characterized as "a small subfield of the social sciences" (Stern et al. 1992, pp. 25, 171) Dichotomizing the subfields of social science among those that "tend to emphasize human reactions to the environment" and those that "have focused on the character of the human-environment relationship *per se*" (pp. 38-39), the NRC committee sets human ecology in the latter camp. What they call environmental social science is placed firmly in the position which human ecology is accustomed to holding: "These research areas [the subfields] taken together constitute a broader field of environmental social science," the committee opines, and the latter is "a cluster of research activities that takes human-environment relationships as its focus" (p. 38). This definition is precisely that by which human ecology knows itself. (A definition for human ecology is given, but is garbled and is distinctly not the one shared by most human ecologists.)

Attempts by social science to capture human ecology go back to the 1920s (Young 1991, 1989, 1986, 1983, 1978, 1974), and it is disheartening to witness the resurrection of this discredited formulation in so important a report. At the same time, however, the facility with which this prestigious committee perpetuates this error says something very significant about the degree to which human ecology remains undeveloped. To the extent that human ecology is *not* a small subfield of social science, it may be said to not yet have been invented— at least not as an applied science that moves beyond theoretical constructions. This situation is reflected in the committee's advocacy of methodological pluralism as the most appropriate strategy for the near term, based on their conclusion that "much more understanding of the underlying processes needs to be developed before great strides can be made in integrative modeling" (Stern et al. 1992, p. 7). This is not to imply that human ecology equates to integrative modeling, but the lack of an integrative base too often applies to human ecology itself (with some notable exceptions; cf. Young 1989).

A clear recognition of the interdisciplinary nature of the challenge is repeated throughout the committee report and, like the NIE, a problem-centered approach is urged. The NRC committee also echoes Howe (see above) in noting the career and funding problems faced by interdisciplinary researchers. A good deal of hard thinking about specific roles, questions, and approaches in interdisciplinary collaboration is evident, particularly in a chapter titled "Problems of Theory and Method." Here, the committee has gone well beyond any of the other programs reviewed in this paper, to the cutting edge of human ecology itself. Their achievements point up the fuzziness in much of the human ecology literature, which merely asserts that interdisciplinary work is necessary but seems baffled about how to go about it. A similar pioneering theoretical synthesis is made in the identification of analogous properties between large, complex human and natural systems.[15] Based on its recognition of the challenges presented by these characteristics, the NRC committee issues what may be the quintessential call for human ecology:

> problems of global change require approaches that treat the earth as a single interactive system and stress the powerful interdependencies among environmental and human systems. Such approaches tend to be interdisciplinary rather than multi-disciplinary and are characterized by holistic analytic premises such as those of ecology or systems analysis. (Stern et al. 1992, p. 32).

These advances notwithstanding, the committee's articulation of interdisciplinarity resolves itself in several troubling formulations that seem to reduce it at times to bland calls for cooperation between natural scientists and social scientists or for incentives to encourage collaboration between social and natural scientists, and assertions such as that social scientists must understand environmental processes. Such simplistic approaches to the practice of interdisciplinary research exemplify the problem discussed above, as each area treats the other as a "neighboring multidisciplinary complex." Thus, when articulating an agenda, the NRC manifesto for social science research is sometimes as narrow and provincial in its way as the SBI is in promoting purely biological research. Some of the sample research questions posed by the committee are myopic in their search for the explanation of one social change by means of another, rather than by attending to ecological processes in human affairs or by distilling the crosscutting characteristics of social changes that play into those processes. In other instances, however, the committee has done exceptional interdisciplinary thinking, as, for example, in their examination of which kinds of social science studies would be most meaningful based on an analysis of the significance of various behaviors as driving forces that effect global biological and physical changes.

Finally, though a general recognition of global changes as consequences of anthropogenic stresses in commons runs through the committee report, little or no heed is paid either to the idea of capacitance as a characteristic of systems or to sustainability as a vision to guide research. Again, this may be due to a degree of focus on social science which, despite broad recognition of environmental change, neglects basic elements that may come more naturally to mind among researchers working with the biological and physical environment.

National "Green Plans":   The Dutch Example

National green plans differ from the routine development and implementation of environmental policy and regulation that is a part of the normal function of government at all levels. They differ in the degree to which the best of them are *comprehensive, integrated,* and *strategic.* These environmental plans address all aspects of the environment in a coordinated manner so that, for example, environmental problems are not merely shoved from one media to another (e.g., from solid waste to air quality through incineration). They explicitly recognize national responsibility for natural values and for environmental change at all scales. The Dutch plan, for example, considers five spatial scales of environmental issues: the global, the continental, the fluvial, the regional, and the local level (The Netherlands 1990).

The national green plans do not seek to affect policy or decision making, as they *are* policy and reflect the outcome of environmental decisions. Similarly, they do not call for something akin to applied human ecology, they go ahead and *do* it. They recognize the same anthropogenic changes in commons and stresses to environmental capacities that underlie the programs reviewed above, though with a wider agenda and particular themes occasioned by geographic circumstances. Both global and national problems are addressed. Whether they attack these problems with the necessary interdisciplinary tools and an appropriate applied human ecology remains to be seen.

Among the national green plans reviewed for this paper were:

- Netherlands National Environmental Policy Plan (NEPP);
- Canadian Green Plan for a Healthy Environment;
- Norwegian Report to the Storting on Environment and Development;
- Britain's Environmental Strategy: This Common Inheritance; and
- Premises and Perspectives for the Development of a National Environment Plan in Austria.

The following discussion concentrates on the Netherlands as an example, but makes limited reference to the others as well. The Dutch plan (NEPP) was occasioned by the Brundtland Report (WCED 1987) and a subsequent national survey called "Concern for Tomorrow."[16] Even though debate over the plan led to the fall of one cabinet, by May 1989 the plan was published. The NEPP is based on the strikingly bold conclusion that even full end-of-pipe environmental controls would not do and, thus, structural changes in production and consumption would be needed. Their recognition of commons problems is reflected by statements such as these:

Where a few decades ago, local health effects and impacts on nature were in the fore, we are now also confronted with damage to the social and economic functions of the environment [i.e., the environment in its capacity as provider of common goods and services]: problems with the drinking water supply, the agricultural production capacity of the soil, forestry, and recreation (de Jongh 1991a, p. 4).

One line of thought in evolutionary theory suggests that patterns that work best for populations as a whole are favored over those advancing the interests of the individual. While this point remains controversial, it at least suggests commons may not be a problem at all but rather one defining condition of evolutionary development. That is, solving the problems of the commons as a group—and not being best at individual exploitation of the commons—may be what guarantees evolutionary success. Recognition of such structural aspects of human ecology vis-à-vis the commons is implied in the national green plans. For example, Hofseth (1992), presenting the Norwegian Green Plan at a recent workshop, noted that the Norwegian approach is based on the principle that individual choice presupposes a prior collective choice, a formulation which is virtually definitive of a functional common property regime.[17]

Theory states that if choices regarding commons are both informed and conscious, so that the collective establishes boundaries for individual choice in the commons, both the collective and the individual may benefit. A presentation on the Netherlands Green Plan by de Jongh (1992) in the same workshop provides an empirical basis. Describing end-of-pipe controls and structural changes in the social and industrial sectors to manage environmental quality, de Jongh noted that *if* the Netherlands were joined by the remainder of the European Economic Community (EEC) in implementing these measures, an increase in wealth would be projected by 2010, as compared to a marginal decrease in wealth under the scenarios of: (1) business as usual, (2) less stringent control, or (3) full control but without common (e.g., EEC) cooperation:

> The outcome was somewhat amazing: if the neighboring countries should follow more or less the same policy, then the sustainable scenario would lead to even more economic growth than was foreseen in the "normal" forecasting of the Dutch economy (de Jongh 1992, p. 2).

Such data indicate that commons problems respond positively to common action, although individual altruism may be penalized, and, further, that environmental quality can be consistent with economic prosperity if both are integrated within a commons framework. The Dutch, recognizing ecological realities in a small country, have taken these analyses to indicate that they must "promote the recognition of global environmental problems [and] reinforce worldwide environmental management structures" (de Jongh 1991a, p. 11) for their own benefit as stakeholders in the commons. This objective is explicitly incorporated in the NEPP and is of obvious concern to other nations, especially such other countries as Canada, Norway, and Austria which find themselves on the cutting edge of green planning. The situation is summarized in the Norwegian program to follow-up to WCED report:

> The challenges we face in environmental politics are mainly related to compliance with Norway's international commitments. In a global context, Norwegian discharges are small, and a great deal of the pollution which causes problems for Norway originates in other countries. It is therefore also in Norway's own interests to be in the forefront of efforts to bring about international agreements concerning the environment (Norway 1989, p. 59).

Comprehensive strategic environmental plans affect the entire economies of countries that implement them. Leaders in green planning risk a loss of competitive position, in addition to facing the continued impacts of "environmental dumping" by other nations that have not implemented similar plans (Schreiber 1992; Hofseth 1992; Norway 1989). At the same time, leaders in these nations realize that their credibility in urging international action rests on their own demonstrated commitment to the programs they advocate:

> If our work for more stringent environmental standards is to have credibility, we must be in the first rank in cleaning up and preventing environmental damage within our own borders (Norway 1989, p. 59).

Returning to the Dutch plan, it also explicitly recognizes carrying capacity in several places (see Appendix D) and places sustainable development as its centerpiece goal. It also includes a control-systems model of human-environmental relationships and, although no calls for human ecology or for interdisciplinarity are issued, the Dutch clearly possess a sophisticated appreciation of the nature and function of feedbacks between human and environmental systems. They discuss a type of feedback moderator which they term roll-off mechanisms. The concept would be familiar to economists by analogy to the idea of externalized costs of public goods and services; it expresses the idea that environmental costs are "rolled off" to other scales (e.g., when local impacts are distributed regionally), to other social groups or to other generations.

These "roll-offs" lead to the accumulation of "environmental debts," which the Dutch propose to reduce or eliminate by influencing system feedback. Feedback would be affected in two ways: first, by an analysis of values, and second, through infrastructure changes, using closed cycles, and efficiency and quality improvements. Identifying the role of values at all is a pioneering advance, let alone giving it first place.

The notions of commons, carrying capacity, and sustainable development come together in the notion of "squandering," one of eight central themes[18] around which the Dutch have built the NEPP:

Squandering [reflects] the need to integrate economic, energy, and resource policies with environmental policies. The environment is considered as a resource stock and the strategy here is aimed at the development of policies for managing stocks of, for example, clean groundwater, soils with buffering capacity, and other environmental stocks which determine the environment's carrying capacity. Within this theme the development of instruments for the promotion of sustainable development has priority, as well as the encouragement of structural measures through experiments directed at the closing of substance cycles, energy conservation and improvement of the quality of products and production processes (de Jongh 1991a, p. 13).

The NEPP identifies target groups[19] for the application of the various goals and prescriptions generated under these themes and asks each of them to contribute substantively—ideas, time, and money—to their realization. Environmental management roles are assigned to each of these groups, and the NEPP contains blueprints to tightly integrate the Dutch government's actions with leadership in each of them. Detailed strategies are put forth for managing technology per se, including the redirection of the development of new technologies toward more environmentally friendly ends and for cradle-to-grave management of the interface between technology and resources. The ultimate goal is a clean environment within one generation.

Turning briefly to the other national green plans, the Canadian and Norwegian plans share much in common with the Dutch model, including: wide involvement of all sectors of society and industry; an integrated strategy to coordinate actions affecting different resources and systems at different spatial and temporal scales; and insight into the systems character of human-environment interactions and feedbacks. The Austrian National Environmental Plan appears to be now arriving at the stage that the Dutch, Norwegians, and Canadians occupied during 1988-1989, as the need for green planning is recognized and the plan's main features take shape within the context of a broad debate on its structure, coverage, and impact on socioeconomic sectors.

Of the five green plans reviewed, the British showed the least evidence of being either integrated or strategic. Its centerpiece is a long White Paper that lists some 350 initiatives and commitments in almost two dozen areas of environmental concern (United Kingdom 1990). Though this is the first comprehensive statement of environmental policies by any British government (Stoker 1992), it is neither programmatically tied together nor underlain by a systematic analysis. The focus is on enumeration rather than integration. Consequently, it seems to represent more of a broad-scale effort to move forward Britain's environmental program on all fronts than an integrated plan. The White Paper's statement of first principles is founded on an argument for growth, taking no heed of Herman Daly's distinction between the concepts of growth (which he asserts cannot continue) and development (which can). There is evidence throughout the British plan of the pro-growth philosophy advanced by the United States, and its related strategy inclines toward more study and less action than the other plans.

Most damning, however, is the omission from the British plan of all reference to the work of the London-based Commonwealth Human Ecology Council (CHEC). CHEC is the longest lived of the world's human ecology organizations and occupies an international leadership position. Since 1951, CHEC has held six international conferences on development and human ecology, while conducting applied human ecology case studies and establishing human ecology councils with policy advisory functions throughout a wide spectrum of the 49 countries of the British Commonwealth (Daysh 1988). The CHEC approach integrates the perspectives of some 37 identified disciplines and provides the sort of framework which the British White Paper sorely needs.

THE MARGINALIZATION OF HUMAN ECOLOGY[20]

The field of human ecology—including the practitioners who have called themselves human ecologists and the body of knowledge they have built up— is simply being left behind: by green planning that explicitly combines the human and natural sciences, by the sustainable biosphere initiatives and human dimensions of global change programs, by UNCED, and by the proposed NIE. As a field, human ecology either needs to assert its legitimacy and unfold its legacy in leading these initiatives by providing the theoretical underpinnings and intellectual structure they need, or resign itself to an increasingly cranky role at the outskirts. Applied human ecology is needed now more than ever— and that need is being met. Applied human ecology is simply being done by those who see the need and do not have time to wait in moving to meet it. As these efforts move forward, that field which has called itself human ecology is in danger of becoming irrelevant.

The programs reviewed above often contain eloquent expressions of the need for human ecology. They are in large part *definitive* of human ecology. Their work is pioneering, deserves applause, and promises to be effective in handling obdurate problems of human ecology. Their problem statements and expressions of need often read like primers in human ecology. Why, then, is the field not mentioned, its legacy left unused? Why are few or no human ecologists cited in their bibliographies? Are we witnessing remarkably bad scholarship on the part of the scientists who lead the international development of these plans and programs?

Although the term human ecology is almost never used, no human ecologist would fail to recognize these programs for what they are. What is odd is the clean sweep of the term itself from these texts; in all but a few, reference to the field that for some decades has made its objectives synonymous with the terms in which these programs are phrased is entirely lacking.

The question as to whether this omission is deliberate cannot be avoided. Has the field's checkered history as the sometime-captive of now this and now that academic discipline contributed to a tacit decision to avoid it? Has its perceived inability to articulate a compelling and pragmatic action plan left it a dying field?

If, on the other hand, the lack of reference to the field is inadvertent, then equally troubling questions must be raised regarding the sophistication of both the proposed programs and their authors. Repeatedly, eloquent calls for the development of a comprehensive research framework are made in terms indistinguishable from those by which human ecology defines itself. If the authors of these calls think they are new or that an integrated framework remains to be formulated, they are appallingly unaware of work that has been going on for some time (cf. Young 1974, 1978, 1983, 1989). For example, an appendix of the SBI lists "cross-cutting issues in ecology" that bear a striking resemblance to themes developed in Young's (1989) interdisciplinary framework for human ecology, but does not acknowledge his much more extensive development of these themes.

The fact that these programs are nevertheless proceeding to create a framework for themselves must be a matter of serious concern to the field of human ecology, for if these efforts succeed, whether or not they must reinvent the wheel in the process, that field will in the end be not merely marginal, but irrelevant.

One reason that human ecology as a field has been overlooked—perhaps the most important one—may be simply that it has always been marginal:

> Human ecology, rather than being firmly established within any one discipline, even in the social sciences, is perched rather precariously on the margins of each and every academic realm involved with study of the human species (Young 1983, p. 2).

Thomas Dietz, a member of the NRC committee and president of the United States Society for Human Ecology, notes that some research agencies have not recruited individuals with key skills for the study of human dimensions of global change:

> The Academy has noted that there is an almost perfect mismatch between the talents and skills available in the lead global change research agencies and those required for human dimensions research. For a variety of reasons, DOE, NASA, NOAA, and EPA have never recruited a significant body of social scientists, let alone specialists in human ecology. Nor have scholars with a significant record of research on human-environment interactions been prominent on advisory and review panels for these agencies (1992, p. 7).

But perhaps a deeper answer is rooted in the inability of human ecologists to get beyond general problem statements and theoretical frameworks. While human ecologists—including a great many who have never paid much attention to the field and would not accept its laurels—have done well in identifying the complex of problems to which attention must be paid, human ecology as a field has been largely ineffectual in actually dealing with the pressing environmental issues of the day. Indeed, the field's stunted development as an applied science has left it with little more role than that of backroom theorizing and the sounding of repeated alarms. And when the alarm is heard and the battle joined, the field of human ecology rarely has been able to contribute anything substantial. The important decisions are taken elsewhere; the key actions are guided by other paradigms. I do not think we may put this down to the stupid intransigence of an uneducable world. The field of human ecology, as yet, has not articulated any very useful action plans (though efforts toward focusing human ecology on the needs of decision-makers are emerging; cf. Pratt 1989).

Environmental crises, we are warned, present themselves on every hand. We are surrounded, it seems, by intractable dilemmas in our environmental relationships. Moreover, these are woven in a "world-knot" fiendishly braided in such a manner that an attempt to undo any part of it plaits new difficulties into its tangle. To make an environmental problem go away, we create a severe economic dislocation. Resolve the economic predicament and a political quandary emerges. Take steps to contain the political situation and several social problems arise. This is the nine-headed hydra of Greek mythology—a dragon whose heads multiply as each is cut off, unless the wound is immediately cauterized.

As a field, human ecology has been a leader in identifying and describing the natural history of this nine-headed dragon. It is no wonder, then, that human ecologists most often define their activities in terms of the practical intricacies of this complex of problems in the "real" world. But as a strategy, how well has that worked?

Faced with applied problems—pollution, population growth, resource exhaustion, extinction of unique species and cultures, or world hunger—the field of human ecology struggles to be an applied science. It has largely failed to bring anything new to such problems on its own terms; it could be argued that human ecology as a field furnishes nothing that is not already supplied by the existing applied fields such as economics, planning, environmental engineering, architecture, home economics, politics, and the rest. In drawing on these fields, human ecology too often reduces itself to competing with them on the grounds of their own competence, a contest from which it cannot benefit. It has never articulated a cogent basis as an applied science and possesses no distinct operational concepts of its own which, placed in the hands of those on the battlelines of world environmental problems, could be used to hew off the dragon's heads or sear its necks. The hard truth is that human ecology has remained a marginal field for over 70 years because, historically, it has offered too little of practical importance to the councils of the pragmatic or the desperation of the embattled. It recognizes the need to be integrative, to be interdisciplinary, but, beyond raising the clarion call, has done too little to actually advance that objective.

CONCLUSION: A CENTRAL ROLE FOR HUMAN ECOLOGY

Marginalized or not, the programs reviewed for this paper lay down a mandate for human ecology. Each and every one of them calls—not once, but repeatedly—for the perspective, framework, and services that human ecology provides. To those working within human ecology, the naiveté revealed by the omission of reference to the legitimate body of work done by human ecologists may seem stunning. It is also irritating:

> Because the amounts of funding are increasing, work on human dimensions is attracting many new researchers. To the extent that this provides new insights and energy it is welcome. But a certain naiveté comes with it. Over the last few years, I have all too frequently reviewed research proposals and papers whose authors, by omission or commission, suggest that nothing has been written on the topic they are studying, when in fact a substantial body of work, spanning several decades and dozens of papers, already exists (Dietz 1992, p. 6).

Is the field of human ecology equipped to fulfill its mandate? According to Dietz, it comprises "a substantial body of methods, theory and substantive knowledge that can be used to guide policy in the short run and that provides the foundation for further research" (1992, p. 6). Moreover, the programs reviewed provide a basis for bringing this fund of knowledge into the mainstream. Each of them takes important steps toward the development of an applied human ecology. However, their approaches often fail to go beyond impacts (cf. Young 1974, 1983). Ecology is about organism-environment relationships and these programs (with notable exceptions) repeatedly fail to bring the human organism fully into their equations and models other than a source of impacts. Until they do, their approach will not be ecological, it will not be satisfactory human ecology, and it will ultimately fail. Dietz asserts:

> Funding for research on human dimensions of global environmental change must not be wasted on naive efforts that ignore the body of existing knowledge and skills (1992, p. 6).

He goes on to cogently summarize the likely outcome if funding is, as he says, wasted on naive efforts:

> This makes it likely that funds expended on human dimensions research by these agencies will be badly allocated and not produce either the short term or cumulative payoff possible (p. 7).

The premise of this paper and the reason for undertaking this detailed review is that these possibilities cannot afford to be squandered. Whether for human dimensions of global change, sustainable biosphere initiatives, or national environmental research programs, the services of human ecologists are needed.

The repeated, nearly identical calls issued by each and every one of these programs for the perspective and framework provided by human ecology make this clear. However, the onus is on human ecologists to inform leaders in all of these programs of their field, their capabilities, and the share that they are prepared to contribute to these efforts.

APPENDIX A: PROBLEM STATEMENTS AND EXPRESSIONS OF NEED FOR HUMAN ECOLOGY

Santa Fe Workshop on Global Change

"To forecast the ecological impact of global change, research initiatives are needed on the explicit role of humans in ecological systems" (Brown and Roughgarden 1990, p. 173).

"There should be support for collaborative studies among ecologists and social scientists on topics such as the growth and resource use of human populations; the ecological basis of sustainable economic development; the effects of different social, economic, and political systems on landscapes and biological diversity; and the reciprocal relationships among human activities, the organization of ecological communities, and biogeochemical ecosystem processes" (Brown and Roughgarden 1990, p. 181).

Sustainable Biosphere Initiative (Ecological Society of America)

"Many of the environmental problems that challenge human society are fundamentally ecological in nature" (Lubchenco et al. 1991, p. 373).

"Ecological understanding of complex phenomena is essential if society is to anticipate and ameliorate the environmental effects of human activities. Human activities may have unanticipated or indirect effects on parts of the Earth's life support systems, often at considerable distances from the site of the activity" (Lubchenco et al. 1991, p. 377).

"Because the science of ecology is devoted to understanding interactions between organisms and their environments, it is particularly appropriate for ecologists to focus on the complex relationships between humans and the biosphere" (Lubchenco et al. 1991, p. 384).

"The SBI recognizes that common ecological processes govern the response of the biosphere to human activities. Therefore, common ecological principles are likely to be involved in the solution of environmental problems....[A] comprehensive research framework is needed...because common ecological principles underlie effective management strategies" (Lubchenco et al. 1991, p. 384, 397).

"Humans depend on natural and managed ecological systems for food, shelter, clothing, and clean air and water. As demands for the goods and services of the biosphere increase, so does the need to understand the complex array of interactions between humans and the biosphere. Ecological approaches to understanding environmental change increasingly will include the roles of humans both as agents of change and as populations responding to change" (Lubchenco et al. 1991, pp. 391-392).

"Today, the discipline of ecology faces the challenges of enlarging ecological perspectives to include human values" (Lubchenco et al. 1991, p. 395).

"A world so altered by human activity offers the opportunity and the challenge to expand the scope of the discipline of ecology" (Lubchenco et al. 1991, p. 395).

"In all of this work, it will be essential to combine studies of human populations with those that examine changing patterns of resource use, air and water quality, or global and regional climates" (Lubchenco et al. 1991, p. 396).

International Sustainable Biosphere Initiative and Related Events

"Environmental problems resulting from human activities threaten the sustainability of global life-support systems.... Activities initiated in pursuit of an improved quality of life, through the production of food, fiber, shelter, consumer goods, recreation, and so forth, frequently lead to unintended results. These negative consequences of humanity's activities all relate to the functioning of ecological systems, and require knowledge and understanding of such processes in natural and transformed environments as keys to their solution" (Huntley et al. 1991, p. 7).

"The problems are not only scientific, but include people's value systems and expectations, education and judgement.... Solving the problems... will require a suite of ecological studies that will differ in scale and application from those addressing the problems of desertification, sedimentation, sanitation, and malnutrition experienced by the Third World" (Huntley et al. 1991, p. 8).

"The ISBI will have to overcome existing attitudes that frequently do not perceive ecologists as offering solutions to problems relating to the quality of life. Ecologists will have to break away from the intellectual and professional traditions that have constrained their involvement in social, economic, and political matters" (Huntley, et al. 1991, p. 9).

"[S]ustainability is a human-centered concept and can only be achieved with the willingness and cooperation of many culturally diverse human societies.... [W]e urge ecologists to investigate the complex interrelationships between urban, agricultural, forest, and natural terrestrial and aquatic ecosystems which together make up the cultural landscapes within the biosphere" (Huntley et al. 1991, p. 10).

[Goals of the Human Dimensions of Sustainability component of the ISBI program include:] "to understand the relationships between the human population and renewable resources. What are the cultural constraints on how people perceive environmental degradation? How does community participation in sustainability planning influence perceptions of the rate and direction of environmental change/degradation? How is human regional migration related to perceptions of trends in environmental quality/degradation? How can traditional knowledge and established production systems be incorporated into strategies for sustained development?" (Huntley et al. 1991, p. 12).

"To understand the role of various beliefs and value systems in generating differences in the dynamics of resource depletion or resource conservation at the local and regional levels. How do local and regional values and belief systems constrain or promote the degradation of natural resources? How can traditional values be incorporated into strategies for maintenance of biological diversity?" (Huntley et al. 1991, p. 12).

"To understand how various life styles and socioeconomic regimes are related to ecological impacts. What is the relationship between equity of resource access/allocation and the sustainable use of natural resources? What are the relative environmental impacts of different human life styles? What are the ecological consequences of alternative industrial technologies?" (Huntley et al. 1991, p. 12).

"[the question of the earth's carrying capacity] is a complex question and must be addressed in terms of differing socioeconomic scenarios, implied living standards, and potential per-capita material and energy use scenarios" (Huntley et al. 1991, p. 12).

"The earth can be subdivided into hierarchies of systems in which humans interact with the environment. Such systems are dynamic, ever-changing and responsive as they react to their changing environments and to changes in energy flow, diversity, information, or controls from higher or lower order systems" (INTECOL 1991, p. 2).

"Fundamentally, the issue of sustainable development involves bringing together, and integration of, all the diverse sources of information, experiences and theories relevant to the human/environment problem in its broadest aspect. It is necessary that we break out of the bounded structures that were created to solve other problems and create new, broader, more integrative points of action to understand and solve problems of sustainable development" (INTECOL 1991, p. 2, 5).

U.S. Man and the Biosphere Human-Dominated Systems Directorate

"The mission of the United States Man and the Biosphere Program is to foster harmonious relationships between humans and the biosphere through an international program of policy-relevant research which integrates social, physical and biological sciences to address actual problems" (USMAB 1991a, p. 1).

"Interdisciplinary research is never easy. Understanding diverse ecosystems, their important characteristics and natural variability, their response to stresses, and their recovery processes is extremely challenging. Adding to this diversity of simultaneous anthropogenic stresses, direct and subtle feedbacks from ecological responses to society, a continuously changing physical and societal environment, and the desire to manipulate and manage societal policies and institutions to achieve a particular ecological outcome is truly daunting. Yet the present scale and intensity of human-caused stresses on the biosphere and the rate at which valuable ecological resources are becoming impoverished nationally and globally, demand an understanding of those relationships and complexities if a high quality of life for humans and the other biota on Earth is to be achieved and sustained" (Harwell et al. 1991, p. 2).

"An organizing paradigm, essentially a control-systems model of coupled human/ecological systems, will provide the overall framework for the activities, the focal point for specific hypothesis testing and data integration and analyses, and the point-of-departure for a continual development and refinement of a conceptual model" (Harwell et al. 1991, p. 1).

"[T]he Directorate will emphasize...the effects of cultural and behavioral factors on ecosystem utilization, and the relationship of human activities to biological diversity" (USMAB 1991a, p. 3).

"Central to the Directorate are interdisciplinary issues at the interface between ecological systems and society" (Harwell et al. 1991, p. 1).

"[L]ittle is known about feedbacks from natural systems to *modern* human systems beyond the fact that such feedbacks exist.... [A] view that includes human institutions as an integral part of the human/biosphere system raises a number of fundamental questions...because of the complexity and geographical scope of the interactions that must be dealt with" (Harwell et al. 1991, p. 19).

United Nations Conference on Environment and Development

"For too many years, and at great cost, governments, agencies, and their specialists have tried to view the environment/development matrix as a series of discrete phenomena which could be analyzed and manipulated independently without repercussions to the larger system. A new era is dawning where holistic, systems-oriented thinking is beginning to emerge as a counter-weight to this anti-ecological approach" (Valentine 1991, p. 4).

"Better scientific understanding of the connections between human activities and the environment and better use of that knowledge must be incorporated into the formulation of policies for development and environmental management" (*Agenda 21,* Sect. IV, ch. 35).

"There is still a considerable lack of awareness regarding the interrelated nature of human activities and the environment" (*Agenda 21,* Sect. IV, ch. 36).

The Earth Covenant: "Recognizing that people's actions toward nature and each other are the source of growing damage to the environment and resources needed to meet human needs and ensure survival and development..." [the beginning of a one-sentence pledge expected to be signed by hundreds of millions of people in support of the Earth Charter].

Proposed National Institutes for the Environment

"NIE-sponsored research would seek to understand...the interactions of people and the environment" (CNIE 1992, p. 5).

"[The mission of the Institute of Human Environments would be] to better understand and improve the interaction of human societies with their environments" (CNIE 1992, p. 8).

"[The mission of the Institute for Ecosystem Management and Restoration would be] to understand how organisms interact...with humans" (CNIE 1992, p. 8).

"[The mission of the Institute of Environmental Change would be] to understand and anticipate the effects of global change on natural and human systems. [An example of a key question would be:] How do people affect environmental change?" (CNIE 1992, p. 8).

"[D]eforestation in tropical and temperate ecosystems occurs without knowing what is being lost or what alternative development schemes might bring; untested ecological theory often substitutes for empirical science, making reliable predictions next to impossible; regional and global changes proceed without comprehensive analysis of the cultural, economic, and diplomatic consequences; humans change nature, without knowing how those changes will affect future generations; exploitative commodity-based resource use for short-term profit neglects the integrated analysis that underlies sustainable resource use" (Howe and Hubbell 1990, pp. 71-72).

"Environmental change will foment or shape the major geopolitical agendas of the new decade and the next century, but the causes and biological, economic, and social consequences are poorly understood" (Howe 1991, p. 3).

"Human beings are becoming the dominant influence on life support systems, but information about the human role and the effects of altered environments on societies lags behind" (Howe 1990, p. 25).

"[The Institute of Human Environments] will concentrate on the human impact on the human environment, and in turn on the impact of altered environments on human responses....[Its] goals will be to predict, prevent, and mitigate [the] damaging effects of diverse human activities on the environment....[Its] research programs will address improved use of existing knowledge about human ecology" (Howe 1990, pp. 26, 29).

"[T]he social dimensions of ecosystem change are rarely addressed beyond reactive measures towards impending catastrophe. Social values are hardly uniform across societies...yet even the most fundamental issues receive only rudimentary attention" (Howe 1990, p. 20).

"[Effective management] will require...a comprehensive understanding of ecological principles brought about by detailed, long-term study, together with an imaginative and proactive economic analysis which can inform policy recommendations. The natural sciences must document the processes involved, economic analysis must assess the consequences of alternative sustainable and non-sustainable practices, and policy scientists must evaluate the social and political implications of different development, management, and *laisse fairez* scenarios" (Howe 1990, p. 22).

"[M]uch of the critical research that needs to be done concerns either social science projections of the consequences of environmental change, or analyses of the policy implications of environmental change" (Howe 1990, p. 30).

"The coming millennium will witness unprecedented alteration of human environments, and unprecedented challenges to societies forced to cope with environments altered and often degraded by their own history of environmental mismanagement, or by the historical and continuing environmental mismanagement of other nations" (Howe 1990, p. 31).

NSF Human Dimensions of Global Change Program

"The HDGC program was established...to encourage...research on the myriad ways that human systems affect and respond to changing natural and physical systems...[and] how individuals and institutions affect and respond to environmental processes at a multinational or global scale" (NSF 1992a, p. 1).

"In order to design effective responses to the global environmental changes that human activity is producing, we must understand how human and environmental systems interact" (*USMAB* 1991c, p. 1).

"The NAS Committee...[recommends] that a study be made to lay the intellectual groundwork for the development of the human dimensions of global change as a well-defined and widely recognized field of study" (*USMAB* 1991c, p. 1).

"The future of [anthropogenic global environmental] changes cannot be adequately predicted by simple extrapolative techniques because the course of human behavior changes with new knowledge and technology....We need an effort to produce new knowledge for explaining and predicting the course of human actions that alter the environment.... The...proximate human causes of global change, such as fossil fuel use and biomass burning, are in turn caused by several driving or social forces, including population growth, economic growth, technological change, political and economic institutions, and human values. We need a better understanding of how these forces work together" (*USMAB* 1991c, p. 3).

"Because human activities interact with physical and biological systems both as driving forces and as critical links in feedback mechanisms, any effort to understand, much less to come to terms with, global environmental change that does not include a sustained commitment to improving our knowledge of the human dimensions cannot succeed....[T]he Committee on Earth and Environmental Sciences flatly states that 'without an understanding of human interactions in global environmental change that is based both on empirical observations of human behavior and on a better understanding of the consequences of human actions, the models of physical and biological processes of change will be incomplete.' As the committee goes on to observe, an especially critical need is the 'identification of the ways that human, physical, and biological systems interact, often through complex feedback mechanisms' " (Stern et al. 1992, p. v).

"How should we allocate our attention between studies of the underlying sources of anthropogenic change and studies of human responses to global environmental change, which figure prominently in the relevant feedback mechanisms?" (Stern et al. 1992, p. vi).

"To explain or predict the course of the present global environmental changes, one must...understand the human sources, consequences, and responses, some of which can alter the course of global change....To understand global environmental change, it is necessary to focus on the interactions of environmental systems, including the atmosphere, the biosphere, the geosphere, and the hydrosphere, and human systems, including economic, political, cultural, and sociotechnical systems. Human systems and environmental systems meet in two places: where human actions proximately cause environmental change, that is, where they directly alter aspects of the environment, and where environmental changes directly affect what humans value. The main questions about human causes concern the underlying sources or social driving forces that give rise to the proximate causes of global change" (Stern et al. 1992, p. 1).

"New theoretical tools are required. Studies of the human dimensions of global change require analysis at spatial and temporal expanses much greater than most social scientific theory encompasses. Social science will need to develop new theoretical tools for analyzing such issues as...relationships between global social changes and the global environment, and links between human-environment relationships at different levels of spatial aggregation" (Stern et al. 1992, p. 6).

"These characteristics of the global environment present serious challenges for scientific research and may call for new theories and methods....[P]roblems of global change require approaches that treat the earth as a single interactive system and stress the powerful interdependencies among environmental and human systems. Such approaches tend to be interdisciplinary rather than multi-disciplinary and are characterized by holistic analytic premises such as those of ecology or systems analysis" (Stern et al. 1992, p. 32).

"Research on the human dimensions of global change strives to understand the interactions between human systems and environmental systems...and to understand the aspects of human systems that affect those interactions" (Stern et al. 1992, p. 33).

"The global environmental changes of greatest current concern are inextricably intertwined with human behavior. They cannot be understood without understanding the human activities that cause them and the ways humans may respond to the awareness of global change" (Stern et al. 1992, p. 42).

"The highest priority for research is to build understanding of the processes connecting human activity and environmental change....[A]n inter-disciplinary environmental social science—a field that examines the environmental effects of the driving forces—is not yet organized. There is a critical need for support of the research that would constitute that field" (Stern et al. 1992, p. 95).

"These elements form a dynamic, interactive system. Over decades or centuries, human societies adapt to their environments as well as influence them; human values tend to promote behavior consistent with adaptation; and values and social organization affect the way humans respond to global change, which may be by changing social organizations, values, or the environment itself" (Stern et al. 1992, p. 102).

National Green Plans

"[T]he federal government...will promote new directions in scientific exploration of both domestic and global environmental problems, the goal being an integrated, ecosystem-based understanding" (Canada 1990, p. 149).

"We live in a complex and integrated environment. All creatures, including humans, interact with and depend on each other. They all draw on the materials and energy of the physical environment to obtain food and recycle wastes. They all affect each other's behavior. In the past, responses to environmental problems paid very little attention to these important inter-relationships. Today, the increasing number and complexity of environmental issues demand that we adopt a more integrated approach" (Canada 1990, p. 18).

APPENDIX B: CALLS FOR INTERDISCIPLINARITY

Santa Fe Workshop on Global Change

"[T]he scale and complexity of global problems requires collaboration among scientists in different disciplines (Brown and Roughgarden 1990, p. 176).

"Conducting ecological research that includes humans calls for increased collaboration among ecologists and social scientists" (Brown and Roughgarden 1990, p. 178).

Sustainable Biosphere Initiative (Ecological Society of America)

"Addressing the topic of sustainable ecological systems will require integration of social, physical, and biological science" (Lubchenco et al. 1991, p. 375).

"Successful implementation of the SBI will require a significant increase in interdisciplinary interactions (Lubchenco et al. 1991, p. 375).

"The establishment of new interdisciplinary connections will facilitate the advancement of ecological understanding" (Lubchenco et al. 1991, p. 378).

"Advances in the physical, chemical, biological, or social sciences are interdependent.... Advances in the political, social, and economic spheres, in agronomy and resource management, as well as in ecology are needed" (Lubchenco et al. 1991, pp. 378, 392).

"[I]nteractions with other disciplines are necessary for a truly comprehensive approach to urgent environmental problems" (Lubchenco et al. 1991, p. 379).

"[S]ustainable human use of Earth's resources will require new alliances between ecology and other disciplines" (Lubchenco et al. 1991, p. 379).

"Ecology, in many ways an interdisciplinary science itself, will play a critical role in accelerating the development of new interdisciplinary approaches" (Lubchenco et al. 1991, p. 379).

"[T]here is an urgent need to forge a new theory that explicitly incorporates economic as well as ecological principles" (Lubchenco et al. 1991, p. 390).

"To promote a sustainable biosphere ecological science must...develop interdisciplinary and multi-disciplinary approaches that integrate ecology, economics and other social sciences" (Lubchenco et al. 1991, p. 393).

"Some of the most important research topics of the coming decade will be at the interface of the social, economic, and ecological sciences. These topics include both the effects of humans on the environment and the consequences of environmental change for human populations and human well-being" (Lubchenco et al. 1991, p. 397).

"SBI proposes the formulation of an integrated research framework.... New interdisciplinary connections will be required" (Lubchenco et al. 1991, pp. 397, 377).

"To fully understand how human populations affect and are affected by ecological processes, the complex interfaces between ecology and social and economic sciences and policy analyses must be developed to a much greater extent" (Lubchenco et al. 1991, p. 398).

International Sustainable Biosphere Initiative and Related Events

"Entirely new ways of organizing research projects and implementing their findings will be needed because the sustainability of ecosystems... requires the integration of social, physical, and biological sciences" (Huntley et al. 1991, p. 8).

"[P]ossible approaches include ...stimulate the emergence of a new breed of research ecologists with training that includes not only the natural sciences but also the social sciences" (Huntley et al. 1991, p. 9).

"Here we again emphasize the need for a closer link between ecologists and our colleagues in the social sciences" (Huntley et al. 1991, p. 10).

"Ecologists and social scientists have traditionally worked separately, using dissimilar approaches to the same or related problems. Achieving sustainability of the biosphere will call upon these separate disciplines to integrate their approaches in a complementary manner" (Huntley et al. 1991, p. 12).

"[N]ew decision support systems...must bring together information on physical, biological, and socioeconomic domains" (Huntley et al. 1991, p. 12).

U.S. Man and the Biosphere Human-Dominated Systems Directorate

"[A]ssure appropriate communications and understandings across disciplines—getting scientists and policy specialists to understand each other's terminology and percepts and facilitating exchange of information is essential to successful execution of interdisciplinary activities" (Harwell et al. 1991, p. 33).

United Nations Conference on Environment and Development

"Around the terms 'environment' and 'development' entire academic and bureaucratic disciplines have been built. Within each there are subcategories of specialists who work in even narrower areas of expertise. This specialization has created an array of differences which often take the form of an unbridgeable gap; a gap which is at the heart of the dilemmas facing the organizers of the Summit" (Valentine 1991, pp. 3-4).

"Developing countries wish to see environmental, economic, and social issues considered in a comprehensive manner.... Many...argue that discussions on improving the global environment are pointless unless they focus on the social, political, and economic problems of which environmental degradation is a natural by-product" (Valentine 1991, p. 4).

"Decision-making in many countries tends to separate economic, social, and environmental factors.... Agenda 21 proposes the full integration of environmental and developmental issues for Government decision-making on economic, social, fiscal, energy, agricultural, transportation, trade, and other policies" (Agenda 21, Sect. I, ch. 8).

"Countries, schools and/or appropriate international and national institutions and organizations should...encourage cross-disciplinary university courses in fields which have an impact upon the environment" (Agenda 21, Sect. IV, ch. 36).

"Of particular importance is the need to integrate the ecological dimension into education and economics" (Strong 1992, p. 8).

Proposed National Institutes for the Environment

"The NIE will...fill critical gaps by sponsoring collaborative efforts across scientific disciplines" (CNIE 1992, p. 4).

"[M]ost significant environmental problems are complex and require an integrated, cross-disciplinary approach for solution. Research sponsored by the NIE would be organized by core problem areas [i.e., as opposed to organization by discipline] such as deforestation, biodiversity, sustainable development, and pollution prevention" (CNIE 1992, p. 5).

"The NIE would...[integrate] multi-disciplinary research efforts around core problem areas...[and] focus on critical environmental problems rather than on scientific disciplines" (CNIE 1992, p. 6).

"The NIE would promote an integrated approach to problem-solving through multi-disciplinary funding" (CNIE 1992, p. 5).

"The assembled group saw little evidence of serious thought to the need for creation of cross-disciplinary efforts that would forge new disciplines that will be required in the next century" (Howe and Hubbell 1990, p. 72).

"[A] major portion of each NIE institute support would go [to] multi-disciplinary teams that make the best use of skills, perspectives, and tools of biological, physical, engineering and policy scientists...the biological component of NIE research priorities would directly benefit and be thoroughly integrated with, economic, engineering, geophysical, and social research" (Howe 1991, p. 5).

"In a siege mentality, much of the environmental research that does occur is narrowly disciplinary, often of no consequence for meeting practical human needs, where multi-disciplinary perspectives leading to practical solutions are absolutely necessary" (Howe 1991, p. 7).

"The NIE is a more ambitious vision than either the NIH or NSF because it will promote the integration of biological, physical, engineering, and policy sciences in addressing broad environmental problems" (Howe 1991, p. 9).

"The NIE effort has four central premises....(3) a successful effort to meet broad environmental challenges must promote multi-disciplinary integration of research among the engineering, natural, and social sciences and relevant humanities; ...Because environmental challenges cut across academic and political boundaries, solutions are inherently multi-disciplinary....Many disciplines will contribute, but strictly disciplinary approaches have not, and will not, solve mammoth interdisciplinary challenges facing society" (Howe 1992, p. 2).

"Because environmental challenges cut across academic and political boundaries, solutions are inherently multidisciplinary.... Many disciplines will contribute, but strictly disciplinary approaches have not, and will not, solve mammoth interdisciplinary challenges facing society" (Howe 1992, pp. 4-5).

NSF Human Dimensions of Global Change Program

"The NAS Committee... [recommends] that [efforts] be made to initiate a mutually rewarding dialogue and basis for collaboration between social scientists and natural scientists working on global environmental change" (USMAB 1991c, pp. 1, 3).

"[D]espite the clear need for better knowledge on [general processes of response in human groups] and other points of human behavior [in respect to global change], the social science community is unlikely to provide the knowledge on its own. There are significant barriers to effective research on the human dimensions of [global environmental] change. They include the effect of disciplinary specialization, which makes interdisciplinary training difficult [and] the fact that scientists' professional incentives favor work in the mainstreams of disciplines rather than at the margins" (USMAB 1991c, p. 3).

"What can we do to break down intellectual and institutional barriers between the social sciences and the natural sciences or, for that matter, among the individual social science disciplines in the interests of deepening our understanding of global environmental change?" (Stern et al. 1992, p. vi).

"Almost all human activity has some potential relevance to global change. Researchers in a number of fields have studied human-environmental interactions, usually within the boundaries of single disciplines.... They have demonstrated that a complex of social, political, economic, technological, and cultural variables, sometimes referred to as driving forces, influences the human activities that proximately cause global change" (Stern et al. 1992, p. 2).

"Single-factor explanations of the anthropogenic sources of global environmental change are apt to be misleading, because the driving forces of global change generally act in combination with each other and the interactions are contingent on place, time, and level of analysis. Understanding the linkages is a major scientific challenge that will require developing new interdisciplinary teams" (Stern et al. 1992, p. 3).

"Interdisciplinary collaboration is essential. A high priority... should be to support problem-centered interaction among social and natural scientists" (Stern et al. 1992, p. 6).

"We recommend that proposals for substantive research... be evaluated on their ability to synthesize interdisciplinary questions" (Stern et al. 1992, p. 10).

"Special attention should be given to proposals that suggest effective methods of enhancing the partnership between the natural sciences and the social sciences or encouraging interdisciplinary research among the social sciences relating to global environmental change" (Stern et al. 1992, p. 12).

"Recommendation 4: The federal government...should establish a national fellowship program through [which] social and natural scientists...could spend up to two years interacting intensively with scientists from other disciplines, especially...across the social science-natural science divide" (Stern et al. 1992, p. 14 et. seq.).

"To the extent that resources continue to be channeled through the familiar disciplines, the disciplines look increasingly like part of the problem" (Stern et al. 1992, p. 32).

"[R]eal success in forging...alliances [between the natural and social sciences] have been few and far between, despite frequent declarations concerning the importance of interdisciplinary studies" (Stern et al. 1992, p. 42).

"The relationship between humanity and global environmental change is among the most interdisciplinary of intellectual topics.... Understanding the human dimensions of global change requires creating bridges between disciplines—both between the social and behavioral sciences and the natural sciences and between the disciplines of social and behavioral science" (Stern et al. 1992, p. 168).

"The global change research agenda, more clearly than many other topics in social science, demands interdisciplinary cooperation...the driving forces of global change involve interactions among the favored variables of all the social sciences" (Stern et al. 1992, p. 171).

National Green Plans

"[T]he Canadian Global Change Program acts to develop, coordinate and promote...comprehensive nation-wide research into all aspects of global change, including both the natural sciences and human sciences" (Canada 1990, p. 149).

APPENDIX C: RECOGNITION OF ANTHROPOGENIC ENVIRONMENTAL CHANGE IN THE COMMONS

Santa Fe Workshop on Global Change

"[T]oday [global] changes are caused by a single species, our own *Homo sapiens*.... While we know that a nuclear war will make the earth uninhabitable, we are just beginning to appreciate that the cumulative effect of our day-to-day activities might be just as severe" (Brown and Roughgarden 1990, pp. 173-174).

"*Homo sapiens* has become *the* dominant species of the planet. Humans have converted about 11% of the earth's land area, and more than 90% of certain productive habitats...to agricultural fields. Most of the remaining land, together with coastal waters and lakes is used to harvest natural resources. Two recent studies estimate that *Homo sapiens* uses 20-40% of the terrestrial primary production. [the discussion continues to consider CO_2 emissions and climate change, loss of biodiversity, and toxic wastes]" (Brown and Roughgarden 1990, p. 174).

Sustainable Biosphere Initiative (Ecological Society of America)

"Human activities are currently leading to unprecedented changes in the Earth's atmospheric, terrestrial, freshwater, and marine environments" (Lubchenco et al. 1991, p. 386).

"[A]n ecological definition of global change also must include large-scale alterations in patterns of land and water use and anthropogenic changes in environmental chemistry" (Lubchenco et al. 1991, p. 386).

"Land-use changes and other human activities have caused massive changes in the biosphere" (Lubchenco et al. 1991, p. 387).

"Virtually every ecosystem on Earth has been influenced, to some extent, by the activities of humans" (Lubchenco et al. 1991, p. 392).

International Sustainable Biosphere Initiative and Related Events

"[T]he status of our natural resources is not only changing as a result of direct human impacts...but is also being changed due to indirect effects of human activity leading to changes in the composition of the atmosphere and most likely to climate change itself" (Huntley et al 1991, p. 11).

"[I]in the past, usage patterns tended to evolve over a longer period of time and impacts were of lower intensity. Thus, decisions were often reversible and often did not limit the options of future generations. Now, impacts are greater in intensity and area" (Huntley et al. 1991, p. 12).

U.S. Man and the Biosphere Human-Dominated Systems Directorate

"There are many circumstances in which human activity has so profoundly altered the underlying ecosystems that a very different environment is created.... These processes create altered and distinct ecologies dominated by humans.... In addition, many of these areas suffer from problems arising from damage to ecological life support systems" (USMAB 1991a, p. 1).

"The goal will be explicitly to...*evaluate patterns of human uses* of environmental resources and other *anthropogenic stresses* imposed upon...ecosystems" (Harwell et al. 1991, p. 1, italic in original).

"The difficulty is that all ecosystems are affected by human activities, even those systems set aside for non-interference, and that a change in a natural stress regime itself constitutes an anthropogenic stress. Ecological sustainability goals must be set with this in mind" (Harwell et al. 1991, p. 15).

"Among anthropogenic stresses it may be useful to consider three types: a) stresses resulting from the *direct extraction* of one or more component from a system or landscape; b) stresses from the *release of residuals* into the environment; and c) *stresses induced indirectly* from the above" (Harwell et al. 1991, p. 16).

United Nations Conference on Environment and Development

"Deeply concerned by the continuing deterioration of the state of the environment and the serious degradation of the global life-support systems....Recognizing also...the global character of environmental problems, including climate change, depletion of the ozone layer, transboundary air and water pollution, the contamination of the oceans and the seas and degradation of land resources, including drought and desertification" (United Nations 1989, pp. 1-2).

"Poverty and underdevelopment compel people, in the interests of immediate survival, to overstress and destroy the resources on which their future development depends" (United Nations 1992d, p. 3).

"The deterioration of the global environment meant setbacks for both rich and poor. Air and water pollution problems, and the cancerous spread of urban poverty and blight made many developing-country cities the most polluted of the world's urban environments. Water contamination, impending shortages of supply and rising tides of toxic substances have been added to degradation of the renewable resources, loss of soil, forest cover and important species of plants and animals" (Strong 1992, p. 2).

Proposed National Institutes for the Environment

"[The mission of the Institute for Pollution Prevention and Mitigation would be] to monitor, understand, and better manage...the impact of pollution on natural and human systems and resources" (CNIE 1992, p. 8).

"Resources are [being] consumed without regard to replacement, and habitats are destroyed without really knowing what resources they hold.... [We are engaged in the] unwitting destruction of resources that are not even recognized as resources. Despite the fact that societies depend on biotic resources for food, fuel, fiber, timber, chemical products, and sources of biological pest control, living species are often treated as expendable....[We are seeing] unprecedented rates of global depletion and extinction of known and potential biotic resources" (Howe 1990, pp. 9, 10, 11).

"Ecosystems are subject to alterations which are often unplanned, undesirable, and sometimes devastating.... Humans... cause inadvertent damage to their own environment... when pollution of the air, soil, waterways, and groundwater destroy the productive base on which human civilization depends" (Howe 1990, pp. 18-19).

"[T]he pace of devastation is accelerating in developed countries like the United States. Moreover, political boundaries are permeable to the effects of environmental degradation.... Misuse of resources, and the contamination of air, rivers, oceans and groundwater and major geopolitical issues. "(Howe 1990, p. 25).

"[T]he scale of anthropogenic alteration of nature—extending to ocean currents, climatic patterns, and global resources of air and oceans—promises to present policy decisions unprecedented in the human experience" (Howe 1990, p. 31).

NSF Human Dimensions of Global Change Program

"People have always sought to transform their surroundings. However, we only now realize that producing food, providing shelter or employment, and increasing our comfort have grave side effects. We are actually changing the global environmental conditions that originally permitted our emergence as a species" (USMAB 1991c, p. 1).

"[G]lobal environmental changes of primary interest today are largely of anthropogenic origin, and include ozone depletion, loss of biological diversity, and climate change" (USMAB 1991c, p. 3).

"The earth has entered a period of hydrological, climatological, and biological change that differs from previous episodes of global change in the extent to which it is human in origin. Human beings, both individually and collectively... for the first time... have begun to play a central role in altering global biogeochemical systems and the earth as a whole" (Stern et al. 1992, p. 1).

"The global changes of greatest interest today, like ozone depletion, climate change, and the loss of biodiversity, are largely anthropogenic in origin" (Stern et al. 1992, p. 24).

"There is a need for research probing the roots of the anthropogenic sources of global change" (Stern et al. 1992, p. 41).

"Short-sighted and self-interested ways of thinking can also act as underlying causes of environmental degradation. The inexorable destruction of an exhaustible resource that is openly available to all, what Hardin called the 'tragedy of the commons,' is, at a psychological level, a logical outcome of this sort of thinking" (Stern et al. 1992, p. 90).

National Green Plans

"Where a few decades ago, local health effects and impacts on nature were in the fore, we are now also confronted with damage to the social and economic functions of the environment [i.e., the environment in its capacity as provider of common goods and services]: problems with the drinking water supply, the agricultural production capacity of the soil, forestry, and recreation" (de Jongh 1991a, p. 4).

"For the first time in history, human activity has the capacity to alter global ecosystems" (Canada 1990, p. 11).

APPENDIX D: RECOGNITION OF STRAINED SUPPORT OR CARRYING CAPACITY

Santa Fe Workshop on Global Change

This theme was not identified by the Workshop.

Sustainable Biosphere Initiative (Ecological Society of America)

"The growing human population and its increasing use and misuse of resources are exerting tremendous pressures on Earth's life support capacity" (Lubchenco et al. 1991, p. 373).

"Human activities may have unanticipated or indirect effects on parts of the Earth's life support systems" (Lubchenco et al. 1991, p. 377).

"Human population growth and human activities have profound effects on the environment" (Lubchenco et al. 1991, p. 384).

International Sustainable Biosphere Initiative and Related Events

"Ultimately, we must address the question of most fundamental importance: that of the Earth's human supporting capacity. This must be accepted as a valid and urgent research priority" (Huntley et al. 1991, p. 12).

"Sustainable development was defined as the maintenance or enhancement of the productive and regenerative capacity of the environment.... [It] depends on maintaining the health of [the] responsive capacities [of environmental systems]. These capacities are currently under serious stress, which in the long-term threatens natural environments and the human populations that depend upon them.... Scientific data on... the capacity of ecological systems to resist insult and to recover... provide a firm basis for our concern and action" (INTECOL 1991b, p. 2).

"Members participating in ASCEND recommended intensified research into natural and anthropogenic forces and their interrelationships, including the carrying capacity of the Earth and ways to slow population growth and reduce overconsumption" (INTECOL 1992, p. 1).

U.S. Man and the Biosphere Human-Dominated Systems Directorate

"[N]not only is the natural ecosystem profoundly and adversely altered, but the consequences for the human inhabitants threaten their health, their well-being, and ultimately often threaten the very objectives for which the modifications were made in the first place, e.g., cities that become unhealthy habitats, agriculture that loses productivity. The carrying capacity of natural systems, and the viability of various types of human interventions need to be better understood" (USMAB 1991a, p. 1).

"[T]he Directorate will emphasize...how ecosystem modification creates stress and how stress affects ecosystems" (USMAB 1991a, p. 3).

"The goal will be explicitly to: *define ecological sustainability...* specified in terms of particular levels of selected ecological endpoints [i.e., carrying capacity thresholds]" (Harwell et al. 1991, p. 1).

"At some point the effects of the anthropogenic contribution to the stress come to be judged by society as reaching an undesirable or pathologic state....Human population density, as well as the nature and intensity of human use of the system, is a key element of whether the contributor to stress reaches a level judged as significant" (Harwell et al. 1991, pp. 16-17).

United Nations Conference on Environment and Development

"Deeply concerned...by trends that, if allowed to continue, could disrupt the global ecological balance, jeopardize the life-sustaining qualities of the earth and lead to an ecological catastrophe" (United Nations 1989 p. 1).

"The earth cannot provide infinite natural resources or endlessly assimilate our wastes" (United Nations 1992d, p. 2).

"We need to value the carrying and absorptive capacities of the earth's natural systems...if we are going to maintain them" (United Nations 1992d, p. 2).

"The relationship between population dynamics and the ecosystems on which the survival and well-being of people depend is decisive in achieving sustainable development" (United Nations 1992d, p. 3).

"Poor people in search of day-to-day sustenance and impoverished nations in need of export earnings to service their debt overexploit their natural resources" (United Nations 1992e, p. 1).

"New concepts of wealth and prosperity should be developed which allow higher standards of living through changed lifestyles that are less dependent on the earth's finite resources and more in harmony with its carrying capacity" (Agenda 21, Sect I, ch. 4).

"The growth of world population and production combined with unsustainable consumption patterns has put increasingly severe stress on the life-supporting capacity of the planet" (Agenda 21, Sect. I, ch. 5).

"Strategies for sustainable development must be based on an accurate assessment of the earth's carrying capacity and resilience to human activity. A deeper understanding of the interconnections between water, nutrient and biogenic cycles and the energy flows of land, oceans and atmosphere is crucial.... Knowledge of the earth's carrying capacity and processes that impair or enhance its ability to support life should be enhanced.... Regular standardized audits of carrying capacity and vulnerable resources are needed at the national, regional, and global levels" (Agenda 21, Sect IV, ch. 35).

"Each country must determine the relationship between the growth and distribution of its own population, its environment and resource base, and the quality of life its development policies and programs are designed to produce for its people" (Strong 1992, p. 8).

Proposed National Institutes for the Environment

"Ecosystem processes provide the soil on which our crops, pastures, and timber resources grow, the air that we breath, the means of ameliorating carbon dioxide build-up, the accumulation, dispersion, and concentration of toxins, and the stability of recreation resources. The Institute for Ecosystem Management and Restoration would support research that explored, monitored, and restored the productive capacity of natural and managed ecosystems" (Howe 1991, p. 8).

"The habitability of the earth is threatened by accelerating environmental change" (Howe 1990, p. 5).

"[O]ur species is reducing the productive capacity of the ecological systems upon which it depends. Many forests, farmlands, lakes, and oceans no longer produce what they once could, while the urban areas that house most of our citizens foul the air, drinking water, and groundwater upon which they directly or indirectly depend. Moreover, as the human population continues to climb, degradation of land and water ecosystems continues a needless and accelerated depreciation of contemporary and future resources. Mindless destruction of productive capacity occurs when human activities irrevocably alter ecosystems without knowledge or understanding of the processes involved.... The human species is not just fouling its nest; it is dismantling it" (Howe 1990, p. 19).

"[We] must...manage ecological systems in ways that derive the greatest possible yields while maintaining the regulatory function of interactions between living and non-living components of the environment" (Howe 1990, pp. 19-20).

"In the United States and abroad, many ecosystems are often stressed by human activities—often to the point of failure in their capacity to support human endeavors" (Howe 1990, p. 25).

NSF Human Dimensions of Global Change Program

This theme was not identified.

National Green Plans

"The main objective of the policy plan is to preserve the carrying capacity of the environment in order to realize sustainable development" (Netherlands 1990, p. 2).

"The carrying capacity of the environment is being affected.... Apart from population growth itself (at the global level) almost all human activities are currently damaging environmental values to some extent: traffic, agriculture, energy supply, building, households, recreation" (de Jongh 1991a, p. 4).

"[E]conomic activities... are overloading much of the world's environment. Deforestation, pollution and extinction of wildlife species are but a few of the well-known consequences of human activity. In turn, as the environment becomes less healthy, the health of individuals and the economy can be adversely affected" (Canada 1990, p. 27).

"[O]ur water, land and air have a finite capacity to absorb waste safely; we must not overburden them. We should not exploit renewable resources such as farmland, fish stocks and forests more rapidly than they can replenish themselves" (Canada 1990, p. 16).

"[O]ur diminishing pool of environmental assets will simply not support more of the resource-hungry kind of prosperity that dominates in developed nations" (Canada 1990, p. 5).

APPENDIX E: CALLS FOR SUSTAINABILITY

Santa Fe Workshop on Global Change

This theme was not identified in the workshop.

Sustainable Biosphere Initiative (Ecological Society of America)

"Research Recommendation #3:   A major new integrated program of research on the sustainability of ecological systems should be established. This program would focus on understanding the underlying ecological processes in natural and human-dominated ecosystems in order to prescribe restoration and management strategies that would enhance the sustainability of the Earth's ecological systems" (Lubchenco et al. 1991, p. 374).

"Current research efforts are inadequate for dealing with sustainable systems that involve multiple resources, multiple ecosystems, and large spatial scales" (Lubchenco et al. 1991, p. 374).

"The sustainability of ecological systems is one of the greatest challenges facing human society, yet it is the one that has received the least attention to date...we call for a greatly accelerated and expanded effort toward developing sustainable ecological systems" (Lubchenco et al. 1991, p. 379).

"[H]uman use of...resources must be made sustainable" (Lubchenco et al. 1991, p. 392).

International Sustainable Biosphere Initiative and Related Events

"The central goal [is] to facilitate the acquisition, dissemination, and utilization of ecological knowledge to ensure the sustainability of the biosphere" (Huntley et al. 1991, p. 7).

U.S. Man and the Biosphere Human-Dominated Systems Directorate

"The activities [of the Directorate] will focus on the central theme of *ecological sustainability,* defining precisely what that means ecologically and examining a variety of human institutions and policies that impinge upon it....The goal will be explicitly to: *define ecological sustainability...; examine societal and institutional factors* influencing ecological sustainability; and *assess their compatibility* with essential characteristics of ecological sustainability" (Harwell et al. 1991, p. 1).

"We believe [that] specification of ecological endpoints and sustainability targets is an essential first step in establishing management policies to protect ecological resources" (Harwell et al. 1991, p. 3).

United Nations Conference on Environment and Development

"[T]he Conference should elaborate strategies and measures to halt and reverse the effects of environmental degradation in the context of strengthened national and international efforts to promote sustainable and environmentally sound development in all countries" (United Nations 1989 p. 3).

"The transition to sustainability is the only way to revitalize the development process" (United Nations 1992d, p. 1).

"Sustainable development cannot be imposed by external pressures; it must be rooted in the culture, the values, the interests and the priorities of the people concerned" (Strong 1992, p. 8).

Proposed National Institutes for the Environment

"[The mission of the Institute for Sustainable Resources and Development would be] to understand the sustainable use of energy, land, soil, water, mineral, and biotic resources" (CNIE 1992, p. 8).

"The NIE charter would be to ensure the integrity of the earth's ecosystems by achieving a healthy and sustainable relationship between human societies and the natural world of which they are a part, and upon which they depend" (Howe 1990, p. 5).

"Societies throughout history have repeatedly misjudged the economic burden of mining potentially renewable resources to exhaustion" (Howe 1990, p. 9).

NSF Human Dimensions of Global Change Program

This theme was not identified.

National Green Plans

"The Netherlands decided to make sustainable development the cornerstone of its integral approach to the environmental question" (Netherlands n.d., p. 17).

"With a reference to the report of the World Commission on Environment and Development (Brundtland), the NEPP has sustainable development as the leading principle" (Netherlands 1990, p. 1).

"The Government...supports the principle of sustainable development" (United Kingdom 1990, p. 47).

"While Canadians accept the merits of sustainable development, we understand it is a philosophy, not an action plan" (Canada 1990, p. 5).

APPENDIX F: OBJECTIVES TO AFFECT ENVIRONMENTAL POLICY AND DECISION-MAKING

Santa Fe Workshop on Global Change

"A new agency is...urgently needed to monitor the ecological state of the nation, and to provide synthetic products to scientists, the general public, and the legislative and executive branches of the government" (Brown and Roughgarden 1990, p. 180).

"[T]he formation of a multi-disciplinary agency, to be called the National Institutes of the Environment (NIE), seems warranted now. The NIE might have five institutes: the U.S. Ecological Survey, an Institute of Basic Ecology, an Institute of Applied Environmental Sciences, an Institute of Human Demography, and an Institute of Sustainable Economics" (Brown and Roughgarden 1990, p. 183).

Sustainable Biosphere Initiative (Ecological Society of America).

"Citizens, policy-makers, resource managers, and leaders of business and industry all need to make decisions concerning the Earth's resources, but such decisions cannot be made without a fundamental understanding of the ways in which the natural systems of Earth are affected by human activities" (Lubchenco et al. 1991, p. 373).

"The SBI calls for the incorporation of [ecological] knowledge into policy and management decisions" (Lubchenco et al. 1991, p. 373).

"Thousands of ecologically based decisions are made annually by policy-makers and regulatory agencies, land and water use planners, resource managers, business and industry, consulting firms, and conservation groups. To be useful to decision-makers, ecological information must be both accessible and relevant" (Lubchenco et al. 1991, p. 375).

International Sustainable Biosphere Initiative and Related Events

"Ecologists must be joined by policy makers, resource managers.... The ISBI... must also link the actions of global decision-makers with those of rural peasants" (Huntley et al. 1991, p. 8).

"The knowledge generated by such studies must be incorporated into policy on and management of natural resources. The development and application of decision-support systems... will be an integral and ongoing component of the program" (Huntley et al. 1991, p. 10).

"Our research program... must also be related to the scale at which management decisions are made" (Huntley et al. 1991, p. 10).

"There is a need for new decision support systems. These systems must bring together information on physical, biological, and socioeconomic domains" (Huntley et al. 1991, p. 12).

U.S. Man and the Biosphere Human-Dominated Systems Directorate

"[Human-Dominated Systems Directorate] research topics include... human decision-making processes and institutions related to ecosystem management... the Directorate will emphasize... environmental management and policy [and] effects on ecosystems of integrating political, social, and environmental factors into decision-making" (USMAB 1991a, pp. 2-3).

"Eventually [the Directorate Core Project] conceptual model will form the basis for an explicitly coupled human systems/ecological systems simulation model designed for use in examining alternative policies" (Harwell et al. 1991, p. 1).

United Nations Conference on Environment and Development

"[Conference objectives include] development and implementation of policies for sustainable and environmentally sound development;...to promote the further development of international law;...to [arrive] at specific agreements and commitments by Governments and by inter-governmental organizations;...to recommend measures to Governments and the relevant bodies of the United Nations;...to promote the development or strengthening of appropriate institutions" (United Nations 1989, pp. 5-7).

"[B]etter communication among scientists, decision-makers, and the general public should be established as part of policy-making" (Agenda 21, Sect. IV, ch. 35).

"The main task of the Rio Conference of 1992 will be to move environment and the development issues into the center of economic policy and decision-making" (United Nations 1992a, p. 4).

"[A]ddressing common global concerns...will require serious examination of the need to extend into the international arena the rule of law and the principle of taxation to finance agreed actions which provide the basis for governance at the national level" (Strong 1992, p. 6).

"The expectation is that the presence of leaders, and representatives of the people they serve, will generate the kind of political will required to take bold decisions" (Strong 1992, p. 3).

"[I]mproving the mechanisms by which science makes available its advice and guidance to policy- and decision-makers...will be significant" (Strong 1992, p. 5).

Proposed National Institutes for the Environment

"A serious gulf exists between what scientists know and what the public and policy-makers understand. The NIE would provide a system whereby policy-makers can articulate research needs, and research is coordinated and made accessible to policy-makers" (CNIE 1992, p. 4).

"[The mission of the Office of Environmental Education would be] to...inform...policy-makers of the current state of the national and global environment, and of progress toward solutions to environmental problems" (CNIE 1992, p. 9).

"The NIE would improve upon the NIH model by directly linking science and policy research.... The objective of the NIE is to ensure that sound natural and policy science underpins environmental policy" (Howe 1991, pp. 3-4).

"[E]ngineering, natural, and social sciences of ... importance to understanding and mitigating environmental problems experience ... neglect ... communication of technical results to policy-makers receives negligible support ..., even good science in quantity, communicated only through the technical literature, does not and probably cannot provide what is needed by society and lawmakers in a timely fashion" (Howe 1992, pp. 3, 4).

"By bringing engineering, natural, and social scientists into direct interaction far more than existing programs do, or attempt to do, the NIE will ensure that policy options square with technical and physical reality, and that the social, human, and economic implications of technical fixes are understood; By focusing social and policy sciences on environmental issues, the NIE will ensure that human alternatives are well-reasoned and well-known, allowing a prescriptive rather than ad hoc response to environmental change.... By translating technical results into language that makes both the facts and implications of environmental research clear, NIE will provide what policymakers... require to create, debate, and support rational policy" (Howe 1992, pp. 14-15).

"NIE objectives are [to] improve environmental research and policy decision-making by improving the process of identifying and ranking problems to set a national environmental agenda" (Howe 1990, p. 7).

"[I]t will be necessary to overcome barriers to the use of scientific information in public and private decision-making and to develop a decision-making calculus that takes into account different kinds of information—scientific, technical, socioeconomic, and political" (Howe 1990, p. 29).

NSF Human Dimensions of Global Change Program

"[We] need to build stronger links between the natural sciences and the social sciences in efforts to understand global environmental changes and to devise public policies to respond to them in an effective manner" (Stern et al. 1992, p. 21).

"[F]eedback process, including policy responses... may mitigate or accelerate natural processes" (Stern et al. 1992, p. 22).

"[H]uman causes of global environmental change quite often depend on decisions made and actions taken without any consideration of the global environment" (Stern et al. 1992, p. 33).

"[S]ocial science can help global change research by... soliciting appropriate outputs for decision-making and policy analysis" (Stern et al. 1992, pp. 169-170).

National Green Plans

"[Strategy #50 of the Netherlands National Environmental Policy Plan is:] Integration of environmental aspects into all relevant national government policy areas" (de Jongh 1991b, p. 3).

"[T]he principles of the environmental policy must be incorporated in other government policies, e.g., on agriculture, traffic, industry, energy, construction, education, the police and in other areas...it was decided to identify several important target groups in environmental policy for whom a special approach would be developed.... The Netherlands has attempted to work out environmental policy in cooperation with the target groups and the authorities concerned.... The instruments of Netherlands environmental policy include legislation; voluntary agreements formally laid down; financial incentives; enforcement, including sanctions; public information, education, and communication" (Netherlands n.d., pp. 21, 37, 45).

"The National Environmental Policy Plan (NEPP) was the first comprehensive, integrated, strategic approach towards environmental management in The Netherlands. Through a 'Government Statement' the Dutch cabinet in 1989 acknowledged the importance of sound environmental policy development and implementation by assigning the environment as the third focal point in policy development at the national level" (Netherlands 1990, p. 1).

"No longer was the issue 'How can we change our environmental policies a little?' but 'How can we change not only our environmental policies, but also the government's policies in general?'" (de Jongh 1991a, p. 4).

"The Government of Canada is prepared to show leadership on environmental matters. The Government will continue to define policy on national environmental issues and to advance Canada's environmental interests in the international community" (Canada 1990, p. 17).

"[W]e must all change the way we make decisions and the way we see our own activities in relation to the environment" (Canada 1990, p. 12).

NOTES

1.   This review encompasses a variety of programs, plans, initiatives, agendas, conferences, and institutional proposals. For the sake of bravity, all of these are included within the term "program" in the following discussion.

2.   Other themes, such as calls to preserve biodiversity, to establish a national environmental data base, or for environmental education are also found in most of the programs reviewed below, but are not considered in this paper. The selection of extracts found in the appendices are not intended to be exhaustive, but only to establish the extent to which these themes permeate the programs reviewed.

3.   The workshop was commissioned by the National Science Foundation (NSF) and Department of Energy (DOE) to consider an ecological research agenda to cope with global change.

4.   Young (1974) identifies numerous other such formulations during the 1950s and 1960s which are not cited here.

5.   Here is another instance of poor scholarship; the idea of "limits to growth" can be traced back to Leibig's "law of the minimum" as well as to the founders of political economics—Adam Smith, T.R. Malthus, and David Ricardo.

6.   Brundtland defines sustainable development as "development that seeks to meet the needs and aspirations of the present without compromising the ability to meet those of the future" (WCED 1987, p. 43).

7. This despite an introductory presentation of human ecology given at the 1989 ESA meeting by the United States Society for Human Ecology and Institute for Human Ecology (Borden and Pratt 1989) the year before the SBI was presented to the ESA membership.

8. The term endpoints is somewhat misleading, as there is nothing of the nature of an "end" in them. These are defined as "specific characteristics or properties of ecosystems that are used for evaluating ecological health" and are measured by "ecological indicators." In some cases, they appear to be very similar to carrying capacity thresholds; in other cases they are merely parameters of interest or are not specified well enough to determine precisely what is measured (Harwell et al. 1991, *passim*).

9. Indeed, one statement appears to reduce the broad topic of "human/biosphere problems" to nothing more than "externality problems in economics" (Harwell et al. 1991, p. a-15).

10. Brown and Roughgarden (1989) call for a "multi-disciplinary agency, to be called the National Institutes of the Environment (NIE)" in their report on the Santa Fe workship discussed above, but this is neither cited nor incorporated in the NIE materials.

11. A very illuminating discussion by Howe and Hubbell (1990) of disciplinary antagonisms encountered in the development of the NIE proposal mirrors the kind of difficulties which have beset attempts by human ecologists to sort out their field (see, e.g., Pratt and Young 1990).

12. Additional funding was supplied by the MacArthur Foundation, the NRC Fund, and the U.S. Geological Survey.

13. The "human response systems" include individual perception, judgement, and action; markets; sociocultural systems; organized responses at the subnational level, such as by communities, social movements, corporations, and so forth; national politics; international cooperation; and global social change.

14. Stern et al. write: "Human ecology incorporates...regional, local, and historical concerns but also attempts to integrate micro-social phenomena and social interactions into an understanding of human-environment relations and draws on evolutionary approaches to social and environmental change" (1992, p. 39).

15. The analogous characteristics identified include: complex interdependencies leading to unanticipated consequences; nonlinear responses triggered when thresholds are crossed, so that small perturbations can have huge effects; irreversible changes; long lag times; and interactions of local systems with relationships across spatial scales.

16. The Brundtland Report was also cited as seminal for the Canadian (Canada 1990) and Austrian (Schreiber 1992) plans, and of course the Norwegian (Hofseth 1992) "green plan." The Austrian plan cites, in addition, the influence of the Club of Rome *Limits to Growth* report. The Canadian plan, like the Dutch, is rooted in a nationwide process involving every sector of society— described as a "national multi-stakeholder consultation process"—and a 1990 background paper, *A Framework for Discussion on the Environment* (Canada 1990).

17. It will immediately be argued that American democracy is based on "prior collective choice," but in fact, frontier Americans are strongly resistent to the recognition of commons let alone the circumscription of individual choice by "prior collective choice; in the regulation of what may—and what may not—be done with commons resources, a fact made all too clear by our recent sorry cameo appearance at Rio.

18. The others are acidification, euthrophication, diffusion (of toxic and radioactive substances), waste disposal, disturbance (affecting the quality of life), climate change, and groundwater overdrafts.

19. These include agriculture, transport, energy supply, industry in general, the chemical industry, the building trades, research and education institutes, consumers and retailers, and the environmental trade.

20. Throughout this section (as throughout the entire paper), a potentially troublesome confusion of language arises in that two things both going under the name "human ecology" must be referenced and kept distinct. On the one hand is the field of human ecology with its body of

literature and practioners who call themselves human ecologists. On the other hand is the practice itself, "applied human ecology," which can be recognized throughout the programs reviewed in this paper though they themselves do not call that practice by its proper name. At the risk of being somewhat pedantic and verbose, I make every effort here to clearly separate the field from the practice.

REFERENCES

Arler, F. 1991a. "Justice in the Greenhouse: Dimensions of a Greenhouse Ethic." Paper presented at Universitet Göteborg and Royal Swedish Academy of Sciences International Conference on Human Ecology, Human Responsibility and Global Change, Göteborg, Sweden, June 9-14, 1991.

_____. 1991b. "Reflections on Humans' Place in Nature." Pp. 63-69 in *Human Ecology: Strategies for the Future. Selected papers from the Fourth Conference of the Society for Human Ecology, Michigan State University, East Lansing, Michigan, April 20-22, 1990*, edited by S. Sontag, S. Wright, G. Young, and M. Grace. Fort Collins, CO: Society for Human Ecology.

Borden, R., and J. Pratt. 1989. "An Agenda for Human Ecologists in a Time of Global Change." Paper presented at the 1989 Annual Meeting of the Ecological Society of America, University of Toronto, Canada, August 6-10.

Boyden, S. 1986. "An Integrative Approach to the Study of Human Ecology." Pp. 3-25 in *Human Ecology: A Gathering of Perspectives. Selected Papers from the First International Conference of the Society for Human Ecology*, edited by R.J. Borden, G.L. Young, and J. Jacobs. Fort Collins, CO: Society for Human Ecology.

Brewer, C.A., K.M. Doyle, J.J. Honaker, J.C. Krumm, W.F.J. Parsons, and T.T. Schulz. 1992. "The Sustainable Biosphere Initiative: A Student Critique and Call to Action." *Bulletin of the Ecological Society of America* 73(1): 23-25.

Brown, J.H., and J. Roughgarden. 1990. "Ecology for a Changing Earth." Technical report accompanying "In Our Hands: Survival on Earth," by J. Roughgarden, J. Brown, E. Lehman, B. Mendelsohn, and J. Unruh, released by Stanford University, 1989. Reprinted in *Bulletin of the Ecological Society of America* 71(1): 173-188.

Canada, Ministry of the Environment. 1990. *Canada's Green Plan for a Healthy Environment.* Ottawa: Ministry of the Environment.

Carpenter, W. 1988. "Human Ecology: The Possibility of an Aesthetic Science." Pp. 1-8 *Human Ecology: Research and Applications. Selected Papers from the Second International Conference of the Society for Human Ecology*, edited by in R.J. Borden, J. Jacobs, and G.L. Young. Fort Collins, CO: Society for Human Ecology.

_____. 1989. "House Logic: Myth and Art in Human Ecology." Paper presented at the Beatrice Paolucci Symposium, Ecological Decision-making for the Future: Interdependence of Public and Private Spheres, Michigan State University, East Lansing, January 19-21, 1989.

Committee for the National Institutes for the Environment (CNIE). 1992. *National Institutes for the Environment: A Proposal.* Washington, DC: Committee for the National Institutes for the Environment.

Crowe, B. 1969. "The Tragedy of the Commons Revisited." *Science* 166: 1103-1107.

Daysh, Z. 1988. "The Work of the Commonwealth Human Ecology Council." Pp. 19-32 in *Human Ecology: Research and Applications. Selected Papers from the Second International Conference of the Society for Human Ecology*, edited by R.J. Borden, J. Jacobs, and G.L. Young. Fort Collins, CO: Society for Human Ecology.

de Jongh, P. (Head, Office for Strategic Planning, Directorate General for Environmental Protection, Ministry of Housing, Physical Planning, and the Environment, The Hague).

1991a. "The Dutch Environmental Policy Plan." Paper presented at Advanced Environmental Sanitation: Environmental Policy and Management Tools conference, International Institute for Hydraulic and Environmental Engineering, Delft, The Netherlands, March 7, 1991.

_____. 1991b. "The Promotion of External Integration in Environmental Policies in The Netherlands." Paper presented at Global Pollution Prevention '91 conference.

_____. 1992. "The Netherlands National Environmental Policy Plan." Paper presented at Green Plans: National Policies Toward a Green Century, An International Environmental Workshop, sponsored by Resource Renewal Institute, March 5-7, 1992, San Rafael, CA.

Dietz, T. 1992. Testimony to the U.S. House of Representatives Committee on Science, Space and Technology, Subcommittee on Environment. Human Ecology Research Group, Department of Sociology and Anthropology, George Mason University. May 5, 1992.

Doherty, J., and A.W. Cooper. 1990. "The Short Life and Early Death of the Institute of Ecology: A Case Study in Institution Building." *Bulletin of the Ecological Society of America* 71: 6-17.

Duncan, O.D., 1959. "Human Ecology and Population Studies." Pp. 681-710 in *The Study of Population: An Inventory and Appraisal*, edited by O.D. Duncan and P.M. Hauser. Chicago: University of Chicago Press.

Ehrlich, P.R. 1985. "Human Ecology for Introductory Biology Courses: An Overview." *American Zoologist* 25: 379-394.

Ehrlich, P.R., and A.H. Ehrlich, 1970. *Populations, Resources, Environment: Issues in Human Ecology*. San Francisco: W.H. Freeman.

Ehrlich, P.R., A.H. Ehrlich, and J.P. Holdren. 1977. *Ecoscience: Populations, Resources, Environment*. San Francisco: W.H. Freeman.

Fulton, D. 1992. "Applying the Conceptual Framework for an Interdisciplinary Human Ecology: The Problem of Cross-cultural Land Ethics." Paper presented at the 4th North American Symposium on Society and Resource Management, Madison, WI, May 17-20.

Hardin, G. 1968. "The Tragedy of the Commons." *Science* 162: 1243-1248.

Harwell, M.A., P. Bradt, W. Chang, J. Hadidian, J. Long, O. Loucks, R. Walker, and J. Wilson. 1991. *Ecological Sustainability and Human Institutions: Case Studies of Three Biosphere Reserves*. Washington, DC: U.S. Man and the Biosphere core project for Human Dominated Systems Directorate.

Hofseth, P. (Special Advisor, Ministry of Environment, Oslo). 1992. "Norway: Follow-up to 'Our Common Future.'" Paper presented at Green Plans: National Policies Toward a Green Century, an International Environmental Workshop sponsored by Resource Renewal Institute, March 5-7, San Rafael, CA.

Howe, H.F. 1990. "National Institutes for the Environment: A Needs Statement.' Testimony of H.F. Howe before the Senate Committee on the Environment and Public Works, 24 April.

_____. 1991. "One Alternative to Environmental Paralysis: The National Institutes for the Environment (NIE)." Unpublished manuscript.

_____. 1992. "Rationale for the National Institutes for the Environment (NIE)." Unpublished manuscript.

Howe, H.F., and S.P. Hubbell. 1990. "Towards the National Institutes for the Environment." *Global Environmental Change* 1(1): 71-74.

Huntley, B.J., E. Ezcurra, E.R. Fuentes, K. Fujii, P.J. Grubb, W. Haber, J.R.E. Harger, M.M. Holland, S.A. Levin, J. Lubchenco, H.A. Mooney, V. Neronov, I. Noble, H.R. Pulliam, P.S. Ramakrishnan, P.G. Risser, O. Sala, J. Sarukhan, and W.G. Sombroek. 1991. "A Sustainable Biosphere: The Global Imperative." Report from the International Sustainable Biosphere Initiative Workshop, Cuernavaca, Mexico, June. *Ecology International* 20(special issue): 5-14.

INTECOL. 1991a. "Editorial: The International Sustainable Biosphere Initiative." *INTECOL Newsletter* 21(3): 3.

INTECOL. 1991b. "Statement of INTECOL/IUBS Workshop on Sustainable Development, 15-17 November 1991, Paris." *INTECOL Newsletter* 21(3): 2-5.

INTECOL. 1992. "ASCEND-21 Recommendations for Earth Summit." *INTECOL Newsletter* 22(1): 1-2.

Janetos, AC. 1992. "The Sustainable Biosphere Initiative and the Federal Agencies." *Bulletin of the Ecological Society of America* 73(1): 25-28.

Jungen, B., 1986. "Integration of Knowledge in Human Ecology." Pp. 26-44 in *Human Ecology: A Gathering of Perspectives. Selected Papers from the First International Conference of the Society for Human Ecology*, edited by R.J. Borden, G.L. Young, and J. Jacobs. Fort Collins, CO: Society for Human Ecology.

Kuhn, T. 1970. *The Structure of Scientific Revolutions*. Foundations of the Unity of Science, Vol. 2(2). 2nd ed. Chicago: University of Chicago Press.

Lindemann, E.C. 1940. "Ecology: An Instrument for the Integration of Science and Philosophy." *Ecological Monographs* 10(3): 367-372.

Liverman, D.M. 1991. "Global Change and Mexico." *Earth and Mineral Sciences* 60: 71-76.

Lubchenco, J., A.M. Olson, L.B. Brubaker, S.R. Carpenter, M.M. Holland, S.P. Hubbell, S.A. Levin, J.A. MacMahon, P.A. Matson, J.M. Melillo, H.A. Mooney, C.H. Peterson, H.R. Pulliam, L.A. Real, P.J. Regal, and P.G. Risser. 1991. "The Sustainable Biosphere Initiative: An Ecological Research Agenda." Ecological Society of America Committee for a Research Agenda for the 1990's. *Ecology* 72(2): 371-412.

McCarthy, T. 1992. "Akio Morita's Voice of Reason." P. 12 in "World Press Review" (April). (From *The Independent* of London, quoting an article from the February issue of *Bungei Shunju*.)

McCay, B.J., and J.M. Acheson. 1988. *The Question of the Commons: Culture and Ecology of Communal Resources*. Tucson: University of Arizona Press.

Meeker, J.W. 1980. *The Comedy of Survival: In Search of an Environmental Ethic*. Los Angeles: Guild of Tutors Press.

National Science Foundation (NSF). 1992a. *Human Dimensions of Global Change: Program Announcement*. Washington, DC: NSF Division of Social and Economic Science.

National Science Foundation. 1992b. *Directorate for Biological, Behavioral and Social Science, Division of Social and Economic Science: Program Announcement*. Washington, DC: NSF.

The Netherlands. 1990. *Summary of the Dutch Environmental Policy Plan*. The Hague: Ministry of Housing, Physical Planning and the Environment.

The Netherlands. n.d. *Environmental Policy in the Netherlands*. The Hague: Ministry of Housing, Physical Planning and the Environment.

Norway, Ministry of Environment. 1989. *Report to the Storting No. 46 (1988-89), Environment and Development: Programme for Norway's Follow-up of the Report of the World Commission on Environment and Development.*

Pratt, J. 1988. "The Revolution in Human Ecology." Institute for Human Ecology Briefing Paper, Spring.

————. 1989. "The Need for a Program to Develop Human Ecology and Apply It to Decision-making and Public Policy." *Human Ecology Bulletin* 6(Fall/Winter): 19-22

————. 1991. "Towards an 'Ecology of Knowing.'" Paper presented at Universitet Göteborg and Royal Swedish Academy of Sciences International Conference on Human Ecology, Human Responsibility and Global Change, Göteborg, Sweden, June 9-14.

————. 1992. "Young's Conceptual Framework for an Interdisciplinary Human Ecology: A Critical Review." *Journal of Human Ecology* 3: 501-520.

_____. 1993. "Ecology of Knowing: A Brief Conceptual Statement." Pp. 94-103 in *Human Ecology: Crossing Boundaries, Selected Papers from the Sixth Conference of the Society for Human Ecology,* edited by S.D. Wright, T. Dietz, R. Borden, G. Young, and G. Guagnaro. Fort Collins, CO: Society for Human Ecology.

_____ In press. "Facilitating Paradigm Emergence in Human Ecology." *Human Ecology and Decision-making: An International and Interdisciplinary Collaboration. Proceedings of the Society for Human Ecology Third International Conference,* Vol. II, edited by J. Pratt, G. Young, and R. Borden. Fort Collins, CO: Society for Human Ecology.

Pratt, J., and G.L. Young. 1990. *Human Ecology: Steps to the Future. Proceedings of the Third International Conference of the Society for Human Ecology,* October 7-9, 1988, Golden Gate National Recreation Area, San Francisco, CA.

Redford, K.H., and S.E. Sanderson. 1992. "The Brief, Barren Marriage of Biodiversity and Sustainability?" *Bulletin of the Ecological Society of America* 73(1): 36-39.

Rothenburg, D. 1990. "The Greenhouse from Down Deep: What Can Philosophy Do for Ecology?" Paper presented at the Fourth Conference of the Society for Human Ecology, Michigan State University, East Lansing, MI, April 20-22.

_____. In press. "Parabola of Being, Song of Existence: Toward a Poetic Conception of Human Action." In *Human Ecology and Decision-making: An International and Interdisciplinary Collaboration. Proceedings of the Society for Human Ecology Third International Conference,* Vol. II, edited by J. Pratt, G. Young, and R. Borden. Fort Collins, CO: Society for Human Ecology.

Schreiber, H. (Director General of the Ministry of the Environment, Youth, and Family, Vienna). 1992. "Premises and Perspectives for the Development of a National Environmental Plan in Austria." Paper presented at Green Plans: National Policies Toward a Green Century, International Environmental Workshop sponsored by Resource Renewal Institute, March 5-7, San Rafael, CA.

Skolimowski, H. 1991. "Ecological Consciousness as a Missing Dimension of Human Ecology." Pp. 70-83 in IHuman Ecology: Strategies for the Future. Selected Papers from the Fourth Conference of the Society for Human Ecology, Michigan State University, East Lansing, Michigan, April 20-22, edited by S. Sontag, S. Wright, G. Young, and M. Grace. Fort Collins, CO: Society for Human Ecology.

Slater, R. (Assistant Deputy Minister of Policy for Environment Canada). 1992. "Canada: Green Plan for a Healthy Environment." Paper presented at Green Plans: National Policies toward a Green Century, International Environmental Workshop sponsored by Resource Renewal Institute, March 5-7, San Rafael, CA.

Steiner, D. 1990. "The Human Ecological Significance of Different Types of Knowledge." Paper presented at International Symposium on Human Ecology: Between Theory and Practice, Bad Herrenalb, Switzerland, August 29-September 2.

Steiner, D., F. Furger, and C. Jaeger. In press. "Mechanisms, Forms, and Systems in Human Ecology." In *Human Ecology and Decision-making: An International and Interdisciplinary Collaboration. Proceedings of the Society for Human Ecology Third International Conference,* Vol. II, edited by J. Pratt, G. Young, and R. Borden. Fort Collins, CO: Society for Human Ecology.

Stern, P,C., O.R. Young, and D. Druckman, eds. 1992. *Global Environmental Change: Understanding the Human Dimensions.* National Research Council Committee on the Human Dimensions of Global Change. Washington, DC: National Academy Press.

Stewart, P. 1986. "Meaning in Human Ecology." Pp. 109-116 in *Human Ecology: A Gathering of Perspectives. Selected Papers from the First International Conference of the Society for Human Ecology,* edited by R.J. Borden, G.L. Young, and J. Jacobs (eds). Fort Collins, CO: Society for Human Ecology.

Stoker, J. (Head, Environment Protection Central Division of Department of Environment, London). 1992. "Britain: 'This Common Inheritance.'" Paper presented at Green Plans: National Policies Toward a Green Century, International Environmental Workshop sponsored by Resource Renewal Institute, March 5-7, 1992, San Rafael, CA.

Strong, M. 1992. *From Stockholm to Rio: A Journey Down a Generation.* Geneva, Switzerland: UNCED.

TeHennepe, E. 1991. "Ecology, Education, and Philosophical Maps." Paper presented at Universitet Göteborg and Royal Swedish Academy of Sciences International Conference on Human Ecology, Human Responsibility and Global Change, Göteborg, Sweden, June 9-14.

Tengström, Emin. 1985. "Human Ecology—A New Discipline?" *Humanekologiska Skrifter* 4. Göteborg, Sweden: Göteborg Universitet Institutionen för fredsforskning och humanekologi.

United Kingdom. 1990. *This Common Inheritance: Britain's Environmental Strategy.* (White Paper presented to Parliament by the Secretaries of State for Education and Science, Employment, Energy, Environment, Health, North Ireland, Scotland, Trade and Industry, Transport, and Wales, and the Minister of Agriculture, Fisheries and Food, September 25. 291 pp. + 36 pp. Summary published separately.) London: HMSO.

United Nations. 1989. *UN General Assembly Resolution 44/228: United Nations Conference on Environment and Development.* (Adopted by UN General Assembly December 22, 1989.)

————. 1992a. *A Reference Booklet about the United Nations Conference on Environment and Development.* Geneva, Switzerland: UNCED.

————. 1992b. *Earth Summit: Press Summary of Agenda 21.* New York: UN Deptartment of Public Information.

————. 1992c. *Earth Summit Press Summaries: Convention on Climate Change, Convention on Biological Diversity, Rio Declaration, Forest Principles.* New York: UN Deptartment of Public Information.

————. 1992d. *Earth Summit Quotable Quotes by Maurice Strong, Secretary-General, UNCED.* New York: UN Deptartment of Public Information.

————. 1992e. *Earth Summit Issues In Brief.* New York: UN Deptartment of Public Information.

U.S. Man and the Biosphere Program (USMAB). 1991a. *Mission of the U.S. Man and the Biosphere Program Directorate on Human-Dominated Systems.* Washington, DC: USMAB Human-Dominated Systems Directorate.

U.S. Man and the Biosphere Program. 1991b. "Request for Proposals, Fiscal Year 1992." *Federal Register* 56(158): 40651-40653.

U.S. Man and the Biosphere Program. 1991c. "Global Environmental Change: Understanding the Human Dimensions." (Book review). *USMAB Bulletin* 15(4): 1-3.

Valentine, M. 1991. *An Introductory Guide to the Earth Summit.* San Francisco: U.S. Citizens Network on the United Nations Conference on Environment and Development (UNCED), June 1-12 1992, Rio de Janeiro, Brazil.

Visvader, J. 1986. "Philosophy and Human Ecology." Pp. 117-127 in *Human Ecology: A Gathering of Perspectives. Selected Papers from the First International Conference of the Society for Human Ecology,* edited by R.J. Borden, G.L. Young, and J. Jacobs. Fort Collins, CO: Society for Human Ecology.

Ward, D. 1991. "Question Mapping in Human Ecology." Paper presented at Universitet Göteborg and Royal Swedish Academy of Sciences International Conference on Human Ecology, Human Responsibility and Global Change, Göteborg, Sweden, June 9-14.

————. 1992. "Mapping Questions and Answers in Human Ecology." Unpublished Masters thesis, Vrije Universiteit Brussel, Belgium, July.

Watson, V. 1991. "Sustainability and Soul Searching in Old San Antonio." *Bulletin of the Ecological Society of America* 72(4, December): 204-206.

Wolanski, N. 1989. "Man-Culture-Ecosystems and Human Ecology: Comment on Young's 'Interdisciplinary Human Ecology.'" *Acta Oecologiae Hominis* 1(1): 144-160.

_____. 1990. "Notion and Contemporary Status of Human Ecology." *Journal of Human Ecology* (India) 1(3): 209-218.

World Commission on Environment and Development (WCED). 1987. *Our Common Future.* Report to United Nations General Assembly. Oxford and New York: Oxford University Press.

Young, G.L. 1974. "Human Ecology as an Interdisciplinary Concept: A Critical Inquiry." *Advances in Ecological Research* 8: 1-105.

_____. 1978. *Human Ecology as an Interdisciplinary Domain: An Epistemological Bibliography.* Monticello, IL: Vance Bibliographies.

_____. 1983. *Benchmark Papers in Ecology,* Vol. 12: *Origins of Human Ecology.* Stroudsberg, PA: Hutchinson & Ross

_____. 1986. "Environment: Term and Concept in the Social Sciences." *Social Science Information* 25: 83-124.

_____. 1989. "Conceptual Framework for an Interdisciplinary Human Ecology." *Acta Oecologiae Hominis* 1(1): 1-136.

_____. 1991. "Minor Heresies in Human Ecology." Pp. 11-25 in *Human Ecology: Strategies for the Future,* edited by S. Sontag, S. Wright, G. Young, and M. Grace. Selected papers from the Fourth Conference of the Society for Human Ecology, Michigan State University, East Lansing, MI, April 20-22. Fort Collins, CO: Society for Human Ecology.

Studies in Symbolic Interaction

Edited by **Norman K. Denzin**, *Department of Sociology, University of Illinois*

Volume 15, 1993, 289 pp.　　　　　　　　　　$73.25
ISBN 1-55938-764-5

CONTENTS: Forward, *Norman K. Denzin.* **PART ONE: FEMINIST DISCOURSE READING POPULAR CULTURE. Negotiating the Woman of Broadcast News,** *Linda A. Detman.* **Up By Her Garter Straps: Reading Working Girl,** *Virginia Husting.* **Favorite Clothes and Gendered Subjectivities: Multiple Readings,** *Susan B. Kaiser, Carla M. Freeman and Joan L. Chandler.* **Feminist Theory and the Study of Popular Music,** *Anahid Kassabian.* **PART TWO: A POSTMODERN SENSIBILITIES I: CONVERSATION AND DIALOGUE. Reflections on Voice in Ethnography,** *Davide L. Altheide and John M. Johnson.* **Travesty,** *Alan Blum.* **Writing McDonalds, Eating the Past: McDonald's as a Postmodern Space,** *Alen Shelton.* **PART THREE: POSTMODERN SENSIBILITIES II: CONTROVERSY AND DIALOGUE. Cornerville as Obdurate Reality: Retooling the Reseaerch Act Through Postmodernism,** *Raymond L. Schmitt.* **Interactionist Ethnography and Postmodern Discourse: Affinities and Disjunctures in Approaching Human Lived Experience,** *Lorne L. Dawson and Robert C. Prus.* **The Postmodern Sensibility,** *Norman K. Denzin.* **Interactionist Ethnography and Postmodern Discourse Revisited,** *Andrea Fontana.* **Human Enterprise, Intersubjectivity, and the Ethnographic Other: A Reply to Denzin and Fontana,** *Lorne L. Dawson and Robert C. Prus.* **PART FOUR: NEW EMPIRICAL STUDIES. Generating and Analyzing Processual Data: The Social Act,** *David T. Bastien and Todd J. Hostager.* **Postmodern Claimstaking: An Abortive Politics?,** *Dickinson McGaw.* **Sad Tales and Other Accounts in Labeling Chronic Mental Illness,** *Kenneth J. Smith.* **PART FIVE: DOMESTIC VIOLENCE. The Myth of Protection Orders,** *Rameshwar P. Adhikari, Dorothy Reinhard and John M. Johnson.* **Treating Domestic Violence: Evaluating the Effectiveness of a Domestic Violence Diversion Program,** *John M. Johnson and Dianne J. Kanzler.*

Also Available:
Volumes 1-6, 8,9,11-14 (1978-1993)
　+ Supplement 1 (1986)　　　　　　　$73.25 each
Volumes 7 (1986) & **10** (1990)
　+ Supplement 2 (1986)　　　　　　　$146.50 each

JAI PRESS INC.

55 Old Post Road # 2 - P.O. Box 1678
Greenwich, Connecticut 06836-1678

Tel: (203) 661-7602　　　Fax:(203) 661-0792

Research in Social Problems and Public Policy

Edited by **William R. Freudenburg,** *Department of Sociology, University of Wisconsin—Madison* and **Ted I.K. Youn,** *School of Education, Boston College*

Volume 5, 1993, 312 pp. $73.25
ISBN 1-55938-879-7

Also Available:

Contemporary Studies in Sociology
Theoretical and Empirical Monographs

Volume 12.

Self, Collective Behavior and Society:
Essays Honoring the Contributions of Ralph H. Turner

Edited by **Gerald M . Platt**, *Department of Sociology, University of Massachusetts* and **Chad Gordon**, *Department of Sociology, Rice University*

1994, 413 pp. $73.25
ISBN: 1-55938-755-6

J A I
P R E S S

Steven L. Gordon. **Learning the Trade from a Master Sociological Craftsman,** *Paul Colomy.* **Ralph H. Turner as Teacher and Mentor,** *K. Jill Kiecolt.* **IV. COLLEAGUE AND CHAIR: ANALYSES OF PERSON, ROLE AND INSTITUTIONAL CHANGE. Role and Person: An Appreciation of Ralph Turner,** *Melvin Seeman.* **Institutional Change: Ralph Turner and Sociological Developments at UCLA, 1956-1969,** *Charles R. Wright.* **Ralph Turner: Friend, Colleague, Department Leader,** *Oscar Grusky.* **V. INTELLECTUAL LEGACY: CONTRIBUTIONS TO THE SYMBOLIC INTERACTION CANON. Roles and Interaction Processes: Toward a More Robust Theory,** *Jonathan H.. Turner.* **VI. CLOSING REMARKS. Epilogue,** *Ralph H. Turner.* **About the Contributors.**

JAI PRESS INC.

55 Old Post Road # 2 - P.O. Box 1678
Greenwich, Connecticut 06836-1678

Tel: (203) 661-7602   Fax:(203) 661-0792

J A I   P R E S S

Advances in Medical Sociology

Edited by **Gary L. Albrecht,** *School of Public Health, University of Illinois at Chicago*

Volume 4, A Reconsideration of Health Behavior Change Models
1994, 280 pp. $73.25
ISBN 1-55938-758-0

CONTENTS: Plausible Explanations of Health Behavior Change, *Gary L. Albrecht.* **A Theory of Triadic Influence: A New Theory of Health Behavior with Implications for Preventive Interventions,** *Brian R. Flay and John Petraitis.* **Models of Preventive Health Behavior: Comparison, Critique and Meta-Analysis,** *Rick S. Zimmerman and Dee Vernberg.* **Lifestyle and its Social Meaning,** *Michael Calnan.* **Some Speculations on the Concept of Rationality,** *Roger Ingham.* **In Search of Physician-Patient Interaction in Models of Healthy Behavior Change,** *Frederic W. Hafferty and Jeffrey Coleman Salloway.* **Older Adult Behavior Change in Response to Symptom Experiences,** *Thomas Prohaska and Michael Glasser.* **The Worried Well Myth: Older Americans and the Use of Health Services,** *Fredric D. Wolinsky, M. Callahan, John Fitzgerald and Robert Johnson.* **Organizational and Community Change As the Scientific Basis for Disease Prevention and Health Promotion Policy,** *C. James Frankish and Lawrence W. Green.* **Adherence to and Assessment of Well Roles Among Adults,** *Deborah C. Glik, Jennie J. Kronenfeld, and Kirby Jackson.* **A Typology of Health Rationality Applied to Third World Health,** *Eugene B. Gallagher.*

Volume 5, Quality of Life in Health Care
In preparation, Fall 1994
ISBN 1-55938-832-2   Approx. $73.25

Edited by **Gary L. Albrecht,** *School of Public Health, University of Illinois at Chicago* and **Ray Fitzpatrick,** *Nuffield College, Oxford University*

CONTENTS: A Sociological Perspective of Health-Related Quality of Life Research, *Gary L. Albrecht and Ray Fitzpatrick.* **A Theoretical Framework for Assessing and Analyzing Health-Related Quality of Life,** *Paul D. Cleary, Ira B. Wilson, and Floyd J. Fowler.* **Health-Related Quality of Life: Origins,**

Gaps and Directions, *Debra J. Lerner and Sol Levine.* **Quality of Life Issues and the Dialectic of Medical Progress: Illustrated by End-Stage Renal Disease Patients,** *Eugene Gallagher.* **Qualitative Research and Quality of Life: The Case of Liver Transplantation,** *Joost Heyink and Tjeerd Tymstra.* **Social Support and Quality of Life: Socio-Cultural Similarity and Effective Social Support Among Korean Immigrants,** *Samuel Noh, Sheng Wu and William R. Avison.* **Quality of Life in Older People,** *Morag Farquhar.* **Quality of Life: Assessing the Individual,** *Ciaron O'Boyle, Hannah McGee and C.R.B. Joyce.* **The Workers' Compensation System as a Quality of Life Problem for Workers' Compensation Claimants,** *Allen Imershein, A. Stephan Hill and Andi Reynolds.* **Outcome Measures for Resource Allocation Decisions in Health Care,** *Erik Nord.* **Practical and Methodological Issues in the Development of the EuroQol: The York Experience,** *Paul Kind.* **Conceptual and Methodological Issues in Selecting and Developing Quality of Life Measures,** *E. Nancy Avis and Kevin W. Smith.* **Methodological and Psychometric Issues in Health Status Assessment Across Populations and Applications,** *Colleen McHorney.*

Also Available:
Volumes 1-3 (1991-1993) $73.25 each

JAI PRESS INC.
55 Old Post Road # 2 - P.O. Box 1678
Greenwich, Connecticut 06836-1678
Tel: (203) 661-7602   Fax:(203) 661-0792

Advances in Human Ecology

Edited by **Lee Freese,** *Department of Sociology, Washington State University*

Volume 1, 1992, 234 pp. $73.25
ISBN 1-55938-091-8

CONTENTS: Preface, *Lee Freese.* **The Last Ancestor: An Ecological Network Model on the Origins of Human Sociality,** *Alexandra Maryanski.* **The Evolution of Macrosociety: Why Are Large Societies Rare?,** *Richard Machalek.* **Separation Versus Unification in Sociological Human Ecology,** *William R. Catton, Jr.* **The Natural Ecology of Human Ecology,** *Jeffrey S. Wicken.* **Between the Atom and the Void: Hierarchy in Human Ecology,** *Gerald L. Young.* **From Entropy to Economy: A Thorny Path,** *C. Dyke.* **The Ethical Foundations of Sustainable Economic Development,** *R. Kerry Turner and David W. Pearce.* **The Energy Consumption Turnaround and Socioeconomic Well-Being in Industrial Societies in the 1980s,** *Marvin E. Olsen.*

Volume 2, 1993, 241 pp. $73.25
ISBN 1-55938-558-5

CONTENTS: Preface, *Lee Freese.* **The Biology of Human Organization,** *Jonathan H. Turner and A.R. Maryanski.* **Components of Socioecological Organization: Tools, Resources, Energy and Power,** *Marvin E. Olsen.* **A Socioecological Perspective on Social Evolution,** *Marvin E. Olsen.* **Sociology, Human Ecology and Ecology,** *Curtis E. Beus.* **Social Entropy Theory: An Application of Nonequilibrium Thermodynamics in Human Ecology,** *Kenneth E. Bailey.* **Sustainable Regional Development: A Path for the Greenhouse Marathon,** *Carlo C. Jaeger.* **Minimum Data for Comparative Human Ecological Studies: Examples From Studies in Amazonia,** *Emilio F. Moran.* **The Elementary Forms of the First Proto-Human Society: An Ecological/Social Network of Approach,** *A.R. Maryanski.*

JAI PRESS INC.

55 Old Post Road # 2 - P.O. Box 1678
Greenwich, Connecticut 06836-1678

Tel: (203) 661-7602   Fax:(203) 661-0792